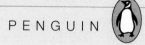 

PENGUIN

DARWIN AND THE BIBLE
THE CULTURAL CONFRONTATION

RICHARD H. ROBBINS

SUNY Plattsburgh

MARK NATHAN COHEN

SUNY Plattsburgh

PEARSON
Education

Boston   New York   San Francisco
Mexico City   Montreal   Toronto   London   Madrid   Munich   Paris
Hong Kong   Singapore   Tokyo   Cape Town   Sydney

Publisher: Nancy Roberts
Marketing Manager: Lindsey Prudhomme
Production Supervisor: Liz Napolitano
Editorial Production Service: GGS Book Services
Composition Buyer: Linda Cox
Manufacturing Buyer: Debbie Rossi
Electronic Composition: GGS Book Services
Photo Researcher: Annie Pickert
Cover Designer: Joel Gendron

For related titles and support materials, visit www.pearsonhighered.com.

Library of Congress Cataloging-in-Publication Data

Darwin and the Bible: the culture confrontation/[edited by] Richard H. Robbins, Mark Nathan Cohen. —1st ed.
     p. cm.
Includes bibliographical references and index.
ISBN-13: 978-0-205-50953-9
ISBN-10: 0-205-50953-3
   1. Evaluation (Biology)—Religious aspects. 2. Intelligent design (Teleology) 3. Creationism. 4. Religion and science. 5. Darwin, Charles, 1809-1882—Criticism and interpretation. I. Robbins, Richard H. (Richard Howard), 1940-II. Cohen, Mark Nathan.

  BL263.D24 2009
  231.7'652—dc22

                                       2007044066

Printed in the United States of America

Dedication

To thoughtful people. . . .
in memory of
Russell Houston Hearn

Table of Contents

List of Contributors

GLENN BRANCH is deputy director of the National Center for Science Education, a non-profit organization affiliated with the American Association for the Advancement of Science that defends the teaching of evolution in the public schools. His articles on creationism and evolution have appeared in such publications as *Academe, The American Biology Teacher, BioScience, Free Inquiry, Geotimes,* and *USA Today.* With Eugenie C. Scott, he is the editor of *Not in Our Classrooms: Why Intelligent Design is Wrong for Our Schools* (Boston: Beacon Press, 2006).

MARK NATHAN COHEN is SUNY University Distinguished Professor of Anthropology (formerly University Distinguished Teaching Professor) at the State University of New York, College at Plattsburgh. His work focuses on cultural evolution and its relationship to human health and demography. His works include *The Food Crisis in Prehistory, Health and the Rise of Civilization, Culture of Intolerance,* and *Teaching Biocultural Anthropology.* He has taught Introduction to Human Evolution for 35 years with growing concern about the mounting threat to science posed by the creationist movement and challenges to the nature of science.

The late STEPHEN J. GOULD was Professor of Geology and Zoology at Harvard University. A prodigious scholar and author, he published a large number of books and articles for both scholarly and popular audiences. He is probably best known for a series of articles published in *Natural History Magazine,* and collections of articles such as *Hen's Teeth and Horses Toes; The Panda's Thumb,* and *Bully for Brontosaurus.* He was an outspoken critic of racism and of attempts to use intelligence measures as indicators of "racial" abilities (*The Mismeasure of Man*). Even though he is sometimes named by creationists as a scientist on "their side" he was also an outspoken critic of creationism, and some methods and presentations of evolutionary theory. His most important contribution to evolutionary theory is probably his development, with Niles Eldridge, of the theory of "punctuated equilibrium" as a partial alternative or supplement to the idea of constant and gradual Darwinian selection as a force for evolutionary change (but within an evolutionary framework). The theory was first presented in an article, "Punctuated equilibria: an alternative to phyletic gradualism" in 1972, and in a series of subsequent articles. His books include *Rocks of Ages: Science and Religion in the Fullness of Life* and *The Structure of Evolutionary Theory.*

WALTER R. HEARN is Professor of Christianity and Science at New College Berkeley in Berkeley, California. He was formerly a professor in the Department of Biochemistry and Biophysics at Iowa State University. He is coauthor of *Teaching Science in a Climate of Controversy* and author of *Being a Christian in Science.*

MARTINEZ HEWLITT is an emeritus professor in the Department of Molecular and Cellular Biology at the University of Arizona in Tucson. He has published 30 scientific papers and is a founding member of the St. Albert the Great Forum on Theology and the Sciences at the University of Arizona. He also serves as an adjunct professor at the Dominican School of Philosophy and Theology at the Graduate Theoretical Union in Berkeley, CA.

PHILLIP E. JOHNSON is Professor of Law Emeritus at the Boalt School of Law, the University of California at Berkeley, and "father" of the Intelligent Design movement. He is co-founder of the Discovery Institute's Center for Science and Culture. He has written extensively about intelligent design as a critique of, and supplement to evolutionary theory. He is author of *Darwin on Trial*; *Reason in the Balance*; and *Defeating Darwinism by Opening Minds*.

EDWARD J. LARSON is Talmadge Chair of Law and Russell Professor of American History at the University of Georgia. He is author of *Trial and Error: the American Controversy over Creation and Evolution*; *Sex Race and Science: Eugenics in the Deep South*; *Summer of the Gods: the Scopes Trial and the America's Continuing Debate over Religion and Science*; and *Evolution: the Remarkable History of a Scientific Theory*. He is the 1998 winner of the Pulitzer Prize in History.

JONATHAN MARKS is Professor of Anthropology at the University of North Carolina at Charlotte. His primary area of research is molecular anthropology—the application of genetic data to illuminate our place in the natural order. He has written extensively on issues of human variation and on human evolution. Marks is editor of Evolutionary Anthropology and author of *Human Biodiversity*, and *What It Means to be 98% Chimpanzee*. He has been awarded the W.W. Howells prize in Biological Anthropology by the American Anthropological Association and the AAA/Mayfield Award for Excellence in Undergraduate Education.

The late ERNST MAYR, former Emeritus Professor of Zoology at Harvard University, was one of the 20th century's leading evolutionary biologists and played a critical role in creating the "modern synthesis" between Genetics and Darwinian theory. He was author of *Systematics and the Origin of Species*, *What Evolution Is*, *Evolution and the Diversity of Life*; and *One Long Argument: Charles Darwin and the Genesis of Modern Evolutionary Thought*.

TED PETERS is Professor of Systematic Theology at Pacific Lutheran Theological Seminary and the Graduate Theological Union in Berkeley California. He is author of *God—The World's Future*, and *Science, Theology and Ethics*. He is editor in chief of *Dialogue, a Journal of Theology*; and he serves as co-editor of *Theology and Science*, published by the Center for Technology and the Natural Sciences in Berkeley.

LAURA PERRAS is a third year student at the SUNY College in Plattsburgh. At the time of writing her chapter, she was a first year student struggling to reconcile her roots in a deeply religious family, her growing dismay with biblical literalism, and her recent exposure to the evidence underlying scientific insistence on the occurrence of evolution.

STEVEN RANDAK teaches biology at Jefferson High in Lafayette Indiana. He has been named National Biology Teacher of the Year. He also received the Presidential Award for Excellence in Science Teaching Biology by the Hoosier Association of Science Teachers and the Evolution Education Award from the National Center for Science Education.

RICHARD ROBBINS is SUNY University Distinguished Teaching Professor of Anthropology at the State University of New York, College at Plattsburgh. He is author of *Cultural Anthropology, a Problem Based Approach* and author of a widely used discussion of contemporary problems, *Global Problems and the Culture of Capitalism*. Edited volumes include *Talking Points on Global Issues: A Reader* and *Globalization and the Environment* (with Gary Kroll). He is also the recipient of the 2005 AAA/McGraw Hill Excellence in Teaching Award from the American Anthropological Association.

The History and Implications of a Cultural Confrontation

by Richard H. Robbins

The year 2009 marks the 150th anniversary of the publication of Charles Darwin's book *On the Origin of Species by Means of Natural Selection, or The Preservation of Favoured Races in the Struggle for Life*. The book contained two basic ideas: first, that the variety of life on the planet was not specially and individually created, but had been gradually modified from existent forms over millions of years, and, second, that the main mechanism of evolution was the process of natural selection.

Darwin, who originally had planned to be a clergyman, realized immediately that his work was controversial, and that it challenged the dominant world view of nineteenth century Great Britain. In 1860 he wrote to Asa Gray, his disciple in America:

> With respect to the theological view of the question. This is always painful to me. I am bewildered. I had no intention to write atheistically. But I own that I cannot see as plainly as others do, and as I should wish to do, evidence of design and beneficence on all sides of us. There seems to me too much misery in the world. I cannot persuade myself that a beneficent and omnipotent God would have designedly created the Ichneumonidae with the express intention of their feeding within the living bodies of caterpillars, or that a cat should play with mice (Darwin, F., 1887, p. 311).

Darwin was very right to be concerned about the reaction of the church to his work. To begin with, it contradicted the accounts of creation contained in the book

1

ON

THE ORIGIN OF SPECIES

BY MEANS OF NATURAL SELECTION,

OR THE

PRESERVATION OF FAVOURED RACES IN THE STRUGGLE
FOR LIFE.

By CHARLES DARWIN, M.A.,

FELLOW OF THE ROYAL, GEOLOGICAL, LINNÆAN, ETC., SOCIETIES;
AUTHOR OF ' JOURNAL OF RESEARCHES DURING H. M. S. BEAGLE'S VOYAGE
ROUND THE WORLD.'

LONDON:
JOHN MURRAY, ALBEMARLE STREET.
1859.

Darwin's *On the Origin of Species* incited a debate about science, religion, nature, and politics that survives to this day.

of Genesis. It also undermined the popular argument for the existence of God. Instead of divine purpose and design in the origin of life, Darwin suggested that human and animal forms had evolved naturally by somewhat random and often bloody processes. Furthermore, his theories implied that man, rather than having fallen from a state of blessedness into a state of sin, had, as David Lack (1957) put it, "risen from the beasts" (p. 16). Finally, it suggested that man's higher intellectual and moral capacities were not, as had been assumed, divine gifts from a God who created man in his own image, but, rather, had evolved by natural means from other animals.

Yet, the problem seemed resolvable if only one assumed, as many theologians did and still do, that there was a divine hand behind evolution. However, for reasons that we will explore in this volume, protagonists on all sides saw threats to their interests. When religionists sought to have their views of divine origin taught in science classes, scientists characterized the threat as a fight for freedom of scientific expression against religious prejudice and dogma. On the other side, theologians defined the issue as a fight against rampant materialism and the need to preserve man's special relationship to God (see Lack, 1957, pp. 12–13). And, when scientists used their public prestige to claim that science, in general, made religion obsolete, or that, in particular, Darwin's work destroyed the need for a belief in God (e.g., Dawkins, 2006), religionists reacted with alarm and sometimes outrage.

Clearly, in spite of almost 150 years of controversy, the debate is still as fierce as ever. In 2005 the National Center for Science Education tracked 78 clashes in 31 states in which school boards were taking steps to teach alternatives to evolution. The major present religious initiative is the "teach the controversy approach" that endorses the teaching of evolution as the centerpiece of any biology curriculum, but only if criticism of Darwin is included (a plan, according to a Zogby poll, that has the support of 71% of the public). Between 34 and 40 percent of the American population say that the Bible is the actual word of God and is to be taken literally. Forty-four percent believe that God created Man in his present form some 10,000 years ago. Furthermore, these figures have been relatively stable for at least thirty years (Witham, 2002, p. 5). In addition, given the spread of a conservative brand of Christianity around the world (e.g., Sugirtharajah, 2001; Jenkins, 2002), along with a similar dilemma for Muslims as well as Jews, the debate is not likely to go away (see Chapter 10 in this volume). The problem is *how are we to understand this confrontation between Darwin and the Bible?*

There are, of course, thousands of books and articles outlining the history of the debate arguing in favor of one perspective or another and many arguing for a greater understanding of the conflicting positions. It would be presumptuous to assume that the selections in this reader can resolve a debate that is as contentious as, (if not more so than), it was 150 years ago. But, as anthropologists, the editors of this volume have the dual responsibilities of arguing for the integrity of scientific research, but, at the same time, attempting to help people understand the perspective and logic of other world views. Neither of the editors of this volume, nor the contributors, doubts at least the basics of Darwin's account of evolution. However, as anthropologists, we cannot discount the views of others, even when they are, as is the case with religious criticism of Darwin, often critical of the whole anthropological and scientific enterprise. Instead, we must seek to understand the cultural roots of the debate.

The purpose, therefore, of this volume is to provide readers with resources to stimulate discussion of why Darwin's theory of evolution appears threatening to some people, and, likewise, to help understand why some scientists often react with such emotion to challenges to their views. The essays in the reader are divided into three sets. The first set addresses how scientists and theologians have tried to resolve the apparent contradictions between Darwin and the Bible. The second set examines the historical and cultural settings that defined, often very differently, the parameters of the debate and the implications they had for both religion and science and the influence of the debate globally. The third set describes how the debate came to center on education and explores the impacts on both teachers and students. All but three of the essays were prepared especially for this volume. Each of the authors in this volume addresses the debate about evolution in his or her own way, either in the classroom or in his or her personal life. Each would not always agree with the others (even the editors, one a physical anthropologist, the other a cultural anthropologist, don't always agree). But the debate often serves as a window into our own culture. Science and religion are key and essential elements of our lives, regardless of how each of us individually perceives them; yet their influence is often contradictory and contentious.

The purpose of this introductory chapter is to provide a brief history of the debate so that readers can gain some understanding of the various issues involved, and to understand the social and cultural dimensions of the debate. Theories and ideas of how the world works have social and cultural consequences; therefore, to understand the intensity of the debate over Darwin's theory of evolution, we need to examine the social implications assumed by detractors.

A Brief History of the Dispute

The debate over Darwin and the Bible can be said to have begun even before Darwin published *Origin of Species*, since Darwin realized as early as 1842 that his theory of species evolution contradicted the biblical idea of God's creation of each life form (Genesis 1:20–27). The debate became a public spectacle in 1860, a year after the publication of the book and two years after Darwin and Alfred Russel Wallace, who had independently developed a theory of evolution by natural selection, jointly had their findings announced before the Linnean Society of London. At that time there was a public debate between Thomas H. Huxley and Anglican bishop Samuel Wilberforce, in which Wilberforce famously asked Huxley whether or not he was descended from a monkey on his mother's side or father's side, and Huxley responded that he would rather be descended from a monkey than to use his gifts to obscure the truth.[1]

Scientists, clergy, and the public soon lined up on one side of the debate or the other, but generally, clergy adopted a position that became known as *theistic evolution* (see Chapters 3 and 4 in this volume) in which evolution was said to be guided by God. Trouble began when scientists and philosophers began to cite Darwin as proof that a belief in a divine hand was unnecessary to understand the formation of life; and, furthermore, that science and scientists offered the greatest hope for humankind. Among these was Francis Galton, a cousin of Darwin, and author of a celebrated book on inherited intelligence, in which he attempted to show that great intelligence ran in family lines, among which was his own. He also invented the term *eugenics*, the idea of the selective breeding of human beings, and turned his not insignificant gifts to propose identifying those individuals who should serve as the breeders of future populations, and setting the field of statistics on a course to make it a major tool of eugenic policy (McKenzie, 1981). A second and related development was Herbert Spencer's characterization of natural selection as the "survival of the fittest," and the development of the doctrine that became known as "Social Darwinism," most associated with Spencer and William Graham Sumner, an ardent opponent of socialism and defender of capitalism. For example, industrialists such as Andrew Carnegie used social Darwinism to justify economic dominance. Politicians in England and Germany used social Darwinism to justify colonialism and military domination and the annihilation of "inferior" races. Thus, during the Herero Revolt in Southwest Africa in 1904, when the German General Lothar von Trotha gave the order to kill all Herero men, women, and children, he justified his actions by citing Darwinian racial struggle as a reason (Weikart, 2004, p. 184).

In response to these developments, along with studies that suggested that teaching evolution encouraged atheism, religionists began to attack Darwin and his theories. These attacks culminated in the crusade in the United States, led largely by three-time Presidential candidate William Jennings Bryan, to ensure that the biblical theory of creation be taught alongside Darwin as another "theory" of human origin. In response, the Tennessee legislature enacted a law (the Butler Act)

---

[1] Actually there was no transcript of the debate, and those oft-repeated lines appeared in Huxley's autobiography.

banning the teaching of evolution in schools. When a Tennessee teacher, John Scopes, volunteered to test the law, the subsequent trial pit Bryan against the most celebrated trial lawyer of his time, Clarence Darrow. The so-called "Scopes Monkey Trial" has been called a turning point in the debate. The popular understanding of the trial was that newspapers ridiculed Bryan, creationism, and Christian Fundamentalists, in general, and seemingly put an end to the debate. That's not quite the case, as we'll see when we examine the Scopes trial in a little more detail in Chapter 7 of this volume.

By the early 1930s, particularly after the publication of Ronald A. Fisher's book, *A Genetical Theory of Natural Selection*, Darwin's version of evolution was generally accepted in the scientific community. However, the majority of the population maintained their faith in the biblical version of creation. Publishers of biology textbooks from the 1930s through the 1950s tried to avoid offending them and made virtually no mention of the theory of evolution.

While public interest in the debate seemed to subside after the Scopes trial, there was, among Fundamentalists themselves, spirited debate regarding such issues as the age of the earth. Some subscribed to what was called the "day age" hypothesis in which the six days of creation in Genesis were said to be of indeterminate length, allowing that the earth might be millions or billions of years old. Others subscribed to the "gap theory" which allowed for multiple cataclysms and creations prior to the six-day Edenic Restoration and Noah's flood. The more orthodox insisted that the earth was only 6,000 to 10,000 years old and that life began with the six-day Edenic creation and a universal flood that occurred some 5,000 years ago.

The flood geologists argued that since there could have been no death prior to Adam's sin, fossils must have been formed after God created Adam and Eve and after the Fall. This idea, first widely disseminated by George McCready Price in the 1920s and 30s, became known as flood or deluge theology, and was revived by Henry M. Morris and John C. Whitcomb in their 1960 book, *The Genesis Flood: The Biblical Record and its Scientific Implications*. According to Morris and Whitcomb, three events dominated early history—the Creation, the Fall, and the Flood. According to their account, God, through methods known and unknown, created the entire universe and populated the earth in six days. For some time Adam and Eve lived in this perfect world without sin or suffering or death. But the Fall led

In his book *The Genesis Flood*, Henry M. Morris sought to demonstrate that the accounts of creation in the Bible could be validated scientifically.

to a period of decay, and was followed by the Flood which was responsible for creating, not only fossils, but also the earth's geologic foundations (Numbers, 1993, p. 203).

Whitcomb and Morris's book claimed to provide scientific proof for biblical events and was greeted enthusiastically by Fundamentalists looking for validation of their biblical view of the world and who were also alarmed at other scientific and political developments. The first was the emergence in biology in the 1950s of what became known as the "New Synthesis," that integrated Darwin's ideas with the emerging field of population genetics. This development, plus the centenary celebration in 1959 of the publication of *Origin of Species*, once again put Darwin and his theories in the public eye.

A second development was the U.S. response to the Soviet Union's launching in 1957 of the space probe "Sputnik." Educators and politicians took this as evidence that the United States was falling behind the soviets in science education, and initiated a reevaluation of how science was being taught. One result was the establishment in 1958 of the Biological Science Curriculum Project (BSCP) headed by Joseph D. McInerney. BSCP produced new textbooks emphasizing evolution and the New Synthesis, but renewed religionists' concerns regarding what was being taught in schools.

Third, religionists also became alarmed regarding legal rulings in the 1960s and 70s such as the banning of prayer in schools and the legalization of abortion, along with what they considered a general breakdown of society. They were angry, also, with claims by biologists, such as William D. Hamilton, Edward Wilson, and Richard Dawkins, that biology, not religion, could account for morality and ethics in human beings (see Chapter 8 in this volume).

Reacting to these and other developments, religionists saw in *The Genesis Flood*, a new strategy for combating what they saw as an attack on their beliefs. By grounding their arguments about biblical creation in scientific terms, creationists could claim, that, as science, it deserved to be taught in schools alongside evolution. Advocates of *scientific creationism* maintain that the events in Genesis can be proved with technical evidence, and without reference to scripture (Toumey, 1994, 7ff).

Some religionists made a related argument that evolution itself was embedded in a quasi-religious ideology called "Secular Humanism." The term itself gained prominence from a 1961 U.S. Supreme Court ruling that failure to believe in God could not be considered grounds for denying someone state employment. In a footnote to that decision, Justice Hugo Black commented that "among the religions in this country which do not teach what would generally be considered a belief in the existence of God are Buddhism, Taoism, Ethical Culture, Secular Humanism, and others" (Toumey, 1994, p. 79). The term "Secular Humanism" was never defined by the court, but it emerged as the target of religionists, some of whom blamed it for sex education, Marxism, evolution, and a general rejection of traditional standards of morality (p. 80). Hostility to secular humanism was encoded in a book *The Battle for the Mind*, by Tim LaHaye (1980). LaHaye defined secular humanism as "man's attempt to solve his problems independently of God," while claiming that "humanists view man as an autonomous, self-centered, godlike person," and that "most of the evils in the world today can be traced to humanism" (Toumey, 1994, p. 82). Also associated with secular humanism were naturalism, evolution, faith in reason and science, relativism, situational ethics, anti-authoritarianism, civil liberties, and globalism (p. 84). But regardless of how it was defined, religionists claimed that, if it was religion, it too should be banned from schools.

Consequently, legislators in Arkansas and Louisiana passed laws requiring teachers to either teach biblical creation alongside evolution or state that evolution was just a theory and remained unproven. However, in 1987, the Supreme Court ruled that scientific creationism represented a religious account, and ruling that these laws were unconstitutional. (For a legal history of the dispute, see Chapter 11.)

However, the debate, for reasons we'll examine next, did not cease. A new account, called Intelligent Design (ID), emerged as another challenger to evolution (see Chapters 5 and 6 in this volume). Intelligent Design was not a new idea; in fact, Alfred Russel Wallace coined the term to describe a belief that life-forms were too complex to evolve on their own through random mutation and natural selection, and, consequently, there must be some sort of intelligent designer responsible for them. The human eye was often used as the major example of something that was too complex to have developed independently of intelligent design. The names most associated with this theory today are Phillip Johnson and Michael Behe. Johnson and his book, *Darwin on Trial* laid out the basis for the latest attack on evolution. As a Berkeley professor of law, Johnson had considerable credibility, and his technique, rooted in a lawyers instinct, was to chastise Darwinism for its gaps and holes. Johnson wrote a series of five books between 1991 and 2000 and lectured widely. A brief contribution from Professor Johnson summarizing his perspectives appears in this volume (see Chapter 5). Michael Behe's contributions hinge on the assertion in his 1996 book, *Darwin's Black Box*, that Darwinian natural selection loses its power to explain organisms at "irreducibly complex" levels, down among the cells and molecules. "At these levels," says Behe, "a class of biochemical systems"—those controlling blood clotting, vision, and various cell functions—look designed because all the pieces have to be there for the system to function" (Witham, 2002, p. 127).

In a more recent development, in 2004, a school board in Dover, Pennsylvania, decided that a four-page disclaimer be read aloud in classes, which described evolution as theory, not fact, and which commended intelligent design (as presented in the book *Of Pandas and People*) to the student's attention. Challenged in court by some of the parents of children at the school, the Federal District Court ruled in December of 2005, that ID was not science, but that it was simply thinly veiled creationism and thus found the school board's policy to be unconstitutional.

Table 1.1 presents a timeline of significant events to date. As we mentioned earlier, this is not likely the end of the matter. Judicial courts, as powerful as they are, are not capable in themselves of ending cultural debates that are as far-reaching as the debate over evolution and creationism/Intelligent Design. Furthermore, the debate is no longer confined to the United States but is gaining global traction (see Chapter 10 in this volume). Therefore, the next question we need to examine is *why does the Bible, understood as the direct word of God, play such an important role for so many people; and why do some groups, particularly scientific creationists, argue that the Bible has standing as scientific evidence? That is, what are the cultural implications of holding to one side of the debate or the other?*

TABLE 1.1

Timeline for the Debate over Darwin and the Bible

Date	Event
1831–1836	Darwin's voyage on the Beagle and his study of the variation of animal life on the Galapagos Islands
ca 1844	Darwin sees how animal breeding and the population theories of Reverend Thomas Malthus can provide a model for evolution and the origin of species
1855	Darwin and Alfred Russel Wallace begin corresponding regarding their respective theories of evolution
1858	Darwin's and Alfred Russel Wallace's findings on evolution are jointly submitted to the Linnean Society of London
1859	Publication of Darwin's book *The Origin of Species by Means of Natural Selection,* or *The Preservation of Favoured Races in the Struggle for Life*
1860	Debate between Thomas Henry Huxley and Bishop Samuel Wilberforce
1864	Publication of Herbert Spencer's *Principles of Biology* in which he first used the term "survival of the fittest" to describe natural selection
1869	Publication of Francis Galton's book, *Hereditary Genius*
1870 to 1900	Codification of Social Darwinism in the writings of Herbert Spencer, William Graham Sumner, and others
1925	Passage of the Butler Act in Tennessee prohibiting the teaching of evolution, and Scopes trial in Dayton, Tennessee, and the resulting confrontation of William Jennings Bryan and Clarence Darrow
1931	The publication of Ronald A. Fisher's book, *A Genetical Theory of Natural Selection* that cemented the importance of Darwin's theories
1957	The launching by the Soviet Union of Sputnik I, the world's first artificial satellite and growing concern in the United States about the quality of science education
1958	Establishment of the Biological Science Curriculum Study to build the new discoveries in biology and the so-called "new synthesis" into school textbooks
1959	Conferences and celebrations centered on the Darwin Centennial
1961	Publication of Henry M. Morris and John C. Whitcomb's book, *The Genesis Flood*
1963	U.S. Supreme Court rules that schools may not require group prayer or religious devotionals for their students
1980	Publication of Tim LaHaye's book, *The Battle for the Mind* outlined the dangers of "secular humanism"
1981	Louisiana and Arkansas pass legislation requiring the "balanced treatment" of scientific creationism and evolution
1987	Supreme Court rejects Louisiana law requiring that scientific creationism be given equal time in schools to evolution

1991	Publication of Philip E. Johnson's book, *Darwin on Trial* in which he attacks the credibility of Darwin's theories
1996	Publication of Michael Behe's book, *Darwin's Black Box* that argues that life at the molecular level is too complex to have evolved without some intelligent designer guiding its development
2005	Pennsylvania court rules in the case of *Kitzmiller v. Dover Area School District* that Intelligent Design is not a scientific theory and that it "cannot uncouple itself from its creationist, and thus religious, antecedents"

Literalism and Contingency in Science and Religion

For most people, the debate over Darwin and the Bible begins with Genesis and the description of God's creation of the world. If, as some people claim, it is literally true, then we are confronted with direct contradictions to the findings of geology, paleontology, biology, and anthropology, among other branches of science. Thus, one question is *why is it so important for some to insist on a literal interpretation of the Bible in spite of the fact that early church leaders such as St. Augustine, Irenaeus, and Clement treated at least part of the Bible as allegory* (Lack, 1957, p. 34)?

In his book, *Serving the Word: Literalism in America from the Pulpit to the Bench*, Vincent Crapanzano (2000) examines what he terms "literalism" in both religion and the law. Literalism, as Crapanzano defines it, is a style of interpretation that, among other things, (1) finds figurative understanding distorting, or even corrupting, (2) views certain texts or books as fundamental to understanding the world, and (3) assumes a "simple, unambiguous, correlation of word and thing" (p. 3).

Literalism is not, says Crapanzano, limited to religion and the law; one also finds it in psychoanalysis or psychotherapy when the aim is to help patients by retrieving "real" traumatic events thought buried in memory, or in accounts of genetics that attribute a specific gene for virtually every trait from homosexuality to baldness. Thus, as we will see, one can also speak of 'scientific literalists' as well as biblical or legal literalists.

The opposite of a literal reading of biblical text might be called a contingent reading. This approach assumes that specific views or, more specifically, texts or writings, must involve interpretation, that descriptions of the world are (1) contingent on the time and place that they were written, (2) on the language in which they are written and the multiple meaning of words, and (3) on the cultural setting and the social interests of the authors.

As we examine the creationism and evolution debate, we need to be aware that there are not simply two perspectives: there are at least four, as well as some variation within those four (see Table 1.2). These are

- *Biblical literalism* claims that every word in the Bible is true, literally true.
- *Biblical contingency* proposes that the Bible should not be read as literal truth, but rather as the attempt of human beings to put into words, however imperfectly, what God intended.

TABLE 1.2

████

Contingency and Non-Contingency in Science and Religion

		Knowledge Dimension	
		Religious Knowledge	Scientific Knowledge
Contingency Dimension	Non-contingent	**Biblical Literalists**	**Scientific Literalists**
		The Bible is the word of God and true in all of its particulars.	Scientific theories say no more than they intend to say and are limited to describing the physical and material universe.
	Contingent	**Biblical Contingency**	**Scientific Contingency**
		The Bible should not be read as literal truth, but rather as the attempt of human beings to put into words, however imperfectly, what God intended. Its messages are contingent on the time and place it was written.	Scientific theories, regardless of how they are described and what they are explicitly intended to describe, carry social and moral messages.

- *Scientific literalism* maintains that scientific theories say no more than they mean to say, that they are limited to descriptions of the physical or material universe, and that they have nothing to say about morality or spirituality.

- *Scientific contingency* assumes that scientific theories, regardless of how they are described and what they are explicitly intended to describe, carry multiple social and moral messages.

One of the difficulties that scientists and religionists have in talking to each other is a consequence of the failure to recognize these divergent positions.

Biblical Literalism and Contingency

When creationists claim that Darwin conflicts with the Bible, they are generally referring to the description of creation in the first three chapters of Genesis. If these descriptions were interpreted as allegory, as did early Church leaders, there is no conflict (Lack, 1957, p. 34; Hearn, this volume)

The problem arises with the notion of biblical inerrancy, the formal view, for example, of the Southern Baptist Convention. The following "Statement of Faith" from John MacArthur's Master's Seminary is a good example of a literalist interpretation of the Bible (Crapanzano, 2000)

1. the Bible is God's written revelation to man, and thus the sixty-six books of the Bible given to us by the Holy Spirit constitute the plenary (inspired equally in all parts) Word of God.

2. the Word of God is an objective revelation, verbally inspired in every word, absolutely inerrant in the original documents, infallible, and God-breathed. We

teach the literal grammatical–historical interpretation of Scripture which affirms the belief that the opening chapters of Genesis present creation in six literal days.

3. the Bible constitutes the only infallible rule of faith and practice.

4. God spoke in His written Word by a process of dual authority. The Holy Spirit so superintended the human authors that, though the individual personalities and different styles of writing, they composed and recorded God's Word to man without error in the whole or in the part.

5. whereas there may be several applications of any given passage of Scripture, there is but one true interpretation. The meaning of scripture is to be found as one diligently applies the literal grammatical–historical method of interpretation under the enlightenment of the Holy Spirit. It is the responsibility of believers to ascertain artfully the true intent and meaning of Scripture, recognizing that proper application is binding on all generations. Yet the truth of Scripture stands in judgment of men; never do men stand in judgment of it. (p. 57)

The Bible, this view implies, has only one meaning, God's meaning, and while people may disagree on the meaning of some passages, the "true" interpretation will be revealed to persons who are under God's enlightenment. There are of course numerous contradictions in the Bible, but biblical literalists manage to rationalize those (e.g., Did Jesus cleanse the Temple at the end of his ministry?—Mark I 1:1-17— Or at the beginning?—Matthew 21:12. The answer is that there were two cleansings). When Crapanzano (2000) asked one of his informants about contradictions in the Bible he said that they only appear as contradictions because we cannot understand God's words fully (p. 79).

Scientists, as well as others, reject the literalists view of the Bible, often in derogatory and dismissive language. Yet there are, for Fundamentalists, logical and forceful arguments for insisting on a literal interpretation of Scripture.

First, Biblical literalists adhere to what is popularly called a "domino approach" to the Bible. If it could be shown, they say, that there was even one error in Scripture, it would destroy faith in the whole. Thus when the Bible says that God created the world in six days, or implies through genealogies (as Bishop Usher did in assuming that the earth was created in 4004 B.C.) that the earth is thousands rather than billions of years old, it must be so. "If the Bible is God given," Henry Morris argued, "it is unthinkable that it should contain scientific mistakes; either it is scientifically accurate whenever it happens to touch on some phase of science, or it is purely the product of human beings and no better than any other book of ethics" (Numbers, 1993, p. 194). "If you accept that the earth is old" as Harvard-educated geologist Kurt Wise (Witham, 2002) argues,

> and if you accept the chronologic column, then Genesis one through eleven—20 percent of the book—must be rejected. . . . You must also reject the 15 percent of Psalms that talks about nature, as well as nearly half of the Old Testament and sundry parts of the New testament where the texts talk of earth history and human history. So you are talking about 20 to 25 percent of the Bible you have to toss out immediately. But it doesn't stop there. The very doctrines we hold true become threatened. (p. 103)

Second, if you open up the Bible to interpretation, you must, therefore, trust human reason and judgment. But Biblical literalists greatly distrust individual judgment. They fear the flawed reasoning of human beings trying to replace God's perfection, and reject it. Human reason is subject to manipulation by Satan and is not to be trusted. They point to war and violence, injustice, hunger, and human misery as consequences of human fallibility. The only alternative, then, is to seek God's judgment; and the only thing that we have of God's is the Bible as His Word. From this perspective, inerrancy makes perfect sense.

The third aspect of biblical literalism is the fact that, according to Crapanzano, history is interpreted differently by biblical literalists. The Fundamentalist understanding of history, says Crapanzano, subsumes all history to Scripture. Thus, for Fundamentalists, the lessons of history are all about morality, not simply a chronology of events. Crapanzano (2000) visited Morris' museum of scientific creationism and says:

> It was only later, as I came to a better understanding of evangelical thought, that I realized that the creationists like Morris had a wholly different understanding of time and history and, therefore, of science. It was not just a question of disjunctive history, one that recognized miracles, one whose end was known, one that was, in a sense, already written; it was a history so morally saturated that morality could not be separated from any other understanding, including the scientific. (p. 189)

Central to the Biblical Literalists idea of history is the <u>Book of Revelation.</u> History, from this perspective, has direction; it may be a premillennial interpretation in which the earth devolves into chaos and the chosen will be raptured while the forces of good and evil do battle prior to the Second Coming; or it may be a postmillennial view in which the Second Coming is preceded by the creation of heaven on earth. <u>Regardless, the future is already written.</u>

Biblical literalists, says Crapanzano (2000, pp. 15–16), note that there is a discrepancy between the way the world is biblically constituted and the way it really is. It is here that the Fundamentalists require explanations, and they find it in man's

The Revelation of John in the Bible contains an account of human history that many people believe is ordained by God.

<u>fallen condition</u>. They are motivated, as we shall see, to make their own lives as biblical as possible—to obliterate the gap between the ideal, literally described and commanded by Scripture, and the real.

Scientific Literalism and Contingency

Scientific literalists make a sharp distinction between science and religion. Science, they say, attempts to discover laws that permit the control of nature for human benefit. Those who recognize the worth of religion at all, say that it addresses human spiritual needs and phenomena that lie outside the realm of science (See Chapters 1 and 2 in this volume). <u>For literalists</u>, as long as religion keeps to its sphere of knowledge and allows science to deal with its sphere, there need be no conflict. However, when religionists claim that biblical authority can explain so-called natural phenomena, scientists strongly object.

But there is another view that holds that scientific knowledge is also contingent upon social and cultural factors. In his classic work, *The Structure of Scientific Revolution* (often used by religionists to critique science), <u>Thomas Kuhn (1961)</u> argued that scientific theories or paradigms are constructed and held until contradictions or insoluble problems overwhelm them and a new paradigm emerges. For example, for almost two thousand years people believed the earth was the center of the universe. Theirs was a two-sphere cosmos consisting of a spherical vaulted heaven that moved eastward across the heavens, and an earthly sphere that was at the center of the universe. There were problems with the system; it was difficult to explain the behavior of the planets that sometimes seemed to reverse their course, or increase and decrease in brightness. But the system worked well enough for thousands of skilled and knowledgeable observers to accept it for hundreds of years. Then, <u>in 1543, Nicholaus Copernicus</u> announced his theory of a sun-centered universe, and a cosmological system that had been sustained in belief for so long slowly began to crumble.

<u>Scientific contingency assumes that even the creation of scientific knowledge cannot be free of cultural bias</u> (Douglas, 1978) or social interests (Barnes, 2002; Bloor, 1991). Thus if one looks at the history of the field of statistics, as Donald McKenzie (1981) suggests, one finds that the statistical tools developed by pioneers such as Francis Galton and Karl Pearson, were developed specifically to further eugenics and the social interests of those who advocated it. Or one can examine the use of language in science. Thus, as Emily Martin (1987) suggests, medical textbooks reflect a strong male bias in how the bodily processes of males and females are described. Thus menstruation is described negatively as "decay" or "degeneration," while sperm production is described using words such as "amazing," and marveling at its "sheer magnitude" (p. 47).

Contingency, as we're using the term, bears a strong relation to "constructivism," a view that, among other things, sees technical terms (e.g., *planet, element, organ, disease, race, gene, or intelligence*) embedded in larger systems or networks of assumptions, rather than isolated elements with discrete meanings (Smith, 2005, pp. 7–8). So-called scientific views, suggests Barbara Herrnstein Smith (2005), are simply beliefs that have become well-established. Thus we have to reject the contrast between "objectively valid scientific knowledge" and "personal opinion" or "popular superstition" and accept the idea that beliefs are more or less contingent, or that they are more or less effective in addressing specific problems (p. 11). After all, maritime navigators, up to the development of Global Positioning Systems (GPS), still operated as if the earth was the center of the solar system. ?

Scientific contingency or constructivism does not imply that science is "wrong." Rather, it says that any social or cultural institution, whether it be religion, government, the family, or science must be limited by the culture, language, and social arrangements that characterize the society from which it emerges.

According to this view, when evolutionists see science as dealing only with the natural world, and assume that scientific theories say only what they "mean" to say, they fail to appreciate the social and cultural implications that others see in evolution. That is, they often fail to appreciate the total system of meanings in which evolution is embedded. While they might like to assume that the domain of science is in explaining natural phenomenon, while religion addresses man's spiritual nature, scientific theories, in fact, say more than that. And that is where the heart of the debate lies. For religionists, the debate over Darwin and the Bible has more to it than simply the truth or falsity of Darwin's theory or the inerrancy of Scripture. The theory of evolution represented a whole new way of conceptualizing some of the basic categories of meaning on which people based their lives. To illustrate, let's examine some of the broader meanings ascribed by religionists to Darwin's book, *Origin of Species* and some of the dilemmas it posed for both theologians and scientists (see also Chapter 9).

The Anthropology of the Debate: Darwin's Metaphor

One source of the debate between Darwin and the Bible has to do with the areas of life to which scientific ideas apply. Scientists, particularly scientific literalists, claim that science in general, and evolution in particular, is concerned only with the material or natural world, while religion, they suggest, should limit itself to contemplation of the supernatural (Scott, 2004, p. 47). Religionists, on the other hand, are concerned about how science and the concept of evolution affects a far wider range of cultural beliefs, practices, and assumptions.

In a 1971 article, Robert Young referred to Darwin's theory as "Darwin's Metaphor." Searching around for some way to conceptualize the processes he was trying to describe, Darwin, in 1838, came across the ideas of the Reverend Thomas Malthus and his writings on population growth. Malthus argued that, in nature, plants and animals reproduce more offspring than can survive, and that many die off from hunger, disease, or predation. From this, Malthus reasoned that unless human beings control their reproductive rate, population would rapidly increase, and famine and war would become epidemic. Reading this, Darwin (1876) wrote in his autobiography that seeing the "struggle for existence" that goes on in nature,

> it at once struck me that under these circumstances favourable variations would tend to be preserved, and unfavourable ones destroyed. The results of this would be the formation of a new species. Here, then I had at last got a theory by which to work. (p. 119–120)

Starting from the idea of struggle that he got from Malthus, Darwin added his knowledge of animal breeding. Thus he wrote to J. D. Hooker in 1844,

> I have read heaps of agricultural and horticultural books, and have never ceased collecting facts. At last gleams of light have come, and I am almost convinced (quite contrary to the opinion I started with) that species are not (it is like confessing a murder) immutable (Young, 1971, p. 453).

In 1858, discovering that both he and A.R. Wallace had drawn on Malthus, Darwin wrote to Wallace:

> You are right, that I came to the conclusion that selection was the principle of change from the study of domesticated productions; and then, reading Malthus, I saw at once how to apply this principle. (Young, 1971, p. 454).

In creating his theory of evolution, Darwin, like all creative scientists, discovered an analogy, a metaphor, that helped him explain how species change. Natural selection, he reasoned, is like the artificial selection that animal breeders had practiced for thousands of years—selectively breeding animals to conserve desired traits. Thus, nature selected in the same fashion that breeders selected. Of course, the metaphor wasn't perfect and contained anomalies. For example, it is one thing to develop a faster horse or a cow that gives more milk; it is quite another to turn either into a new species (an apparent problem that creationists and advocates of Intelligent Design dwell on). Furthermore, the idea of selection implied that someone (e.g., the animal breeder) or something (e.g., a divine or impersonal force) was doing the selecting. Darwin rejected that idea, but many of his contemporaries, including Alfred Russel Wallace, took the metaphor literally to mean that some intelligence with specific purpose was guiding the selective process.

Others, such as Francis Galton and Herbert Spencer took Darwin's metaphor, which he used only to try to explain how species changed, and extended it to the workings of human society. Galton assumed that human beings, like animal breeders, could decide which human traits (e.g., *intelligence*) deserved to be preserved and which traits (e.g., *criminality*) must be eliminated, and breed people accordingly. Others took the metaphor of "survival of the fittest" and extended it to the economic or military realm where they took it to mean that the richest individuals or the militarily-strongest country must be the most fit and, consequently, most deserved to rule.

Thus a scientific theory, like any metaphor, is more than an adherence to the truth of some particular phenomenon the metaphor is supposed to make comprehensible. If Darwin's metaphor was used to explain biological evolution only, it could hardly cause widespread social consternation. But theories or metaphors never remain attached solely to the phenomena they were developed to understand; they migrate, jump, are pushed or pulled to other realms of experience where, often, their implications have dramatic relevance to people's lives.

Thus when Darwin's metaphor, and the concepts of 'selection', 'struggle', and 'fitness' on which it is based, was assumed to be an accurate description of nature and society (as well as simply the evolution of species) the consequences were profound. Viewed through the window of Darwin's metaphor, notions of evil, life, death, marriage, sex, and the desired structure of society, as we shall examine, appeared very different from the way they looked through a biblical frame. This is not to imply that Darwin's theories were directly responsible for the changes in world view that we will be talking about (although see Chapter 9 in this volume). But Darwin's theories could be used to give scientific legitimacy to economic, social, and political arrangements that some people found, for one reason or another, advantageous, while others found them dangerous.

The point of this is to demonstrate that, particularly for religionists, the debate over Darwin and the Bible has to do with more than how life evolved or what the Bible says. It has to do with the sort of assumptions people make or ideas that they hold, about social and moral categories and how they are supposed to live their lives. Darwin's theories, justifiably or not, became a symbol of new ways of thinking about things that many found and still find, threatening or problematical. To illustrate, let's take a brief look at how Darwin's theory became linked to new ways of looking at life, death, evil, marriage, sex, inequality, and morality. Not every person of faith, of course, was equally threatened by these new perspectives; but enough were, and are, concerned to keep the debate over Darwin and the Bible very much alive.

Life and Death

For many Christians and other people of faith, life is sacred: it is God given and should be preserved, regardless of the condition under which a person might live. Death, on the other hand, is unnatural; religious salvation, after all, means everlasting life, a victory over death.

But for many evolutionists, death and destruction, rather than being evil, represented an engine of progress; it was the death and elimination of "less fit" organisms that created space for the "more fit." That's why Darwin's reading of Malthus was critical in the development of his theory. Malthus theorized that death was how populations remained in balance, implying that it would be the poor and weak who would die. Thus Darwin (1859) wrote in the penultimate sentence of *Origin of Species*

> Thus, from the war of nature, from famine and death, the most exalted object which we are capable of conceiving, namely, the production of the higher animals, directly follows. (p. 528).

The Darwinian idea of death as a natural engine of evolutionary progress represented a radical shift from the Christian conception of death as an unnatural, evil foe to be conquered. Death for a Christian, after all, is the price we pay for Adam and Eve's sin. It also furthered the debate about the sanctity of life and debates regarding abortion, infanticide, assisted death, and the like. Richard Weikart (2004) suggests there was no real debate over the sanctity of human life before the advent of Darwinism. Judeo-Christian ethics forbid murder, infanticide, abortion, and suicide. But some evolutionists, suggests Weikart (2004) initiated debate that led to movements for abortion, infanticide, assisted suicide, and even involuntary euthanasia (pp. 145–146). Not all Darwinians or eugenicists went as far as biologist Ernst Haeckel's call for "rational" extermination of the disabled, writes Weikart (2004), but

> it is striking that the vast majority of those who did press for abortion, infanticide, and euthanasia in the late nineteenth and early twentieth century were fervent proponents of a naturalistic Darwinian worldview. Some did not overtly link their views on killing the feeble to Darwinism, though many did. Even those not directly

appealing to Darwinism were usually building their views on eugenics, which was founded on Darwinian principles. (p. 149)

Marriage and Sex

For many Christians, marriage implies a lifetime union ordained by God of one man and one woman. Darwinism saw it very differently. Some Darwinists suggested that sexual activity should advance the positive traits of the coming generation; while monogamy is preferred, polygamy is morally acceptable in cases where a husband with good genes marries an infertile woman; adultery is acceptable when a man with good genes marries a woman with bad genes; homosexuality is neutral (and therefore acceptable) because it is neutral on genetic inheritance.

There was a debate among Darwinists over birth control, however; some saw it as a danger through the elimination of quantity, while others saw it as the way to ensure the reproduction of the most fit, whatever that might mean. "More children from the fit; less from the unfit—that is the chief issue of birth control," said Margaret Sanger (Weikart, 2002, p. 143).[2]

Marriage also needed to be redefined so that only the most biologically fit married; a favorite reform of the early twentieth century was requiring health examinations before marriage to determine the fitness for marriage. Others argued to loosen the marriage bond to honor the normally polygamous male. In the view, of evolutionists, Weikert (2004) writes,

> sexual morality—like all morality—was only valid inasmuch as it was useful to advance the evolutionary process. No matter how much Judeo-Christian baggage some of them still carried about, they had effectively replaced God with evolution as the source and arbiter of sexual morality. (p. 144)

Equality and Inequality

But perhaps Darwin's theory generated the most resistance by challenging Christian notions of charity and equality. Many Christians, particularly those believing in the Social Gospel (see Chapter 7), taught that everyone was equal before God. Inequality was unChristian, and the poor, who suffered in life, would be rewarded in the afterlife. For some Darwinists, on the other hand, inequality and difference were essential; without fit and unfit to choose from, there could be no progress. Ernst Haeckel, argued, for example, that the differences between human societies were greater than that between humans and other animals (Witham, 2002, p. 90). Some social Darwinists even argued against socialism because it reduced necessary inequality. For social Darwinists, individuals had to be given free rein to succeed or fail in order to identify those who were genetically fit and those who were not.

---

[2] Opponents of Planned Parenthood, which Sanger founded, often cite Sanger's views on eugenics and birth control to delegitimize the organization. In fairness to Sanger, however, it must be pointed out that virtually all social workers, indeed progressives, as well as scientists, believed in the worth of eugenics. Since the prevalent scientific view was that undesirable traits (e.g., criminality, idiocy, etc.) were inherited, society could prevent the suffering associated with these traits by discouraging those who possessed them from having children. Others of course went much further than progressives and defined traits such as ethnic or religious group membership as equally undesirable and worthy of elimination.

Alexander Tille, Professor of German Language and Literature at Glasgow University, who considered writing about evolution his true calling, laid out the Darwinian position in 1895 when he wrote:

> From the doctrine that all men are children of God and equal before him, the ideal of humanitarianism and socialism has grown, that all humans have the same right to exist and the same value, and this ideal has greatly influenced behavior in the last two centuries. This idea is irreconcilable with the theory of evolution. It [evolution] recognizes only fit and unfit, healthy and sick, genius and atavist (Weikart, 2004, p. 94).

Another category of the unfit for many Darwinians is the non-European "races." For Christians, all humankind being descended from Adam and Eve were worthy of salvation. Some, of course, had fallen, but could be "saved" by conversion, thus providing employment for the thousands of missionaries dispersed by European nations around the world.

For Darwinists, however, there was doubt over whether "inferior" races could ever be redeemed. Darwinists believed that the power of heredity included not only physical traits, but mental and moral traits as well. Thus, altruism, selfishness, bravery, cowardice, diligence, laziness, and frugality could be removed or introduced into a population only over a long period of time. They thus rejected the influence of education, training, and the environment on shaping or changing human nature (Weikart, 2004, p. 105).

Ethics, Values, and Morality

Finally, there is the question of the source of morality and ethics. For Darwinists, ethics were a product of nature. For Darwin, morality was a biological instinct that contributed to the survival of the species. Survival worked best in groups. Group interaction taught the benefits of cooperating, and human conscience sprang forth. Religion and morality were simply weapons in the struggle for existence. It didn't help the Darwinists' cause when wealthy industrialists, such as Andrew Carnegie said "I got rid of theology and the supernatural but I had found the truth of evolution" (Witham, 2002, p. 245). Biologists have attempted to resolve this dilemma by suggesting that there is a genetic basis for morality (see Chapter 8 in this volume) and even religion itself (Wilson, 1998).

For most people of faith, on the other hand, morality, ethics, and religion are gifts from God. To admit otherwise is to recognize that morality and ethics are relative, and can change according to environmental circumstances. God shaped human nature in the "divine image" and put an eternal soul inside a perishable body. Without God, there could be no absolute meaning.

Each side in the debate, scientists and religionists, face their own dilemma. If theologians accept evolution (or science in general), must they also accept the viewpoint expressed by Stephen Weinberg, the Nobel Prize winner in Physics. Weinberg (1999) stated, "The more the universe seems comprehensible, the more it also seems pointless." Or do they reject that viewpoint and choose a confrontation with science?

Scientists have their own dilemmas, particularly when they seek to arouse public interest in environmental and other social issues. For example, in 1990, American astronomer and astrobiologist Carl Sagan led members of the scientific community in writing a letter to the religious community seeking cooperation between scientists and religious leaders to promote environmental sustainability and stop the spread of global environmental destruction. The letter read, in part

> As scientists, many of us have had profound experiences of awe and reverence before the universe. We understand that what is regarded as sacred is more likely to be treated with care and respect. Our planetary home should be so regarded. Efforts to safeguard and cherish the environment need to be infused with a vision of the sacred. At the same time, a much wider and deeper understanding of science and technology is needed. If we do not understand the problem, it is unlikely we will be able to fix it. Thus, there is a vital role for both religion and science.[3]

The letter led to a meeting in May of 1992 in Washington, D.C., hosted by then U.S. Vice-President Al Gore. The meeting brought together leading scientists, including Sagan, and biologists Stephen Jay Gould and Edward O. Wilson, along with a few religious leaders with the goal of crafting a joint statement in support of environmental sustainability.

As economist Herman Daly who attended the conference, points out, the problem is that scientists were recruiting religious leaders to provide a moral imperative lacking in science, while, at the same time, in other writings, dismissing these religious leaders for their "distorted" view of reality. Stephen Jay Gould (1991) for example, said that

> We cannot win this battle to save species and environments without forging an emotional bond between ourselves and nature as well—for we will not fight to save what we do not love. (p. 14)

But where, asked Daly, does this "love" come from? Where is this spirituality supposed to originate? There is a disconnection in the idea that scientists can use love as a tool for saving what for them is an accidental and pointless universe. In the words of Daly (1996),

> There is something fundamentally silly about biologists teaching on Monday, Wednesday, and Friday that everything, including our sense of value and reason, is a mechanical product only of genetic chance and environmental necessity, with no purpose whatsoever, and then on Tuesday and Thursday trying to convince the public that they should love some accidental piece of this meaningless puzzle enough to fight and sacrifice to save it. (p. 21)

---

[3] This letter is online at http://earthrenewal.org/pen_letter_to_the_religious_community.htm. Retrieved on October 30, 2007.

PART I

Attempting to Resolve the Debate

CHAPTER 1

The Need for Science; the Need for Faith—Separately

by Mark Nathan Cohen

Mark Cohen defines two separate cultures, a culture of science and a culture of faith, each of which provides for essential human needs, but which need to be clearly separated from one another, each defended against unwarranted attacks by the other. The issue isn't faith but attempts to insinuate faith into science, as well as attempts by some scientists to attack faith in unwarranted ways. Cohen defines science in terms of two central properties: (1) an open market of competing ideas ultimately refining our knowledge; and (2) the absolute insistence on "uniformitarian" logic (without magic, miracles, or divine interventions), as the central rule of the competition. He argues that creationists simply miss or ignore these principles and that, whatever they are doing, it isn't science. Pretending that creationism is science undermines the understanding of all science and threatens to undermine its great value. Cohen gives a basic outline of what evolution means and rebuts attempts to undermine the argument or the evidence provided in support. He also argues for the importance of another faith-, emotion-, or social-based paradigm, perhaps the result of evolved human mental abilities, to which students should be exposed—but not in science classes.

The issue isn't primarily about evolution and creation. It is about science as a way of knowing, and rational thought as a way of solving problems. We are threatened with the death of science at the hands of a religious and political agenda that would subordinate thought and human responsibility to faith and obedience to authority—which may in fact well be its goal. We are also threatened with a further dilution of science skills among American students, already falling well behind those of other countries, even though science increasingly is also under attack in many other parts of the world. Yet, many Americans demand teaching creationism as science even though it further erodes all science skills. One cannot defeat evolution in the manner proposed by creationists without destroying science. Evolution is the Trojan horse; science is the citadel to be destroyed.

The issue isn't religious faith, which, as discussed in the following text, is as important as science, but in a context and for purposes that are distinct from science. The problem is creationism foisted off as science often with the use of political force. "Creation Science" is an oxymoron (i.e., the phrase is self-contradictory) because its methods deny the very essence of science and rational problem solving.

I should define what Darwin's theory of evolution, badly understood by many, actually says (in highly simplified form but sufficient for our purposes). First, he argued that all of life is part of an enormous family tree extending over vast periods of time. That is, all living forms are distant cousins. (We are not descended from apes as commonly portrayed, or from any other modern organisms.) Second, he argued that the process involved (family) descent with modification from generation to generation through thousands of generations, the modifications eventually adding up to produce very different organisms. Third, he argued that natural selection, the differential reproductive success of individuals, was the major (but not the only) mechanism of change.

In outline, natural selection is very simple and most of it should be quite obvious—and unthreatening—to most readers. It results from several things that Darwin noticed: fairly obvious things that others could see, but only Darwin assembled into a coherent package. It results also from fairly simple and obvious deductions he made from his observations that other people had not thought about. None of the observations or deductions by themselves are startling.

> **Observation 1:** Animals produce many babies. For example, a mother cat can easily produce eight or more daughters, one mother becoming eight daughters, sixty-four granddaughters, and so on in very few years. Were this to continue, the world would very soon be physically packed with an ever-expanding mass of cats.

> **Observation 2:** The populations of any species aren't expanding at the rate that their reproductive rate would predict. We are not packed with cats.

> **Deduction 1:** By simple subtraction, that means that there must be a very high failure rate in order to account for the difference between birthrates and the actual growth of the species (i.e., most of the kittens apparently do not reproduce successfully).

> **Observation 3:** Animals vary. Just as people all look different and are different in myriad other ways (shape, chemistry, bone structure, etc.), so do members of all other species.

> **Deduction 2** (the first bit that is even mildly controversial and the key one): Some members of a species are more successful *at reproducing* than others, and their success often is not mere luck; it results from design variations that are better adapted for survival and reproduction *in a particular environment*. The measure of relative reproductive success is called "fitness," which is purely and

simply a measure of the relative number of successful offspring—and ultimately the number of descendents—that a parent produces. (That is the *only* thing that "fitness" means in Darwinian terms, no matter how the concept was distorted by later scholars and politicians, as will be discussed.) It is worth noting that natural selection does *not* mean "Nature Red in Tooth and Claw" as it is often envisioned, because the overwhelming majority of reasons for fitness are fairly passive. Natural selection doesn't necessarily even involve direct competition. The features that make an animal fit are situational. Selection refers to success in a particular environment with a particular challenge. The features contributing to an organism's fitness come in an enormous variety, and are situational, depending on the barriers to an organism's success at a particular time. For weeds, fitness can mean chemical resistance to competitors, parasites, pesticides, or poor soil. It can mean resembling a protected plant so it is missed in the weeding process. It can mean having roots too strong to be pulled out, or a stem so weak that it breaks when pulled, leaving the living roots intact. For animals, fitness can involve protective coloration; powerful, accurate senses; good behavioral instincts; proper mating rituals; appropriate care of offspring; disease resistance; and myriad others. For people it may include the cuteness of babies and the god-awful noise they make (carrot and stick) to stimulate and command attention, or a mother's instinctive attention or ability to nurse. A quiet, ugly baby might well not receive adequate care. Fitness, often perceived as a scary concept, is in fact an everyday matter-of-fact quality, visible all around us.

Observation 4: Offspring tend to resemble their parents (in internal as well as visible characteristics), a fact obvious to anyone who looks.

Deduction 3: Therefore, because "fit" parents produce more successful offspring than others, more members of the next generation will resemble those parents and (hopefully) carry on the traits that made the parents successful. The result is that the relative *frequency* of (possibly new mutant) fit and unfit traits in a *population* will change in favor of the fitter designs.
   That's it!

Science

To begin to explain the controversy over the Darwinian model, I need to define science. Science isn't Ph.D.'s; it isn't test tubes, white coats, field or laboratory techniques, or correct procedures. It is not simply biology, chemistry, physics, or anthropology. Science isn't defined simply by testable hypotheses or "scientific method." Confusion over the definition opens doors to creationists and other pseudoscientists who can claim one or more of those attributes. Many creationists and other pseudoscientists have Ph.D.'s in one of the sciences and purport to use scientific methods. But they aren't doing science when they pursue creationist goals.

   Real science is defined by two central properties. If these conditions aren't met, there is no science.

The Scientific Marketplace

First, science is a marketplace of competing ideas about the workings of nature and our potential use of nature's processes. The market is hardly perfect, and some of its imperfections relate to its inevitable ties to values and politics (both internal and external) that can result in distraction, misdirection, and abuse.

Moreover, as many people point out in this volume, science is never as free of values, expectations, politics, and economics as we would like. Social atrocities like eugenics, racism, and ethnic cleansing have often been *defended* on the grounds of misguided and misapplied evolutionary theory. But they are *caused* most often by distorted religious or political beliefs. Remember the Inquisition or any number of recent and historic wars? (The teachings of Jesus are as easily twisted as those of Darwin, and historically, the distortion of Jesus' teachings have been far more numerous and more destructive.) But in the long run, the science market is self-correcting; it comes closer to being a fair market than most we know.

Science resembles the childhood game of "king of the mountain." Scientists compete and try to improve or replace explanations they don't believe. That is our job. We criticize each other's ideas to hone, or perhaps ultimately displace them ("knock them off the mountain") in a constant pursuit of "truth."

Success generally hinges on six main factors:

1. Whether a theory makes sense in light of related knowledge. For example, it fits the known laws and other observations of the scientific field in question rather than defying them.

2. Whether it makes explicit or implicit testable predictions (i.e., predictions about existing conditions not yet fully described, that can be studied and tested, not vague future conditions that obviously cannot be checked) and makes more accurate testable predictions than competing theories. For example, in the fifteenth century, the theory of a round earth predicted (or at least accounted for the fact) that a ship sailing away would not suddenly disappear as if falling off the edge of the earth, but rather would disappear gradually, hull first, mast last, as if it were going over a very large hill, a pattern for which flat earth theory could not account.

3. Whether the theory is "elegant" or "parsimonious" (i.e., whether it can explain all observed phenomena in terms requiring the fewest logical leaps or untested assumptions). For example, if you are late arriving somewhere it is probably because you stopped or your car broke down, not because you were kidnapped by Martians or stopped by an earthquake. It makes no sense to invoke the improbable if a simpler explanation can be found that fits easily into existing experience.

4. Whether successful tests of the theory can be replicated by other scientists. For example, a specific experiment in a laboratory consistently produces similar results when done by other people, or a pattern of fossils is found repeatedly. Recently, two scientists thought that they had demonstrated cold fusion—potentially a source of enormous amounts of energy—in a laboratory. But no one else could make it work, so the claim was dismissed.

5. Whether results can be crosschecked with results derived from other test methods, as when the once controversial results of radiocarbon dating were matched by dates provided by other methods such as calendar dates associated with previously dated objects.

6. Whether apparent exceptions can be explained satisfactorily. (Exceptions *test* or *probe*, not *prove*, the rule. The Latin has been mistranslated.) Eskimos have darker skin than would be predicted by a common theory of skin color related to ultraviolet radiation and the production of vitamin D in the body. This puzzled scientists and challenged the theory, a fact that might have led to the dismissal of the whole theory—until it was realized that the apparent exception could be explained by the fact that the Eskimo's fish-based diet provided rich sources of vitamin D, making their color irrelevant.

A particular theory remains on top of the mountain only as long as a consensus of knowledgeable scientists in related fields concur that, judged by those rules, it is the best explanation of an observation yet devised. What may start as a hypothesis *approaches* the status of truth or fact as it is questioned but withstands all challenges. But, further challenge is never precluded; the game never ends. We never get at final truth or fact. Hopefully, we get closer. Almost everyone on both sides of the evolution–creation debate uses the words *fact* and *truth* inappropriately. What we are taught in classes or textbooks is not the truth; it is whatever idea or theory is accepted (on top of the mountain) at the time the lecture is given or the text written.

I don't think that evolution (as any other complicated idea or conclusion) is fact because, unlike trivia, complicated ideas and concepts never become fact. (It is a fact that I am writing this on a computer, but it is also trivial.) Darwin's model of evolution, originally a mere theory, has been attacked and criticized in the scientific marketplace almost constantly for 150 years. It has been modified many times so that, hopefully, our knowledge gets more and more accurate.

But the core of Darwin's argument, described previously, hasn't yet been refuted, although many people have tried. We are, after all, highly motivated to challenge it because a successful challenge would bring great fame. But, the theory elegantly, parsimoniously explains many observations (such as those of the fossil record and strange features of anatomical design, discussed below) and it has made many successful predictions about what we would and did observe in nature. It is as close to fact or truth as a complex concept ever gets.

But, if you aren't competing in the scientific marketplace and abiding reasonably by its rules and "decisions," you aren't being a scientist. You can disagree with a market decision and challenge it, and you can modify your theory or add new evidence to sway a market decision, but you can't just ignore the decision, or attempt to circumvent it by political rather than scientific means.

Doing science is time and context specific. I am a scientist when I submit my ideas to the market, as I have many times with mixed or sometimes temporary success. But my political opinions are not science nor are the opinions of so-called creation scientists despite our Ph.D.'s, just because we behave as scientists in other contexts. (A trained physicist, even a Nobel Prize winner in physics offering an idea about biology isn't being a scientist unless he or she submits the arguments to his or her adopted part of the market and abides by its decisions.)

It is precisely the reasoning involved in the research, the methods by which the market operates, and the recognition of bad or "pseudo" (fake) science that our students *must* learn if they are to begin to compete again in the world scientific market and if the world as a whole is to proceed to rational solutions to its problems. Teaching bad science simply adds confusion, delaying the development of scientific maturity.

Creationist arguments do enter the market. Some force scientific response, but their efforts to overturn evolution on scientific grounds fail repeatedly and disappear from the market. Attempts to modify creationist ideas to make them more palatable to the scientific market have repeatedly failed. Modern "scientific" creationists want to use appealing slogans ("fairness," "equal time," "balanced presentation") or political force to thrive in a market where they have lost repeatedly. Fairness does not dictate that good and bad meat be sold equally. Creationism being forced politically on the public, as science, is like politicians demanding that meat that has failed inspection be sold anyway to a consumer population not trained to make good choices. In attempts to put creationism in science classes, the inspections are not being done or are being overruled—and the meat is bad and damaging to our scientific health.

Uniformitarianism

The second major principle of all science *by definition* is uniformitarianism. Any attempt at science *must* abide by it. Uniformitarianism means that the world operates by natural laws that, at their core, are unchanging, even if they may be shaped by individual circumstances. It means that there are no miracles in defiance of those laws. If there is a God who created, He doesn't interfere, so we can rely on the laws to be unchanging, hence predictable and usable—or, in the case of prehistory or evolution, reconstructable—if we know enough and think clearly. Laws of gravity, for example, predict that things will fall *down* until they land on an existing surface. So, the lowest layers in a geological or archaeological deposit must be the oldest, newer layers landing progressively on top of them, aiding us in establishing the relative order of fossils embedded in the various layers.

By these same principles, we know that some things are impossible because they defy natural laws. If a great flood once occurred, it could not, by scientific reckoning, have been a miracle. It must have resulted from natural processes we can understand—and it must have left residues that we know accompany flooding. There are many known mechanisms, such as rivers overflowing their banks, that can produce a flood in one location. And they produce the expected residues, generally undifferentiated mud, or gradients of particle size resulting from the fact that heavier particles tend to settle faster in water than fine particles. They do not produce clear layers made of different materials, sometimes with abruptly different particle sizes, sometimes made by different processes as are commonly found in the prehistoric record. We also know from experience that no flood can produce or move the kinds of very large, jagged rocks that we see in the earth's surface. Besides, there are no known natural mechanisms that can produce a flood on the scale of that suggested by a literal interpretation of the Bible. Nor are there visible residues on the necessary scale. Moreover, Noah couldn't possibly have built an ark out of any material known then or now, big enough to house the many thousands of species that are known to exist (not just the few pairs of mammals usually depicted). The assumption that Noah's worldwide flood is a metaphor, or a local flood interpreted as universal, by people who knew very little of the rest of the world, makes much more sense. It is far more in line with what we know about natural laws and how people's minds work, than to assume a flood violating nature's laws or operating by its own magical principles. We know that people tell stories as metaphors and maintain myths. The metaphor theory is therefore the much more elegant and parsimonious theory. One doesn't have to believe that explanation, but doubting it is a matter of faith, not science.

Not only science, but *all* of our knowledge and rational actions depend on the reliability of natural laws. A steel beam of certain strength will support a ceiling of a certain weight; an airplane of correct design will fly. The driving time from New York to Philadelphia (or a walk to class) by a specific route will remain approximately the same. If our expectations fail, there is a natural reason. If an airplane crashes or a ceiling collapses it is because of knowable—and correctable—human or mechanical error, or natural forces such as hurricanes. Known processes do occasionally over-turn earth's layers on a local scale, but the effects are evident. (Imagine a layer cake that falls over and then is fixed up as much as possible, perhaps with new frosting. There may be some remnants of the original layers, upside down, but they don't look like undisturbed layers.) A slow trip from New York to Philadelphia reflects driving habits and road conditions. If we can find no explanation, it means that we don't know enough, not that the outcome was magic. Imagine the impossibility of con-ducting our lives, if we could not rely on nature's rules.

But, our knowledge is imperfect. In keeping with the self-critical, competitive nature of science, we constantly recognize principles that we had not previously understood. We have recently realized that Darwin's theory of evolution as origi-nally formulated is incomplete and in error in some points. It is the job of science to refine and expand our knowledge of natural processes as well as to apply it. Creationists still haven't succeeded in convincingly expanding our knowledge except, perhaps, by promoting negative responses by scientists.

It is very important to understand that these scientific procedures are a spe-cialized realm of human thought that, by agreement, works by these principles. Those rules may be thought by some to be arbitrary, and indeed to an extent they are, but they are the rules by which science has provided enormous benefits to humankind and will continue to do so if it is allowed to remain pure in its special-ized procedures and not denied or badly abused by politics or faith. The rules of sci-ence can in this very narrow sense be compared to the rules of baseball; you can carry your football, but if you do, you are not playing baseball, no matter how good the game of football is. If students are to contribute, they must learn scientific rules and procedures. In other words, maintaining the integrity of science is far more than a philosophical issue: it is an issue of enormous importance to all of us. Teaching pseudoscience—particularly because it provides no grounds for serious analysis—undermines the practical abilities of science.

The evolutionary model is simply a uniformitarian explanation of the origin of varied life-forms. Darwin's idea of a branching tree of living (and fossil) forms is a tree like those we know, involving grandparents, parents, children, grandchildren, siblings, cousins, and so on. But it is an immense family tree developed over myr-iad generations. The mechanisms by which life evolves are the ones we see daily. Children differ from parents and siblings. Differences add up over generations. Each branch of the family undergoes its own pattern of change, so that distant cousins and descendants of one family gradually come to be different from one another. This also provides a uniformitarian, evolutionary explanation of how one species or "kind" can split into two or more. Branches of a family that are prevented from breeding together for long periods of geological time (thousands or millions of generations) will accumulate their own separate sets of modifications to the point where they cannot or will not breed together even if they reencounter each other.

The Evidence for Evolution

Many kinds of evidence exist for evolution. In my mind, two stand out: homology (and its correlate, nonfunctioning or vestigial pieces of anatomy and physiology) and fossils.

Homology

Homologies are similarities in deep structure (not superficial functional similarities) among organisms leading very different lives, which may no longer fit the lives the organisms now lead. The scientific explanation is that such nonsensical deep similarities are family resemblances that have not been lost as different branches of the family have evolved different lifestyles, just as two siblings will retain similar biological structure, even as they take on the trappings of very different lifestyles or professions.

There is enormous deep structural similarity in basic anatomy and physiology of all organisms, no matter what their lifestyles. Many of these similarities make no sense from a design point of view—in fact, many of the similarities are no longer functional (vestiges), are dysfunctional, or are less than perfectly functional in their modern contexts. Organisms commonly have serious design flaws and anachronistic structures (i.e., structures adapted to ancestral lifestyles that no longer work correctly), contradicting the idea of purposeful creation by an intelligent designer. Examples are myriad. There are seven vertebrae of the neck in all mammals whether people, mice, giraffes, or even whales, which have no necks. Five jointed bony fingers are a common design among mammals—even those that have wings or flippers instead of hands or paws. (See Figure 1.1.) Fingernails, claws, horse hooves, and fish scales are all the same material despite their markedly different functions, although it is hard to imagine that the material used is best for all of them. Whales and some snakes have (vestigial) pelvises, although they have no legs. In general, whales and dolphins retain the structure of land mammals from which they are descended, not of fish, although superficially they resemble the latter and lead similar lives.

One human example is the spine. Four-legged animals commonly have an arched backbone and the vertical suspension of organs from it that serve them well. But, the structure became dysfunctional when people began to walk upright. The arch had to be "straightened" (actually bent again) by adding the backward (lumbar) curve. But the vertebrae of our lower back are not perfectly designed for the new, reverse curve, causing lower-back problems such as the pinching of intervertebral disks. Internal organs are not supported against gravity because they are still attached (but now horizontally) to the spine. They sag in the body cavity producing abdominal pressure. If we are designed in God's image, then He has a terrible lower back and is hernia prone. God must also have high blood pressure and diabetes. His system, like ours, is not designed to function in the modern environment.

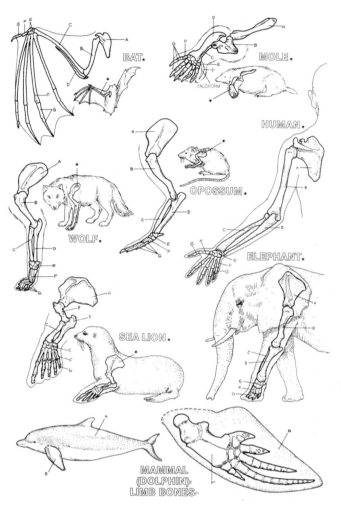

Figure 1.1
The homology of bones in mammalian toes and fingers. Note the bones in the dolphin and bat that have no distinct toes. Courtesy of *The Human Evolution Coloring Book*, by Adrienne Zihlman

Fossils

Evidence also comes from fossils that can be dated to various ages by radioactive techniques and the vertical sequence of layers of the earth. Fossils are extremely rare fragments of prehistoric organisms that give us glimpses of gradual changes in which animals with family resemblances can often be traced back through graded changes to common ancestral organisms. The more fossils we find, the more the evolutionary branches are filled. (See the following discussion.)

Part of the evidence for evolution is that an enormous number of species (in fact, the great majority) are now extinct and clearly met their demise at very different times and are found in different layers of the earth. Either God or evolutionary processes created far more losers than winners, a pattern more compatible with a trial-and-error evolutionary process than with an intelligent designer. If God had designed organisms, he presumably wouldn't have wasted time on so many losers or designed the survivors so badly. On the other hand, known genetic or evolutionary processes are quite likely to produce imperfect or anachronistic designs because new variations appear by chance, and natural selection can choose only the best *available* design which is not necessarily an optimal one.

Creationist Responses

Creationism comes in a variety of forms (summarized in Alters & Alters, 2001, and by Branch, Chapter 10 in this volume) that make various claims about the accuracy and reliability of biblical teachings. I will focus on two forms: young-earth creationism and intelligent design.

Young-earth creationism (YEC), assumes the Bible should be taken literally. Its tenets are that the biblical story of creation is true; that the earth is very young; that the kinds of animals on earth were miraculously and separately created more or less in modern form; and that two kinds of organisms don't come from one. YEC attempts to pass itself off as science, yet its "research" aims at proving foregone biblical conclusions.

Intelligent design (ID) proponents eschew religion and argue that scientists themselves will ultimately arrive at the conclusion that evolution is not an adequate explanation of life-forms. They argue, for example, that some biological organs are too complex to have evolved without a thoughtful divine designer. (See, e.g. Johnson 1993, 1997, this volume, Chapter 5). But in doing so, they are still appealing to an unnatural force outside the realm of scientific inquiry. Both YEC and ID advocates demand miracles, defying uniformitarianism. Neither is susceptible to scientific procedures. So, by definition, they cannot be science. To force them into science classes is to perpetrate a fraud.

Creationist attacks on evidence supporting evolution, as judged by their debating techniques, combine nitpicking; peculiar definitions of evolution that miss the point; cherry-picking (i.e., pulling particular bits out of context); plays on words; quotations out of context; distortion; misunderstanding or (deliberate?) misrepresentation of the principles and evidence; or downright deception. (See various websites from the Institute for Creation Research, the Discovery Institute, Answers in Genesis, Focus on the Family, and a variety of published works by authors such as D. Morris, H. Morris, and D. T. Gish, to list only a few. For a rebuttal see Berra, 1990; Alters & Alters, 2001.) Creationists have attempted to present carefully selected words of a staunch supporter of evolution, Stephen J. Gould, as a defense of their position. Gould is responsible for some modifications of Darwin's theory related to the significance of natural selection and the pace of the process (Eldredge & Gould, 1972), and may therefore appear critical of Darwin. But he has never denied the reality of evolution itself.

Creationists (e.g., Gish, 1995; various organizations' websites) argue that evolutionary lines cannot be traced because there are no fossils "intermediate" in structure between living organisms (i.e., no "missing links"). (In fact, because evolution occurs from generation to generation, each generation is a link. There is no one missing link.) There are myriad well-documented examples of such intermediate fossil sequences, including the evolution of the horse from a small, five-toed animal to a very large one with a single hoof (and two vestigial "toes" further up its leg); evidence that rhinos, tapirs, and horses are descended from a common ancestor; and the emergence of amphibians from fish, reptiles from amphibians, birds and mammals from reptiles, and whales from land mammals. (See, e.g., Hunt 1994–1997; Nedin, 1996.) We even have a rather well-defined sequence of forms intermediate between modern human beings and more apelike ancestors that can be viewed in any recent text in human evolution and that tell the same broadly consistent story. (See Figures 1.2 and 1.3.) We know, for example, the rough order in which special human features appeared in our fossil line. There are human ancestors whose anatomy suggests that they could both walk upright and swing from trees. Walking upright, the altered spine, the evolution of feet from the rear "hands" of other primates, appearance of humanlike teeth (e.g., the loss of fangs) all preceded the use of tools, and all preceded most of the incremental evolution of the large brain.

Of course there are gaps, given the enormous odds against finding fossils. Far less than one in many million organisms produces a fossil. Far fewer are recovered. We can estimate that about five million years separates our evolutionary line from that of chimps (determined both from fossil dating and from estimates of genetic divergence cross-checking each other). If we allow twenty to twenty-five years per generation, there must have been 200,000 to 250,000 generations from the emergence of our line to the time (about 10,000–12,000 years ago and thereafter) when farming replaced hunting and gathering as the primary human economy. If, very conservatively estimated and on average, each generation of the protohuman population numbered from say 10,000 to 10,000,000 individuals including cousins (certainly at the lower end of that range in the early groups, the higher estimate, carefully derived for the later groups just before farming began), we are talking about perhaps 25 billion organisms or more in our own specific branch of the tree. Of these we have a few hundred fossils, at best. This means that perhaps one fossil has been found per 50 million or more of our near ancestors that died. The estimates are crude, but the point is clear. (Moreover, human fossils tend to be in recent, well-preserved strata, relatively dense in fossil content, and they are subject to very intense search, so the frequency with which *human* fossils are found may significantly overestimate the likelihood of finding fossils of most other organisms.)

We also know, as Eldredge and Gould (1972) have pointed out, that a great deal of evolution takes place in small local populations that evolve relatively rapidly in short bursts ("punctuated equilibrium") so that transitional forms may be particularly hard to find. Animals migrating out from a tiny center may appear as brand-new forms in their new homes (where in consequence there might appear to be no intermediate forms locally). The scarcity, not absence, of intermediate forms recovered can be explained parsimoniously within the evolutionary model.

Creationists note that many fossils have been misidentified and others have been frauds, implying that a tiny sample of known fossils reflect the quality of the entire collection—as if one hypocritical Christian taints Christianity itself. The Piltdown fossil *was* a fraud. The so-called Nebraska Man *was* a bad mistake, but mistakes and frauds are very few—and evolutionary scientists corrected the mistakes and unmasked the frauds themselves, long before creationists pointed them out.

Creationists also note that a fossil once considered an ancestor may no longer be considered one, implying that previous mistakes prove the whole thing false. But science self-corrects as new evidence comes to light.

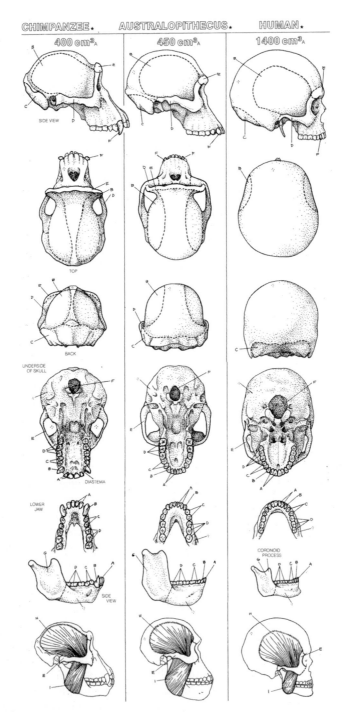

Figure 1.2

A comparison of one intermediate from—an Australopithecine—to a chimp skull (left) and a human skull (right.)

Courtesy of *The Human Evolution Coloring Book* by Adrienne Zihlman

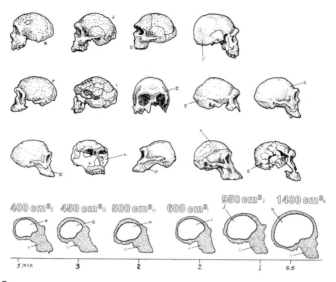

Figure 1.3

A composite of stages in the development of the human cranium and brain in rough stratigraphic sequence.
Courtesy of The Human Evolution Coloring Book by Adrienne Zihlman

The evolutionary family tree, like any family tree, involves diverging families with siblings and cousins, not straight lines like the biblical "begats." Imagine yourself in a room full of your ancestors, never photographed or painted; not wearing any clothes or talking. Most are only skeletons. The vast majority of the ancestors aren't there because they haven't been located. You must distinguish your great-great-great-(etc.) grandfather from his siblings and cousins. But for every ancestor there are myriad cousins. What is the likelihood of choosing accurately the first time? What is the likelihood that scientists might have to change their thoughts about possibly ancestral fossils in the same way?

Creationists often argue that "survival of the fittest" (a phrase mistakenly attributed to Darwin) is a tautology (success of the successful or the survival of the surviving) and therefore meaningless. But, by defining fitness as *differential reproductive success* (i.e., the relative number of descendants an organism has) and by recognizing that fitness consists of many qualities relative to specific environments, Darwin produced a model that has had enormous, successful explanatory power.

Creationists claim that natural principles such as the laws of thermodynamics prevent evolution, an outrageous "misunderstanding" by supposed scientists. Supposedly thermodynamic laws preclude evolution because entropy (crudely, the loss of useful energy) does not permit things to get more complex, as evolution often (but not always) implies. But, if this were true, neither a child nor a tree could grow from a seed nor a building be built, because each is an example of complexity produced from simplicity. The creationist argument might be valid in a world with no outside source of energy to counteract entropy. But on earth, of course, the sun constantly provides new energy, powering the emergence of complexity despite the effects of entropy.

Another creationist argument is that because helium, lighter than air, is lost quickly from the earth's atmosphere, yet some remains, the earth must be very young. But that ignores the fact that helium is constantly being produced on earth by radioactive decay of uranium, replenishing the supply, and that much is trapped underground.

Creationists argue that techniques such as carbon (C-14) dating involve untested assumptions and therefore are on very shaky ground. But they ignore the fact, already suggested, that the results are validated by replication and by cross-checking. In fact, C-14 dates are constantly being cross-checked against each other and against dates from other sources such as dates known from historical sources or tree-ring counts.

A particularly striking example came from attempts to date the Shroud of Turin, supposedly the burial shroud of Christ, which appeared in medieval times and came to be housed in the cathedral at Turin. The obvious question: Was the shroud 2,000 years (hence, potentially that of Christ) or only 500–700 years old? To decide this question, tiny fragments of the shroud were sent for C-14 dating to three labs (replication). Each lab was also sent pieces of linen of known historic dates (cross-checking). The known dates were not given to the research teams (blind-testing). The labs did not know which piece of cloth was presumed to be the shroud because they were not identified. Without communicating, the three labs produced dates that all agreed with one another and with the known historical dates of each piece. All also agreed on the date of the shroud, all concluding that it was medieval.

Creationists argue that we have never actually seen one species become two. But, sexual organisms reproduce slowly, relative to the time we have been watching. Consider the dilemma of chihuahuas and great danes that have evolved separately over a period of a few thousand years from a wolflike ancestor. If they were put into contact at the right time, the scent signals would be correct, so that the animals might be aroused. But they can't do anything about it. They are now perpetually isolated by size and no longer affect each other's genetic patterns. They are effectively two species of animal. The evolution of one will no longer affect the other so they will gradually accumulate different groups of traits. This example, of course, comes in part from human selective breeding, but it also shows the mechanisms of speciation in action.

Intelligent design is not necessary to explain complex organisms. We can actually see the development of complex biological organs by looking at our cousins and fossils. Both the very complex human hand and the human eye are demonstrably the product of incremental changes. The hand, despite its flexibility and complexity, is foreshadowed by the hand of other members of our branch of our family tree—the primates—with five flexible fingers, opposable thumbs, the ability to grip (but not with the precision that human hands can), fingernails, palms, and fingerprints. They are foreshadowed in our larger family—the mammals—by "paws," usually with five-jointed toes with claws.

Our binocular eyes that have depth perception and see color are shared with the rest of our primate family, but are foreshadowed by nonbinocular "color-blind" eyes of most mammals and by light and image sensors of varying quality in our wider family. Our brains, probably the ultimate example of human complexity, are demonstrably built in stages, anatomically, out of the brains of less-intelligent, prehistoric animals. Their anatomy shows clear layering with new structures built on top of old ones visible in the brains of other animals. Behaviors associated with the different parts of the brain can be traced in graded forms through our wider family, with a gradual increase in behavior flexibility and learning.

We also know that many structures serve more than one purpose. For example, feathers serve both as insulation and as flying mechanisms. Initially they may have served only for insulation, but were then gradually perfected for gliding, then flight. Adaptive evolution does not need to be dismissed just because a structure appears to have no obvious advantage for one particular function until it is perfected.

In addition, computer simulations (computer analogues of evolutionary processes) have now shown in repeated experiments that complex designs can arise from simpler designs by purely random processes as implied in evolutionary theory, without the intervention of a designer (Ofria, & Collier, Adami, 2000).

The Attraction of Creationist Arguments

Why is creationism given so much weight and evolution on such fragile political ground when evolution is so soundly based in science and the creationist challenges are so weak?

Part of the problem is the way science presents itself as an exclusive and superior club, which tends to exclude most other people, thereby offending them. Part of the problem is that the core meanings of evolution have been distorted into dangerous political doctrines. It has been used by some *social* scientists and politicians ("social Darwinism") to justify political domination of others, sterilization of the "unfit," or even genocide. But among other misuses of Darwinian selection inherent in such crimes, Darwinian fitness has nothing to do with domination or "quality" as defined by ruling classes (as described previously).

A larger problem isn't fear of evolution, but of uniformitarianism itself. Faith won't solve environmental problems despite the attitude of our government, but uniformitarian reasoning can help. Faith doesn't create cures or vaccines for new diseases. These come through uniformitarian understanding of biology and chemistry. Scientists rely, among other things, on understanding evolutionary principles used to track and predict the evolution of disease organisms in order to design vaccines and remedies.

But uniformitarian reasoning is not clearly understood, or at least consciously recognized by most people outside the scientific community. And it is so taken for granted by scientists that they usually don't teach or discuss it explicitly.

Such reasoning undermines absolute faith in the literal and authoritarian interpretation of the Bible that provides comfort by simplifying decisions. Uniformitarianism means that we are not special, but part of, and subject to, natural laws and processes. Uniformitarian reasoning means that there are no guarantees. God does not intervene. (Being above nature and conquering it are Judeo-Christian ideas. Most world cultures perceive themselves, more accurately, as integral parts of nature and subject to its rules.) In our culture, not being special damages self-esteem both because of the Judeo-Christian heritage and because of our enormous sense of our own superiority.

Faith in God and in country go hand in hand, particularly when leaders wrap themselves simultaneously in flag and Bible. Faith in God is often a kind of patriotism; denying it is a form of treason, particularly at times when other forms of patriotism are threatened. In the United States we are in such times. The resurgence of public displays of religious faith is no coincidence.

Uniformitarian thinking takes effort, taking time to know natural principles and struggling to understand and use them. It is easier to follow authorities that preach faith. Politicians and religious leaders don't want thinking to occur because it produces skepticism of the leaders and of the status quo. The combination of a populace too lazy for uniformitarian thought and eager for simple guidance, and leaders eager to exploit their laziness by creating faith-based dependence is dangerous indeed. President George W. Bush doesn't believe in evolution and advocates teaching creation. The far bigger problem is that he doesn't believe in uniformitarian science at all and is trying fairly successfully to exclude it from decision making. His position not only excuses the country from uniformitarian problem solving; it also excuses individual people.

Scientists face a struggle and can't give an inch. Science does not kowtow to public opinion or political expediency, nor does it bow to democracy or "fairness," no matter how "popular" creationist ideas are and no matter how desirable those values may be in other contexts. Even the Supreme Court can't mandate the teaching of creationism or permit a majority to decide, any more than it can mandate the teaching of bad mathematics. "Free speech," "balanced treatment," and "academic freedom" (to the degree implied) don't apply in classrooms. Accepting privileged, licensed positions as teachers or professors means that individuals sacrifice some freedoms matching the responsibilities of the position. I am free to "hit on" many men and women. But, as a professor, I renounce my freedom to make advances toward my students. Professors and teachers renounce their right to teach incompetently or in defiance of the subject matter, no matter what their personal beliefs. They can no more teach their own version of pseudoscience in science classes than they can teach their own versions of math or grammar. There is no such thing as balanced treatment or equal time in science classes when so many possible explanations of the development of life have been proclaimed around the world, not just two, or when the balance involves positions that are incompetent or outside the definition of the subject (science) being discussed. There can be no opening the doors to Trojan horses. Far too much is at stake.

But What of Human Behavior?

The real battle refers not to the design of the human body or its origin, but to the origins, design, and function of the human mind and the images and behaviors it creates. What actually happened in the emergence of human mind (and soul?) that distinguishes us from all other animals is not clear to anyone whether he or she comes from a background in science or in faith; and it is in this arena where the two worlds most collide. Those of faith propose a clear and simple solution to the origin as God's handiwork, of course, but without much thought about the actual content, abilities, or properties of the human mind.

Modern sociobiologists and evolutionary psychologists (e.g., Dawkins, 1976; Wilson, 1975) seem to represent a faith of their own that attacks other kinds of faith in an overly aggressive manner, often laying claim to explaining everything about people and going out of its way to debunk God and religion. They add to the confusion, without apparently having a sense of what actually evolved in human behavior any more sophisticated than that of other faiths. Their aggressiveness also probably accounts for a good deal of the backlash of those of other faiths against science.

Sociobiologists argue that all of human behavior and the function of the human mind, including the emotions and altruism that most of us value, are directed at the fitness of our genes. All actions, they argue, even the apparently altruistic ones, are essentially selfish in the sense of promoting one's own fitness. If our bodies have been honed by evolution for reproductive success, they ask, doesn't it make sense that our behavior has also been molded by evolution for the same purpose? (By putting explanations of behavior back into the realm of genetic determinism, sociobiology appears to reopen doors to social and political abuses, such as a resurgence of social Darwinism. A modern example is the use of IQ studies in which the purported natural, genetic superiority of the powerful [Herrnstein & Murray, 1994] justifies an exploitative status quo.) Scientists need to be a lot more careful and precise about their claims, and more aware of how their claims sound to others. They must also be far more careful to separate the realities of biology and biological evolution from sociological interpretations.

Among many problems, sociobiologists ignore some obvious facets of human thought and emotion, whether derived through evolution (as I believe) or through inspiration. The key point is that even if behaviors ultimately may be conditioned by genes in the largest sense, they are actually motivated and molded by more proximate mechanisms including our own feelings and senses, just as we jerk our hands away from a fire not on the theoretical grounds that it may do us damage, but because it *hurts*. The proximate mechanisms can actually control behavior in ways that operate *against* genetic demands because they are the emotional guidelines to which we respond. We feel the emotions; we don't perceive the underlying genetic motivation. An excellent example is adoption. Apparently, the need for affect and the urge to protect children (presumably evolved in a general way to increase fitness by maximizing the chances that one's offspring survive) can be displaced onto children that are not kin and have no relation to biological fitness, because they feel good. As Goldschmidt (2005) has put it, "affect trumps the selfish gene."

Goldschmidt (2005) argues that the need for the emotional bonds (or "affect," as in the word *affection*) generated in childhood and then expanded to include the whole of one's society are the keys to human behaviors within the broad outlines of fitness requirements.

The power of his point becomes obvious when we consider the evolved mental powers that characterize people (although some appear in rudimentary form in other apes).

1. Fitness is always served by physical, chemical, and behavioral *flexibility*. One of the greatest advantages of the human species is the flexibility of our behavior, resulting from the gradual evolution of unprogrammed but flexible "computer" brains that require programming (i.e., learning) out of inflexible, preprogrammed "calculator" brains that have a very limited repertoire of responses. All mammals have computer brains to some degree, but the computer becomes far more powerful

in the human branch. Learning, play-based or on-the-job training, replaces prepro-gramming as a basis for behavior, requiring increased involvement in family and community. So, within the general constraints of fitness, human beings have enor-mous freedom to explore alternative behaviors.

2. Human beings carry (and communicate) mental images or "symbols" of things in our heads, that we can use even if the things they represent are not actually present (yesterday, tomorrow, out of sight) and may, in fact, exist only in the abstract, like "love" or "honor"—categories that we can communicate about although we can never touch, or see, or even define.

We can mix the symbols in our heads to solve problems mentally or to think about problems in the past or future, or simply out of sight. For example, we *plan* an action by combining symbols rather than relying on physical trial and error. This is probably the essence of what we call "thinking."

3. Human beings have a symbol (i.e., mental image) of *self*, and like other sym-bols we can manipulate it, imagining ourselves in different times or places or mixed with other things or other people. It may be that the ability to imagine our-selves separated from the actual current state of our own bodies is the essence of our perception of a "soul" or what is often translated as one's "shade" (shadow) in other cultures. We can *imagine* alternative behaviors. (During class, many of my stu-dents are mentally having, recalling, or expecting sex or sunning in Florida.)

4. Yet they *are* in class. Imaginative freedom must be curtailed to achieve goals and to make one's behavior reasonably predictable and comprehensible to other peo-ple. Restricting operational responses to fantasies means establishing social rules, sanctions, socialization (learning), and reinforcement. But they also require certain qualities in the individual involving emotional ties to others and what might be called "conscience," itself an emotional response to the reactions of others, to their antici-pated reactions, or to the past reactions of others that we have internalized.

5. Aware of alternatives to the immediate situation, people have a universal need for explanations of "why" things are as they are. "Why" often may not (ever?) have a scientific answer. The answers come from moral, psychological, or social understandings and values, or some would say, divine inspiration, that differ markedly between groups but are almost always infused with belief in the super-natural that acts as a reservoir of answers for the unexplained. Supernatural expla-nations (i.e., faith) always answer "why" and reaffirm the need for appropriate behavior, even if they don't do so in rational or scientific terms. The specific expla-nation of "why" has to be shared in any group, but it doesn't have to be right, and in fact it differs markedly in varied groups.

6. There are many other things essential to human life in groups including arbitrary definitions of proper motivation, behavior, and even perception. (For a more complete definition and a fuller discussion of these needs and how they are defined see Cohen, 1998.) The form of these things *cannot be* genetic. They vary too much and change too fast. We know from very broad experience that a child of any normal genetic pattern will acquire the behavior, thought patterns, and language of any society in which it is reared. In short, they are clearly learned from the accumu-lated knowledge ("culture") of the group.

It is at this level that the tension between *sociocultural* (not biological or scien-tific) explanations and faith-based explanations of variations in behavior becomes critical. Even if one believes that the abilities are evolved and the solutions cultural and subject to rational analysis, there is clearly a great deal of latitude in trying to explain them. Clearly, in the minds of the great majority of human beings in our own society and around the world, these choices are grounded in faith, in a super-natural, and in beliefs, values, and emotions that transcend science and even transcend rational human understanding. Faith (whether or not in God) is essential to all human beings. As such, it is essential that we understand it. Whether or not behavioral scientists believe that faith actually originates with God, it is clear that this major aspect of human need, thought, and behavior deserves study on its own terms. These concerns are discussed in several chapters of this book, so I will not elaborate further. But it is clear that these patterns of thought and behavior not explained by science are in their own way as important as science and must be addressed as such, while the separateness of scientific and faith- or culture-based explanations is maintained. The two sets of explanation can, in fact must, be made to interact in a positive way.

Science sometimes appears to interfere with or even preclude discussion of social- or faith-determined models, just as religious faith sometimes appears to pre-clude discussions of science. By taking the stance they have, some scientists seem to deny the validity of social- or faith-based behavior choices—even though (almost?) all scientists actually straddle the two camps. In practice, we are, for the most part, both scientists and moral, emotional members of our group. If scientists were willing explicitly to accept and recognize the importance of another paradigm—another means (perhaps more emotional or faith based) to understand our world and our own thoughts and actions—they might be able to separate the two. And by paying respect to the "other" set of explanations, they might be more successful in insisting that science proceed by its own rules.

We must teach the importance of two separate cultures that complement each other rather than competing. We must allow and encourage experts in those areas to teach them in accordance with the principles of each. But that is a problem for general education, not science classes. We must continue to insist on the sanctity of the scientific culture and the rules by which it operates.

Creationism: A Distinctly American Violation of NOMA*

by Stephen Jay Gould

Because of the popularity of his articles on science that appeared in the magazine Natural History, *paleontologist Stephen Jay Gould often found himself in the forefront of the debate over Darwin and the Bible. He was often asked to testify at major court battles over the teaching of evolution and creationism, and devoted a number of his columns, along with a book, to the issue. In his book* Rock of Ages: Science and Religion in the Fullness of Life *(1999), Gould argues that both religion and science have their distinctive place, but that they each must apply what he calls the principle of noninterference, or, as he puts it Non-Overlapping Magisteria, or NOMA for short. Magisterium is a term commonly used in theology that Gould (1999, p. 5) applies to mean "a domain where one form of teaching holds the appropriate tools for meaningful discourse and resolution." Gould proposes that the magisterium of religion and the magisterium of science do not overlap and that each addresses issues unique to it. As he puts it, "science studies how the heavens go, religion how to go to heaven" (1999, p. 6). When scientists start drawing conclusions about religion from their work, or religionists start applying their body of knowledge to the natural world, it represents a violation of NOMA. In the following selection from* Rock of Ages, *Gould argues that the debate is not between science and religion. A great majority of scientists and religionists support NOMA, but a small minority have tried to impose their beliefs on others.*

* Reprinted with permission from *Rock of Ages: Science and Religion in the Fullness of Life* (pp. 125–150), by Stephen Jay Gould, 1999, New York: Ballantine.

The myth of Columbus and the flat earth supports NOMA by the negative strategy of showing how the opposite model of warfare between science and religion often invents battles that never occurred, but arise only as forced inferences from the fictional model. Christian scholars never proclaimed a flat earth against the findings of science and the knowledge of antiquity, and Columbus fought no battles with ecclesiastical authorities over this nonissue. Modern creationism, alas, has provoked a real battle, thus supporting NOMA, with a positive example of the principle that all apparent struggles between science, and religion really arise from violations of NOMA, when a small group allied to one magisterium tries to impose its irrelevant and illegitimate will upon the other's domain. Such genuine historical battles, therefore, do not pit science against religion, and can only represent a power play by zealots formally allied to one side, and trying to impose their idiosyncratic and decidedly minority views upon the magisterium of the other side.

The saga of attempts by creationists to ban the teaching of evolution, or to force their own fundamentalist version of life's history into science curricula of public schools, represents one of the most interesting, distinctive, and persistent episodes in the cultural history of twentieth-century America. The story features a tempestuous beginning, starring two of the great characters of the 1920s, and also a gratifying end in the favorable Supreme Court decision of 1987. The larger struggle, however, has not terminated, but only shifted ground—as creationist zealots find other ways to impose their will and nonsense, now that the Court's defense of the First Amendment precludes their old strategy of enforcing creationism by state legislation!

Please note that I am discussing only a particular historical episode—fundamentalist attempts to impose creationism on public school curricula by legislative fiat—and not all nuances of argument included under the ambiguous term "creationism." Some personal versions of creation fall entirely within the spirit of

Stephen Jay Gould often found himself in the forefront of the debate over Darwin and the Bible.

NOMA [*Non-Overlapping Magisteria*] and bear no relationship to this story—the belief, for example, that God works through laws of evolution over the long time scale determined by geology, and that this style of superintendence may be regarded as a mode of creation.

As a matter of fact, not a necessity of logic, the activists of the creationist movement against the teaching of evolution have been young-earth fundamentalists who believe that the Bible must be literally true, that the earth cannot be more than ten thousand years old, and that God created all species, separately and *ex nihilo*, in six days of twenty-four hours. These people then display a form of ultimate hubris (or maybe just simple ignorance) in equating these marginal and long-discredited factual claims with the entire domain of "religion." I have no quarrel with fundamentalists who believe in teaching their doctrine in homes and churches, and not by forced imposition upon public schools. I am quite sure that they are wrong about the age of the earth and the history of life, and I will be happy to remonstrate with any advocate who maintains an open mind on these questions (not a common commodity within the movement). Lord knows, we have the right to be wrong, even to be stupid, in a democracy! Thus, I have no problem with the largest and most potentially influential of all creationist groups in America, the Jehovah's Witnesses, for they do not try to impose their theological beliefs upon public school science curricula, and they agree with my view that churches and homes are the proper venue for teaching such private and partisan doctrines. In other words, our struggle with creationism is political and specific, not religious at all, and not even intellectual in any genuine sense. (Sorry to be harsh, but young-earth creationism offers nothing of intellectual merit that I have ever been able to discern but just a hodgepodge of claims properly judged within the magisterium of science, and conclusively disproved more than a century ago.) Before presenting a capsule history, I would summarize the peculiarities of our contemporary struggle with creationism in two propositions:

1. The forceful and persistent attempt by young-earth creationists to insinuate their partisan and minority theological dogma into the science curricula of American public schools cannot be read, in any legitimate way, as an episode in any supposedly general warfare between science and religion. If the issue must be dichotomized at all, the two sides might be characterized as supporters versus opponents of NOMA; as defenders of the First Amendment for separation of church and state versus theocrats who would incorporate their certainties as official state policy; or, most generally, as defenders of free inquiry and the right of teachers to present their best understanding of subjects in the light of their professional training versus the setting of curricula by local sensibilities or beliefs (or just by those who make the most noise or gain transitory power), whatever the state of natural knowledge, or the expertise of teachers.

In any case, however we choose to parse this controversy, the two sides cannot be labeled as science and religion on the most basic criterion of empirical evidence. For the great majority of professional clergy and religious scholars stand on the same side with the great majority of scientists—as defenders of NOMA and the First Amendment, and against the imposition of any specific theological doctrine, especially such a partisan and minority view, upon the science curricula of public schools. For example, the long list of official plaintiffs who successfully challenged the Arkansas creationism statute in 1981 included some scientists and educators, but even more ordained clergy of all major faiths, and scholars of religion.

2. This controversy is as locally and distinctively American as apple pie and Uncle Sam. No other Western nation faces such an incubus as a serious political movement (rather than a few powerless cranks at the fringes). The movement to impose creationism upon public school science curricula arises from a set of distinctively American contrasts, or generalities expressed in a peculiarly American context: North versus South, urban versus rural, rich versus poor, local or state control versus federal standards. Moreover, young-earth creationism can be favored only by so-called fundamentalists who accept the Bible as literally true in every word—a marginal belief among all major Western religions these days, and a doctrine only well developed within the distinctively American context of Protestant church pluralism. Such a fundamentalist perspective would make no sense in any predominantly Catholic nation, where no tradition for reading the Bible literally (or much at all, for that matter) has ever existed. Jewish traditions, even among the orthodox, may revere the Torah as the absolutely accurate word of God, where neither one jot nor tittle of text can ever be altered, but few scholars would ever think of interpreting this unchangeable text literally.[1]

3. Protestantism has always stressed personal Bible study, and justification by faith, rather than through saints or the interpretations of priests—and literalism becomes conceivable under these practices. But, again, the vast majority of modern Protestants would not choose to read their sacred texts in such a dogmatic and uncompromising manner—particularly in European nations with a limited diversity of mainly liberal styles.

But American Protestantism has diversified into a uniquely rich range of sects, spanning the full gamut of conceivable forms of worship and belief. The vast majority, of course, pursue the same allegorical and spiritual style of reading as their Catholic and Jewish neighbors, but a few groups—mostly Southern, rural, and poor, to cite the distinctive dichotomies mentioned above—have dug in against all "modernism" with a literalist reading not subject to change, or even argument:

"Gimme that old-time religion. It was good enough for grandpa, and it's good enough for me." (Through personal ignorance, I am not considering here the

---

[1] I am no biblical expert or exegete, and cannot engage this issue in any serious manner. But I must say that I simply don't understand what reading the Bible "literally" can mean, since the text, cobbled together from so many sources, contains frequent and inevitable contradictions. These variant readings pose no problem to the vast majority of religious people who view the Bible as an inspired document full of moral truth, and not as an accurate chronicle of human history or a perfect account of nature's factuality. For the most obvious example, how can "literalists" reconcile the plainly different creation stories of Genesis I and II, which, according to all biblical scholars I have ever consulted, clearly derive from different sources. In the more familiar Genesis I, God creates sequentially in six days, moving from light to the division of waters and firmament, to land and plants, to the sun and moon, and finally to animal life of increasing complexity. On the sixth day he creates human beings, both male and female together: "So God created man in his own image, in the image of God created he him; male and female created he them." In Genesis II, God creates the earth and heavens and then makes a man "of the dust of the ground." He then creates plants and animals, bringing all the beasts to Adam and granting his first man naming rights. But Adam is lonely, so God creates a female companion from one of his ribs: "And the Lord God caused a deep sleep to fall upon Adam, and he slept; and he took one of his ribs, and closed up the flesh thereof; and the rib, which the Lord God had taken from man, made he the woman, and brought her unto the man. And Adam said, This is now bone of my bones, and flesh of my flesh: she shall be called Woman." Our traditional reading conflates these two stories, taking the basic sequence, with humans last, from Genesis I, but borrowing the rib scenario for the subsequent creation of Eve from Genesis II. I often surprise people by pointing out this contradiction and conflation (for even highly devout people don't always study the Bible much these days). They think that I must be nuts, or hallucinating, so I just tell them to check it out (at least most homes still have the basic data, no matter how otherwise bookless!)—and they get mighty surprised. Always be wary of what you think you know best.

traditions of Islam and non-Western religions.) To cite just one example of fundamentalism's distinctly American base, and of the puzzlement that creationism evokes in the rest of the religious world, I once stayed at the Casa del Clerico in Rome, a hotel maintained by the Vatican, mostly for itinerant priests. One day in the lunchroom, a group of French and Italian Jesuits called me over. They belonged to a group of practicing scientists, visiting Rome for a convention on science and the Church. They had been reading about the growth of "scientific creationism" in America, and were deeply confused. They thought that evolution had been adequately proven, and certainly posed no challenge to religion in any case (both by their own reasoning and by papal pronouncement). So what, they asked, was going on chez moi?

Had good scientific arguments for young-earth creationism really been developed, and by lay fundamentalists rather than professional scientists? A wonderful polyglot of conversation ensued for the next half hour in all three languages. I told them that no new (or any) good arguments existed, and that the issues were both entirely political and uniquely American. They left satisfied, and perhaps with a better sense of the conundrum that America represents to the rest of the world.

Trouble in Our Own House: A Brief Legal Survey from Scopes to Scalia

The fundamentalist movement may be as old as America, and its opposition to teaching evolution must be as old as Darwin. But this marginal, politically disenfranchised, and largely regional movement could muster no clout to press a legislative agenda until one of the great figures of American history, William Jennings Bryan . . . decided to make his last hurrah on this issue. Bryan gave the creationist movement both influence and contacts.

In the early 1920s, several Southern states passed flat out anti-evolution statutes. The Tennessee law, for example, declared it a crime to teach that "man had descended from a lower order of animals." American liberals, including many clergymen, were embarrassed and caught off guard by the quick (if local) successes of this movement. In a challenge to the constitutionality of these statutes, the American Civil Liberties Union (ACLU) instigated the famous Scopes trial in Dayton, Tennessee, in 1925. John Scopes, a young freethinker, but quite popular among his largely fundamentalist students, worked as the physics teacher and track coach of the local high school. He had substituted for the fundamentalist biology teacher during an illness, and had assigned the chapters on evolution from the class textbook, A Civic Biology, by George William Hunter. Scopes consented to be the guinea pig or stalking horse (choose your zoological metaphor) for a legal challenge to the constitutionality of Tennessee's recently enacted anti-evolution law—and the rest is history, largely filtered and distorted, for most Americans, through the fictionalized account of a wonderful play, Inherit the Wind, written in 1955 by Jerome Lawrence and Robert Edwin Lee, and performed by some of America's best actors in several versions. (I had the great privilege, as a teenager, to see Paul Muni at the end of his career playing Clarence Darrow in the original Broadway production, with an equally impressive Ed Begley as William Jennings Bryan. Two film versions featured similar talent, with Spencer Tracy as Darrow and Fredric March as Bryan in the first, and Kirk Douglas as Darrow with Jason Robards as Bryan in the later remake for television.) Contrary to the play, Scopes was not persecuted by Bible-thumpers, and never spent a second in jail. The trial did have its epic moments—particularly when Bryan, in his major speech, virtually denied that humans were mammals; and, in the most famous episode, when Judge Raulston convened his court on the lawn (for temperatures had risen into triple digits and cracks had developed in the ceiling on the floor below the crowded courtroom), and allowed Darrow to put Bryan on the stand as a witness for the defense. But the usual reading of the trial as an epic struggle between benighted Yahooism and resplendent virtue simply cannot suffice—however strongly this impression has been fostered both by *Inherit the Wind* and by the famous reporting of H. L. Mencken, who attended the trial and, to say the least, professed little respect for Bryan, whom he called "a tinpot pope in the Coca-Cola belt." Scopes was recruited for a particular job—both by the ACLU and by Dayton fundamentalists, who saw the trial as an otherwise unobtainable opportunity to put their little town "on the map" and not proactively persecuted in any way. The ACLU wanted a quick process and a sure conviction, not a media circus. (The Scopes trial initiated live broadcast by radio, and might therefore be designated as the inception of a trajectory leading to O. J. Simpson and other extravaganzas of arguable merit.) The local judge held no power to determine the constitutionality of the statute, and the ACLU therefore sought an unproblematical conviction, designated for appeal to a higher court. They may have loved Clarence Darrow as a personality, but they sure as hell didn't want him in Dayton. However, when Bryan announced that he would appear for the state of Tennessee to rout Satan from Dayton, the die was cast, and Darrow's counteroffer could hardly be refused.

The basic facts have been well reported, but the outcome has almost always been misunderstood. Darrow did bring several eminent scientists to testify, and the judge did refuse to let them take the stand. In so deciding, he was not playing the country bumpkin, but making a proper ruling that his court could judge Scopes's guilt or innocence only under the given statute—and Scopes was guilty as charged—not the legitimacy or constitutionality of the law itself. Testimony by experts about the validity or importance of evolution therefore became irrelevant. In this context, historians have never understood why Judge Raulston then allowed Bryan to testify as an expert for the other side.

But this most famous episode has also been misread.

First of all, the judge later struck the entire testimony from the record. Second, Darrow may have come out slightly ahead, but Bryan parried fairly well, and certainly didn't embarrass himself. The most celebrated moment—when Darrow supposedly forced Bryan to admit that the days of creation might have spanned more than twenty-four hours—represented Bryan's free-will statement about his own and well-known personal beliefs (he had never been a strict biblical literalist), not a fatal inconsistency, exposed by Darrow's relentless questioning.

To correct the other most famous incident of the trial, Bryan did indeed drop dead of heart failure in Dayton—not dramatically on the courtroom floor (as fiction requires for maximal effect), but rather a week later, after stuffing himself at a church dinner. However, the most serious misunderstanding lies with the verdict itself, and the subsequent history of creationism. *Inherit the Wind* presents a tale of free inquiry triumphant over dogmatism. As an exercise in public relations, the Scopes trial may be read as a victory for our side. But the legal consequences could hardly have been more disastrous. Scopes was, of course, convicted—no surprises there. But the case was subsequently declared moot and therefore unappealable— by the judge's error of fining Scopes one hundred dollars (as the creationism statute specified), whereas Tennessee law required that all fines over fifty dollars be set by the jury. (Perhaps sleepy little towns like Dayton never fined anyone more than fifty bucks for anything, and the judge had simply forgotten this detail of unapplied law.) In any case, this error provides a good argument against using "outside agitators" like Darrow as sole representatives in local trials. The fancy plaintiff's team, lead by Darrow and New York lawyer Dudley Field Malone, included no one with enough local knowledge to challenge the judge and assure proper procedure.

Thus, Scopes's conviction was overturned on a technicality—an outcome that has usually been depicted as a victory, but was actually a bitter procedural defeat that stalled the real purpose of the entire enterprise: to test the law's constitutionality. In order to reach the appropriate higher court, the entire process would have to start again, with a retrial of Scopes. But history could not be rolled back, for Bryan was dead, and Scopes, now enrolled as a graduate student in geology at the University of Chicago, had no desire to revisit this part of his life. (Scopes, a splendidly modest and honorable man, became a successful, oil geologist in Shreveport, Louisiana. He never sought any profit from what he recognized as his accidental and transitory fame, and he never wavered in defending freedom of inquiry and the rights of teachers.)

So the Tennessee law (and similar statutes in other states) remained on the books—not actively enforced, to be sure, but ever-present as a weapon against the proper teaching of biology. Textbook publishers, the most cowardly arm of the printing industry, generally succumbed and either left evolution out or relegated the subject to a small chapter at the back of the book. I own a copy of the text that I used in 1956 at a public high school in New York City, a liberal constituency with no compunction about teaching evolution. This text, *Modern Biology*, by Moon, Mann, and Otto, dominated the market and taught more than half of America's high school students. Evolution occupies only 18 of the book's 662 pages—as Chapter 58 out of 60.

(Many readers, remembering the realities of high school, will immediately know that most classes never got to this chapter at all.) Moreover, the text never mentions the dreaded "E" word, and refers to Darwin's theory as "the hypothesis of racial development." But the first edition of this textbook, published in 1921, before the Scopes trial, featured Darwin on the frontispiece (my 1956 version substitutes a crowd of industrious beavers for the most celebrated of all naturalists), and includes several chapters treating evolution as both a proven fact and the primary organizing theme for all biological sciences.

This sorry situation persisted until 1968, when Susan Epperson, a courageous teacher from Arkansas, challenged a similar statute in the Supreme Court—and won the long-sought verdict of unconstitutionality on obvious First Amendment grounds. (A lovely woman approached me after a talk in Denver last year. She thanked me for my work in fighting creationism and then introduced herself as Susan Epperson. She had attended my lecture with her daughter, who, as a graduate student in evolutionary biology, had reaped the fruits of her mother's courage. I could only reply that the major thrust of thanks must flow in the other direction.)

But nothing can stop a true believer. The creationists regrouped, and came back fighting with a new strategy designed to circumvent constitutional problems. They had always honorably identified their alternative system as explicitly theological, and doctrinally based in a literal reading of the Bible. But now they expurgated their texts, inventing the oxymoronic concept of "creation science." Religion, it seems, and contrary to all previous pronouncements, has no bearing upon the subject at all. The latest discoveries of pure science now reveal a factual world that just happens to correlate perfectly with the literal pronouncements of the Book of Genesis. If virtually all professionally trained scientists regard such a view as nonsensical, and based on either pure ignorance or outright prevarication, then we can only conclude that credentialed members of this discipline cannot recognize the cutting edge of their own subject. In such a circumstance, legislative intervention becomes necessary. And besides, the creationists continued, we're not asking schools to ban evolution anymore (that argument went down the tubes with the Epperson decision). Now we are only demanding "equal time" for "creation science" in any classroom that also teaches evolution. (Of course, if they decide not to teach evolution at all . . . well, then . . .) However ludicrous such an argument might be, and however obviously self-serving as a strategy to cloak a real aim (the imposition of fundamentalist theological doctrine) in new language that might pass constitutional muster, two states actually did pass nearly identical "equal time" laws in the late 1970s—Arkansas and Louisiana. A consortium of the ACLU and many professional organizations, both scientific and religious, challenged the Arkansas statute in a trial labeled by the press (not inappropriately) as "Scopes II," before Federal Judge William R. Overton in Little Rock during December 1981. Judge Overton, in a beautifully crafted decision (explaining the essence of science, and the proper role of religion, so well that *Science*, our leading professional journal, published the text verbatim), found the Arkansas equal-time law unconstitutional in January 1982.

The state of Arkansas, now back under the liberal leadership of Bill Clinton, decided not to appeal. Another federal judge then voided the nearly identical Louisiana law by summary judgment, stating that the case had been conclusively made in Arkansas. Louisiana, however, did appeal to the U.S. Supreme Court in *Edwards* v. *Aguillard*, where, in 1987, we won a strong and final victory by a seven-to-two majority, with (predictably) Rehnquist and Scalia in opposition (Thomas, a probable third vote today, had not yet joined the court).

I testified at the Arkansas trial as one of six "expert witnesses" in biology, philosophy of science, and theology—with my direct examination centered upon creationist distortion of scientific work on the length of geological time and the proof of evolutionary transformation in the fossil record, and my cross-examination fairly perfunctory. (The attorney general of Arkansas, compelled by the ethics of his profession to defend a law that he evidently deemed both silly and embarrassing to his state, did a competent job, but just didn't have his heart in the enterprise.) As a group, by the way, we did not try to prove evolution in our testimony. Courtrooms are scarcely the appropriate venue for adjudicating such issues under the magisterium of science. We confined our efforts to the only legal issue before us: to proving, by an analysis of their texts and other activities, that "creation science" is nothing but a smoke screen, a meaningless and oxymoronic phrase invented as sheep's clothing for the old wolf of Genesis literalism, already identified in the

Epperson case as a partisan theological doctrine, not a scientific concept at all—and clearly in violation of First Amendment guarantees for separation of church and state if imposed by legislative order upon the science curricula of public schools.

I can't claim that the trial represented any acme of tension in my life. The outcome seemed scarcely in doubt, and we held our victory party on the second day of a two-week trial. But cynicism does not run strongly in my temperament—and I expect that when I am ready to intone my *Nunc Dimittis*, or rather my Sh'ma Yisroel, I will list among my sources of pride the fact that I joined a group of scholars to present the only testimony ever provided by expert witnesses before a court of law during this interesting episode of American cultural history—the legal battle over creationism that raged from *Scopes* in 1925 to *Edwards* v. *Aguillard* in 1987. Judge Raulston did not allow Darrow's experts to testify at the Scopes trial, and the Louisiana law was dismissed by summary judgment and never tried; live arguments before the Supreme Court last only for an hour, and include no witnesses. It was, for me, a great joy and privilege to play a tiny role in a historical tale that featured such giant figures as Bryan and Darrow.

The Arkansas trial may have been a no-brainer, but many anecdotes, both comic and serious, still strike me as illuminating or instructive. In the former category, I may cite my two favorite moments of the trial. First, I remember the testimony of a second-grade teacher who described an exercise he uses to convey the immense age of the earth to his students: he stretches a string across his classroom, and then places the children at appropriate points to mark the origin of life, the death of dinosaurs, and human beginnings tight next to the wall at the string's end. In cross-examination, the assistant attorney general asked a question, that he later regretted: What would you do under the equal-time law if you had to present the alternative view that the earth is only ten thousand years old? "I guess I'd have to get a short string," the teacher replied. The courtroom burst into laughter, evidently all motivated by the same image that had immediately popped into my mind: the thought of twenty earnest second-graders all scrunched up along one millimeter of string.

In a second key moment, the creationist side understood so little about the subject of evolution that they brought, all the way from Sri Lanka, a fine scientist named Chandra Wickramasinghe, who happens to disagree with Darwinian theory (but who is not an anti-evolutionist, and certainly not a young-earth creationist—a set of distinctions that seemed lost on intellectual leaders of this side). Their lawyer asked him, "What do you think of Darwin's theory?" and Wickramasinghe replied, in the crisp English of his native land, "Nonsense." In cross-examination, our lawyer asked him: "And what do you think of the idea that the earth is only ten thousand years old?" "Worse nonsense," he tersely replied.

On the plane back home, I got up to stretch my legs (all right, I was going to take a pee), and a familiar looking man, sitting in an aisle seat of the coach section, stopped me and said in the local accent, "Mr. Gould, I wanna' thank you for comin' on down here and heppin' us out with this little problem." "Glad to do it," I replied, "but what's your particular interest in the case? Are you a scientist?" He chuckled and denied the suggestion. "Are you a businessman?" I continued.

"Oh no," he finally replied, "I used to be the governor. I'd have vetoed that bill." I had been talking with Bill Clinton. In an odd contingency of history that allowed this drama to proceed to its end at the Supreme Court, Clinton had become a bit too complacent as boywonder governor, and had not campaigned hard enough to win reelection in 1980—a mistake that he never made again, right up to the presidency. The creationism bill, which he would surely have vetoed, passed during his interregnum, and was signed by a more conservative governor.

But such humor served only as balance for the serious and poignant moments of the trial—none so moving as the dignity of committed teachers who testified that they could not practice their profession honorably if the law were upheld. One teacher pointed to a passage in his chemistry text that attributed great age to fossil fuels. Since the Arkansas act specifically included "a relatively recent age of the earth" among the definitions of creation science requiring "balanced treatment," this passage would have to be changed. The teacher claimed that he did not know how to make such an alteration.

Why not? retorted the assistant attorney general in his cross-examination. You only need to insert a simple sentence: "Some scientists, however, believe that fossil fuels are relatively young." Then, in the most impressive statement of the entire trial, the teacher responded: I could, he argued, insert such a sentence in mechanical compliance with the act. But I cannot, as a conscientious teacher, do so. For "balanced treatment" must mean "equal dignity," and I would therefore have to justify the insertion. And this I cannot do, for I have heard no valid arguments that would support such a position.

Another teacher spoke of similar dilemmas in providing balanced treatment in a conscientious rather than a mechanical way. What then, he was asked, would he do if the law were upheld? He looked up and said, in a calm and dignified voice: It would be my tendency not to comply. I am not a revolutionary or a martyr, but I have responsibilities to my students, and I cannot forgo them.

And now, led back by this serious note, I realize that I have been a bit too sanguine during this little trip down memory lane. Yes, we won a narrow and specific victory after sixty years of contention: creationists can no longer hope to realize their aims by official legislation. But these well-funded and committed zealots will not therefore surrender. Instead they have changed their tactics, often to effective strategies that cannot be legally curtailed. They continue to pressure textbook publishers for deletion or weakening of chapters about evolution. (But we can also fight back—and have done so effectively in several parts of the country—by urging school boards to reject textbooks that lack adequate coverage of this most fundamental topic in the biological sciences.) They agitate before local school boards, or run their own candidates in elections that rarely inspire large turnouts, and can therefore be controlled by committed minorities who know their own voters and get them to the polls. (But scientists are also parents, and "all politics is local," as my own former congressman from Cambridge, MA, used to say.) Above all, in an effective tactic far more difficult to combat because it works so insidiously and invisibly, they can simply agitate in vociferous and even mildly-threatening ways. Most of us, including most teachers, are not particularly courageous, and do not choose to become martyrs. Who wants trouble? If little Billy tells his parents that I'm teaching evolution, and they then cause a predictable and enormous public fuss (particularly in parts of America where creationism is strong and indigenous) . . . well, then, what happens to me, my family, and my job? So maybe I just won't teach evolution this year. What the hell. Who needs such a mess? Which leads me to reiterate an obvious and final point: We misidentify the protagonists of this battle in the worst possible way when we depict evolution versus creationism as a major skirmish in a general war between science and religion. Almost all scientists and almost all religious leaders have joined forces on the same side—against the creationists. And the chief theme of this book provides the common currency of agreement—NOMA, and the call for respectful and supportive dialogue between two distinct magisteria, each inhabiting a major mansion of human life, and each operating best by shoring up its own home while admiring the other guy's domicile and enjoying a warm friendship filled with illuminating visits and discussions.

Creationists do not represent the magisterium of religion. They zealously promote a particular theological doctrine—an intellectually marginal and demographically minority view of religion that they long to impose upon the entire world. And the teachers of Arkansas represent far more than "science." They stand for toleration, professional competence, freedom of inquiry, and support for the Constitution of the United States, a worthy set of goals shared by the vast majority of professional scientists and theologians in modern America.

The enemy is not religion but dogmatism and intolerance, a tradition as old as humankind, and impossible to extinguish without eternal vigilance, which is, as a famous epigram proclaims, the price of liberty. We may laugh at a marginal movement like young-earth creationism, but only at our peril—for history features the principle that risible stalking horses, if unchecked at the starting gate, often grow into powerful champions of darkness. Let us give the last word to Clarence Darrow, who stated in his summation at the Scopes trial in 1925:

> If today you can take a thing like evolution and make it a crime to teach it in the public schools, tomorrow you can make it a crime to teach it in the private schools and next year you can make it a crime to teach it to the hustings or in the church. At the next session you may ban books and the newspapers. . . . Ignorance and fanaticism are ever busy and need feeding. Always feeding and gloating for more. Today it is the public school teachers; tomorrow the private. The next day the preachers and the lecturers, the magazines, the books, the newspapers. After a while, Your Honor, it is the setting of man against man and creed against creed until with flying banners and beating drums we are marching backward to the glorious ages of the sixteenth century when bigots lighted fagots to burn the men who dared to bring any intelligence and enlightenment and culture to the human mind.

CHAPTER 3

Creation Matters

by Walter Hearn

Walter Hearn, a biochemist and evangelical Christian, discusses the degree to which the evolution–creation debate is distorted by the choice of words used to describe each. Different word choices, such as the use of -ism, tend to prejudge the issues at hand. He discusses a variety of ways that people can interpret the Bible, and ways that people who believe in both science and faith have attempted to reconcile or blend the two. He makes clear that he believes in the validity of science and of evolutionary reconstruction despite his own faith, which does not promote literal interpretation of the Bible.

Millions of us, including the pope and the archbishop of Canterbury, seriously believe that the universe and all that is in it have been created by God. Yet we resist being called creationists.

We can properly be called theists, a term that takes in Muslims and Jews as well as Christians.

Many theists, including the pope and the archbishop, consider evolution a reasonable scientific theory of how we came into existence. Yet we don't much like to be called evolutionists, either.

"Houston, we have a problem"—a vocabulary problem.

Choosing the Right Word

To start with, words ending in -*ist* are notoriously slippery. Some may define practitioners of a certain profession or hobby, like a physicist or a philatelist. But an -*ist* word may also designate a person with a specific belief or ideology, like a Baptist, a Marxist, or an atheist. The word *creationist* belongs in the latter category, but what about *evolutionist*? That's part of the problem: It's a word with a dual meaning, like naturalist. Is a naturalist an observer of nature who loves to be outdoors (picture someone with a butterfly net), or a person with a definite conviction that nature (or, as Carl Sagan put it, the cosmos) is all there is? That's why theistic evolutionists add that qualifying adjective when they label themselves. They want to make it clear that to take evolution (hence, nature and science) seriously does not eclipse their fundamental belief in God as creator. Of course, they don't want to be known as fundamentalists, either.

In the second place, a word with which we might identify our own position can have a different ring when used against us. When a label has a range of connotations, people tend to apply the best meaning to themselves and assign the worst to others. Take liberal and conservative, for example. In politics or religion, do you consider yourself one or the other? Basically, conservatives stress that what we have is worth keeping; liberals insist on freedom to find a better way.

Who wouldn't want to be regarded as conservative on some issues, liberal on others? When I'm branded as a conservative, I try substituting "conservationist," a term with the same meaning but acceptable even to the liberal-minded. When I'm denigrated as a liberal, I admit to being a "freedom lover" or "freedom fighter," terms appreciated by political conservatives.

A lot of the "warfare" between creation and evolution is really over the meanings of words. I'm not much of a warrior, but over the years I've been a participant of a sort—with the scars to show for it. Jesus said, "Blessed are the peacemakers," but peacemakers can also get blasted. To be effective, we have to show up on the battlefield and take a position between the combatants. As nonpartisans standing in the middle, we look to each side like someone in the vanguard of the other side, so peacemakers can get shot at by both sides.

I was born the year after the famous Scopes "monkey trial," giving me a good sixty adult years to ponder creation, evolution, and their relation to each other. In my first career (up to 1972) I was a practicing biochemist—just when biochemical discoveries were on the verge of shifting evolutionary focus from species and higher taxa to proteins and DNA. Even before that, I was (and still am) a practicing evangelical Christian—when evangelicals were developing a view of the Bible distinct from that of both fundamentalists and liberal Protestants.

To people who asked "Which side are you on?" my favorite answer was, "I'm a Christian serious about evolution and a scientist serious about creation." That takes longer to say than "theistic evolutionist," but it boils down to pretty much the same idea. I try to avoid pairing a specifically religious term with a strictly scientific one, as in "theistic evolution" or "creation science." But I admit that it's hard to pin down exactly what someone means by evolution or creation even in those realms where the meaning of each should be clearest.

Within science, for instance, despite evolution's rather precise biological definition, astronomers talk about the evolution of stars, and anthropologists about the evolution of human languages. Biologists restrict evolutionary theory to genetic changes since the first viable organism appeared, but you can bet they'll extend their definition to include chemical evolution ("abiogenesis") if relevant experiments ever pan out. I've kept my eye on that field since 1959, when I predicted in a chapter titled "The Origin of Life" that exciting results were just around the corner. That was the Darwin Centennial year and the book was *Evolution and Christian Thought Today*, edited by Russell L. Mixter. (Over forty years later, writing that chapter led in a roundabout way to my brief appearance in the final segment of *Evolution*, an eight-hour PBS television series aired in 2001.) I'm still waiting for those definitive results.

Likewise, in religion, theologians distinguish between an original creative act (*creatio ex nihilo*, "out of nothing") and a kind of ongoing creation (*creatio continuo*). We're obviously dealing with complex technical terminology, but a big problem is that creation and evolution are also used in ordinary parlance. Both words have picked up connotations that muddy their basic meaning. In everyday speech, even a biologist may refer to "the evolution of computers," applying a term that is almost the antithesis of goal-seeking to the work of engineers continually redesigning a basic invention with definite goals in mind. And if scientists ever do the right experiments to show that life arose on its own from chemicals, will they have modeled mindless evolution? Hardly, because they used their intelligent minds to design the experiments.

In much popular usage, *creation* conveys the idea of something being suddenly zapped into existence. Professional cosmologists are likely to call the Big Bang a creation event; to hear them talk you'd think that the most significant stuff happened in the very earliest part of the very first second. That's pretty sudden. Yet artists are likely to speak of creation as a process, even if punctuated by sudden insights. My concept of divine creation is broadened by thinking of it as analogous to my experiences in trying to write poetry. It takes time to create a good poem, even with moments of strong inspiration. I see a parallel even to the two-stage process of neo-Darwinian evolution: first, a more or less random search of possible words to complete a line, followed by a selection of the one word that best fits a pattern already established. But that poem did not just happen. I know, because I wrote it. (A verse in the New Testament, by the way, refers to followers of Jesus as God's "workmanship," a translation of the Greek word *poema*.)

A very significant difference between *creation* and *evolution* is that, in their verb forms, the first is transitive, the second intransitive. Some verbs can be either, like *change*. One can say, "I changed the *clock*," but also, "The times keep changing." The verb *create* takes both a subject and an object. Until recently, the verb *evolve* was always intransitive, without an object. Things simply evolved. Today, though, some research papers are beginning to use the same verb in a transitive way, as in "We evolved new species of RNA molecules in vitro." Translation: "We put precursors in a test tube and found some new RNA sequences in it after a period of time."

Despite this difference, both words are set forth as the answer to the same question, namely, "How did we get here?" We're here now, but at one time we were not. So, what happened in between? We're talking not about two different things but about one thing—whatever it was that actually happened in going from one state to the other. One thing happened, but we have two different words to describe it. With the intransitive verb, we say only that it happened. We also have a transitive verb, to assert (or strongly imply) that something or someone *made it happen*, or set up conditions so that it would happen. That insight helps us choose the right word to use in any given situation. What is the focus of our attention? Are we concentrating on the "How?" questions, on the physical processes by which it happened? Evolution is available to us for that use. To focus instead (or in addition) on the "How come?" questions, inquiring about the purpose or meaning of what exists, about what is behind those physical processes, the word *creation* is at our disposal. It's a perfectly good word.

In 1984 the National Academy of Sciences (NAS) entered the controversy over public education by mailing free copies of its 28-page booklet, *Science and Creationism* (pictured), to some 40,000 high school science teachers.

The NAS is a private, nonprofit, self-perpetuating society of distinguished scholars engaged in scientific and engineering research. It was chartered by Congress during the Civil War to advise the federal government on scientific and technical matters. The NAS today numbers several thousand members and publishes a prestigious weekly technical journal, *Proceedings of the National Academy of Science*. The 1999 edition of *Science and Creationism*, a more substantial booklet on *Teaching about Evolution and the Nature of Science*, and other useful NAS publications can be found at www.nationalacademies.org.

Framing the Controversy

When the words *evolution* and *creation* are used in the same sentence or paragraph, as discussed, people generally expect to see a *versus* between them. That is, these are fighting words. Controversy over them is not likely to go away, though we can hope that efforts like this book will raise it to a higher intellectual level. To that end, let's consider how it might be framed. The controversy one sees in the news usually takes the form of evolution versus creationism, with evolution defined as the current biological theory, model, or working hypothesis (take your pick, more or less) known as the neo-Darwinian synthesis. The modern synthesis includes an understanding of genetic mutation as the source of apparently random biological variation. That's something Darwin could only guess at in 1859 when he finally published his carefully thought-out theory of natural selection as the key to *The Origin of Species*. The *-ism* attached to the word *creation* pegs the other side of the argument as a kind of competing model called scientific creationism or creation science by its proponents, particularly the members of such institutions as the Institute for Creation Research (ICR) and the Creation Research Society (CRS).

Many of the church-going folks who provided early support for ICR were drawn together by the 1961 publication of a profoundly influential book *The Genesis Flood and Its Scientific Implications*, by conservative theologian John C. Whitcomb, Jr., and civil engineering professor Henry M. Morris (who died in 2006 at age eighty-eight). That book attempted to compress millions of years of geological ages into a few thousand years and to explain almost all stratigraphic phenomena by a single catastrophic event. Although they tried to use scientific reasoning to promote their point of view, the authors admitted that their commitment to "flood geology" stemmed from a strictly literal reading of Genesis. Their work was essentially a refinement of geological ideas expressed in earlier books by a self-taught Seventh-day Adventist writer, George McCready Price, especially in his massive volume *The New Geology*, published in 1923. Even so, Whitcomb and Morris hardly referred to Price at all, either to avoid identification with his somewhat off-brand theology or because they realized that his lack of scientific credentials would make it even harder for readers to accept their off-brand science.

Emboldened by what looked like scientific validation of their position in *The Genesis Flood* and a subsequent stream of ICR publications, creationists who believed that the earth must be only a few thousand years old (whatever the rocks say) became a growing antievolution social force. Their argument was that gradual evolution ("from amoeba to man") simply could not be true. For one thing, there had not been enough time for it to occur. That argument was put forth in one-sided lectures in church circles and in debates on university campuses whenever an evolutionist could be found willing to debate. Such debates were advertised in conservative churches and the audiences were often composed largely of church people. The creationists always claimed to have won those debates, and no doubt a number of evolutionists later regretted having stuck their necks out. Yet even the most vigorous debates were local events that remained pretty much under the radar until the early 1980s.

The controversy went public in a big way in 1981 when then-presidential candidate Ronald Reagan made a negative comment about evolution, and when Arkansas and Louisiana passed state laws mandating the teaching of a "two-model" approach to biology in their public schools. The scientific establishment began to sit up and take notice, suddenly discovering that many citizens are suspicious of evolution and even of science in general. When the Arkansas "balanced treatment" law was tried in *McLean v. Arkansas Board of Education*, the American Civil Liberties Union (ACLU)

In 1986–87 the American Scientific Affiliation (ASA) responded to *Science and Creationism* by mailing free copies of its 48-page booklet, *Teaching Science in a Climate of Controversy* to the same National Science Teachers Association list of teachers who had received the NAS booklet. The ASA worried that explicit rejection of "special creation" in the NAS booklet might be regarded by readers as also a rejection of "a divine Creator." Although most teachers who received the ASA booklet found it helpful, some critics considered it "creationist propaganda," others, "evolutionist propaganda." The ASA is a national fellowship of Christians in scientific and technical work, founded in 1941. Today it numbers several thousand members and publishes a quarterly scholarly journal, *Perspectives on Science and Christian Faith*. The 1993 edition of *Teaching Science in a Climate of Controversy* (pictured) is one of many helpful resources on creation, evolution, and other science/faith topics available at www.asa3.org.

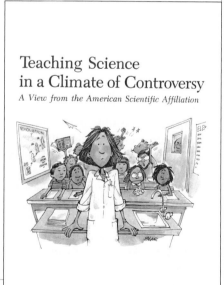

Teaching Science
in a Climate of Controversy
A View from the American Scientific Affiliation

led the case for the plaintiff before U.S. District Court Judge William R. Overton. Many scientists probably breathed a sigh of relief in January 1982 when Judge Overton struck down the statute, declaring that creation science (a.k.a. scientific creationism) was not science and differed in no important way from the account of creation in the Bible. The ACLU then turned its guns on the Louisiana statute, eventually thrown out in 1987 by the U.S. Supreme Court in *Edwards* v. *Aguillard*. Since those two decisions, the unmodified term *creationism* has become synonymous with belief in a young earth, legally as well as in popular usage.

Two excellent sources for digging into these matters are *Trial and Error: The American Controversy over Creation and Evolution* (1985) by legal scholar and science historian Edward J. Larson; and especially *The Creationists: The Evolution of Scientific Creationism* (1992) by science historian Ronald L. Numbers. (For over ten years I thought I was the only person asked by both sides to consider being an expert witness for the McLean trial in Little Rock. Then I heard Ron Numbers say in a lecture that his testimony had been sought by both defendant and plaintiff. Each of us had our reasons for saying no and staying out of the fray.)

Few could have been surprised at the legal outcome, once the scientific community had mustered itself to defend what it considered real science against a pseudoscientific challenger. The plaintiffs included among their expert witnesses religious leaders who identified creationism as a fundamentalist twist based on a naive belief in biblical inerrancy. Researchers from various fields of science documented the creationists' lack of credible scientific evidence. Science is closely associated with technology, and we all know how well technology works. Would we rather fly in an airplane maintained by trained technicians using a schematic diagram, or in one maintained by preachers using the Bible as a reference? What do we want our kids to learn in science classes? How about authentic science? With the question framed that way, the answer was hardly in doubt. On the other hand, what if the *-ism* was on the other foot, so to speak, and the controversy was framed as evolutionism versus creation? That is, what if evolution was regarded as the impostor, a pseudoreligious challenger to a basic religious doctrine? Framed that way, the courts would be much more reluctant to take up the controversy, because our government wants to have nothing to do with religion, either to hinder it or to foster it. And the controversy wouldn't center on what should be taught in public schools. Or would it?

Polls show that a large majority of U.S. citizens believes that the universe did not come into being by itself but was created by a supreme being. Most of them get that belief from the Bible, though some may come by it simply because "there must be a reason for things to exist." Whether out of personal faith, religious heritage, or simply "common sense," many individuals are convinced that a transcendent, spiritual, supernatural creative power exists beyond the capacity of science to explain or explain away. Theists generally believe that God not only initiated creation but also sustains the world and cares for it, showing at least some attributes of a beneficent person who can interact with human persons. Theists are people who pray. Today even the most devout parents in the United States hardly expect the public schools to teach their version of religion to their children, though they will object to any putdown of religious faith by their children's teachers. Most educated parents probably understand that scientific knowledge embraces only natural explanations of the physical world. Individual scientists are expected to put aside whatever personal beliefs they hold when reporting their scientific work. Science teachers should not only respect the religious convictions of their students, but also teach their students that science is restricted to natural explanations. That's the way the system is supposed to work. Often it works that way.

Not always. An atheistic or agnostic science teacher may give the impression that science has rendered faith in God impossible or hopelessly out of date. Why does evolution continue to be the target of so many Christian groups? Partly because some prominent scientists (and a good many other academics) continually use Darwinian evolution as justification for their atheism. Their books and television appearances catch the eye and raise the ire of the Christian public. The popular writings of an atheist like British biologist Richard Dawkins serve as a lightning rod, drawing public attention to the question of whether extrapolation from evolutionary science has become an antidote to belief in God. When evolution serves as a surrogate religion, it can appropriately be called evolutionism. And who wants such a religion, or any other religion, taught in our public schools?

While on sabbatical in London in 1987, University of California law professor Phillip E. Johnson (now emeritus) began reading what prominent scientists were saying about evolution. Letters to the weekly journal *Nature* showed that some objected strongly to a new exhibit on Charles Darwin at the British Museum. The objectors were afraid the exhibit might suggest to the public that Darwin's "grand idea" went beyond the evidence to back it up. Johnson had only a layperson's knowledge of science, but he was a scholar used to dissecting arguments. He concluded that claims for the creative power of natural selection did indeed go beyond the evidence, and that many scientists were behaving more like believers in a doctrine than like dispassionate investigators. His books criticizing scientists for letting this occur, beginning with *Darwin on Trial* (1991), have served as something of a lightning rod themselves. They draw dire warnings from the scientific establishment that science is once again under attack. His books have also drawn together some younger scholars trained in science and philosophy, more or less united under the banner of Intelligent Design (ID). Johnson intended to open up discussion at the university level of the philosophy behind evolutionary science, but some high school teachers and school board members began to wave the ID flag, often quite naively. Whatever the merits or deficiencies of ID as either science or theology (discussed elsewhere in this book), the ID movement has attracted more public scrutiny to the scientific status of evolution than creationism ever did. What about evolution? As a biological theory, is it well supported by the evidence? Has it become an ideology? Has evolutionism, or belief in evolution, taken over the culture? If so, does mandating the teaching of evolution to school children amount to indoctrinating them in a state-approved ideology? Public interest picked up in August 2005 when President George W. Bush told reporters that he thought schools should teach ID alongside evolution. Interest may have peaked during a trial in Harrisburg, Pennsylvania, over the decision of a school board in the small town of Dover to do just that. Once again a federal judge ruled against those who wanted an alternative to evolution taught in science classes, saying that they clearly did so out of religious motives.

Science historian Edward B. Davis, who attended much of that trial and wrote a balanced account of it (2006), offered this assessment: "ID currently consists only of an interesting philosophical critique of the explanatory efficacy of Darwinian

Francis S. Collins, a leading scientist and member of both NAS and ASA, believes that the scientific evidence points to the common descent of all living creatures, yet also trusts in the biblical doctrine that God cares about us and intervenes in human affairs. Since 1993 he has been director of the National Human Genome Research Institute at the National Institutes of Health, which published a working draft of the human genome sequence in 2001 and a complete sequence in 2003. In his 2006 book, *The Language of God*, Collins explains how his view of the Bible has been enhanced by his scientific discoveries. Learn more about him at www.genome.gov/10000779

evolution, combined with an appeal for scientists to add 'design' to the set of explanatory principles they employ in biology and other sciences."

Another way of framing the public controversy would be to consider evolutionism versus creationism. Although the controversy is never actually framed that way, that's the way it often plays out. Religious people who know little about how scientists function can get in heated arguments with science-oriented people who may know little of what it means to be devout. When pseudoreligion contends against pseudoscience, who cares who wins? Finally, though, we come to authentic science and authentic religion, represented by the biological theory of evolution by natural selection on one hand, and the theological doctrine of divine creation on the other. Now we can drop the *versus* and take both concepts with equal seriousness, as they deserve. Most people in the developed world see why evolution should matter to ordinary citizens, because we live in a culture dependent on the technological applications of modern science. But does creation matter? If we had lived a few centuries ago, you and I would have known the answer to that question, as part of a cultural heritage steeped in theism, even if we ourselves were not particularly religious. What has changed since then?

Thinking, Feeling, Believing, Knowing

By drastically compressing cultural history, we can squeeze two significant turning points into one paragraph. First, go back about two thousand years. A tiny fellowship of courageous individuals rooted in an older Jewish culture surprises the world with its intense fascination with otherworldly concerns: eternal life, for instance. Within three or four centuries, Christianity grows into a movement so entwined with powerful governments that it becomes a dominant cultural force, an enduring "establishment" of religion permeating everyday life. Now, fast-forward to the sixteenth and seventeenth centuries. Behold, another tiny fellowship of courageous individuals, rooted in the then-dominant Christian culture, begins to surprise the world with its fascination with a set of different but equally "otherworldly" concerns: the movements of stars and planets, for instance. Within another three or four centuries (that's today), science has likewise become so entwined with governments that it is considered necessary for the survival of powerful regimes. The influence of the scientific establishment is now so pervasive that religion has to be explained to people. With these parallels in their history, and with an alleged antagonism between science and Christianity, should we think of them as totally different pursuits? Well, yes and no.

In other words, we could stress either differences or similarities between science and religion (for me, the Christian religion). One similarity obvious to me is that the perspective I get from doing them is different from an outsider's perspective. Another is how limited even an insider's perspective can be. None of us knows either science or religion as a whole, only the specific area of those grand enterprises to which we commit ourselves. I know personally what it means to do biochemistry; I know only a little about astronomy or anthropology. I know what it is to be an evangelical Protestant; I know Roman Catholicism and Judaism only from friends and books. So be warned that this is my own version of "science and religion"—and an abbreviated (perhaps distorted) one at that.

I view science and religion as two perspectives on reality, two "ways of knowing," two different commitments leading to two types of truth. In science, conclusions must be stated in an objective way that permits them to be checked by others. Curiosity and checking have been called the distinguishing characteristics of science. Scientific work stems from curiosity about the natural world, and scientific knowledge rests on quantitative observations of that world. Openness to the unexpected and honesty in reporting observations are taken for granted. Personal religious beliefs or political leanings are edited out of scientific papers as irrelevant to the work at hand. The research system, with its peer reviews of grant requests and of papers submitted for publication, may not work perfectly, but any infraction of the rules causes an uproar. Data fudging is hard to conceal from fellow scientists trying to replicate a piece of work.

It would be satisfying to think of science and religion as separate paths to the same truth. Theists, however, envision a more transcendent notion of truth (Truth with a capital *T*, as it were) than scientists do. Telling the truth (i.e., not lying) is as important in science as it is in the Ten Commandments, but scientists seldom talk about seeking truth. Instead they talk about drawing conclusions based on empirical evidence. Because the possibility always exists of finding more evidence in the future, the best that scientists can do is to arrive at tentative approximations of partial truth. We could call that proximate truth as opposed to the ultimate truth with which religious believers are concerned. To theists, ultimate truth—including wisdom and perhaps even direct knowledge of what is really true—comes from God. Here we're up against another vocabulary problem. *Creation* and *evolution* cause confusion because they're different words used to describe one thing, but the single word *knowledge* causes confusion because it's used for different kinds of knowledge. Sometimes it refers exclusively to what can be learned by the methods of science; in fact, our word *science* comes from *conscientia*, a Latin word for knowledge.

Scientific knowledge is highly reliable (for certain purposes, at least) primarily because of its built-in verification processes—that "checking" part. It is knowledge with an impersonal, publicly verifiable, probabilistic, statistical quality. Can there be any other kind of knowledge? You bet, say theists. We've alluded to a difference between "knowing" and "knowing about." What makes the difference? The degree of personal experience.

Long before postmodernists started casting doubt on the objectivity claimed for science, chemist-turned-philosopher Michael Polanyi argued that even the most objective knowledge of which we are capable has a personal component. In *Personal Knowledge* (1958) and other writings, Polanyi emphasized that facts are not knowledge unless held by human persons. Scientists in the most rigorously mathematical disciplines are nevertheless purposeful human beings, living personal lives beyond their work, and probably attracted to that work for nonscientific reasons. They may think of themselves as single-minded, but the human mind is a complex piece of equipment. Human beings do things for various reasons and must cope with more than one kind of knowledge. I think like a scientist when I try to keep myself out of investigations as much as possible, but when I think like a Christian (or a poet, for that matter), I am bound to include myself as much as possible in any project I undertake. For me, science is one way of getting a grasp on what will ultimately turn out to be true.

In fact, with its conclusions always stated as approximations or probabilities, science is better suited for detecting errors in specific truth-claims than for discovering truth. Further, its scope is limited to exploring physical or material things. The very qualities that make scientific knowledge reliable enough to serve as a basis for engineering and technology keep it from being of much value to us in other ways. In particular, it's not a good way to get to know other persons, a kind of knowledge based on mutual discovery rooted in mutual trust. Jewish theologian Martin Buber famously distinguished between "I-it" knowledge (science) and "I-thou" knowledge. One can obtain a certain kind of knowledge of another person by using the methods of science (if permitted by law) by treating that person as an object (an "it"), perhaps by extrapolating from experiments with nonhuman organisms. Yet that's hardly the way we come to know the people we care about, such as our families and loved ones. Interpersonal knowledge serves as a model for knowing God as a "Thou." Indeed, *trust* is a synonym for the faith or belief implicit in religious commitment. Trust, commitment, inspiration, and emotion all play a role in the practice of science, but we seldom hear about that. In my Christian life, however, they're recognized as part of the process from beginning to end. Logic is also part of the process, without playing the dominant role it plays in science. Knowing the scientific truth about a thing essentially means being able to describe how it works. Religious knowledge is about far more than description, or even explanation. It includes not only attributing worth (which is what *worship* really means), but also dedication to care for (which is what *love* really means) what is right and good. In religious faith, knowing the truth includes a moral obligation to do the truth.

In my experience, neither way of knowing is ever complete. I've found it not only satisfying but also enriching to engage in both. Because I find it hard to blend them into a single perspective, it is immensely challenging to switch back and forth from one mode of thinking to the other. If I were an emotionless computer rather than a whole person, I might stick to logic and skip religion altogether. Would the concept ever flit through my circuitry or lodge in my central processing unit that I might have been built for a purpose by someone or something greater than myself? Probably not. But the thought makes me wonder if trying to explain *purpose* to a computer would be any harder than trying to justify *creation* to some readers of this book.

In the world of human beings, religious belief has been around a lot longer than scientific investigation. Both are here to stay. Scientists like to think of the sciences as capable of unifying the world's peoples because belief is not an issue. Actually, religions may be more universal because admission to them is more open. For example, Christianity welcomes into its fellowship individuals without an advanced degree or even a course in calculus, the major requirement being acknowledgment of a need for forgiveness and a desire to "follow Jesus." With such a low intellectual threshold for entry, practicing a religious faith entails rather simple "technologies" like prayer, Bible study, even singing. Yet for me it has not been true that science is all rationality, religion all emotionality, nor that science alone deals with facts, religion with fictitious unreality. Both are empirically grounded in actual human experience, though science discounts all individual and collective "spiritual" experience. *Spirit* is the usual translation of the New Testament Greek word *pneuma*, which can also be translated "air" or "gas." That hints at an elusive quality, just as in science a gas seems more elusive or ephemeral than the liquid or solid phases of the same substance. All three phases have mass and occupy space, but as a solid the substance has a fixed volume and shape. As a liquid it has a definite volume but flows to take on the shape of the lower part of its container. As a gas it has no fixed volume and hence fills the total space of any container. It reaches everywhere, which is what Christians say about God's spirit (or the Holy Spirit). This is not a perfect analogy, but I find it helpful, recalling that it took a long time for chemists to recognize that gases are as "real" as solid things. Science is better thought of as a process than as a body of knowledge. Yet, like religion, science depends on what has gone before. Scientists are expected to know the literature in their particular field and to cite earlier work that helped shape a current investigation. So scientists as well as religious believers show respect for the writings of those who have gone before, recorded for our benefit. The primary scientific literature scores high on technical reliability but not so high on general application to broad human concerns. It's a literature for specialists. Religious explorations lack the quantitative techniques of verification that give scientific literature its credibility, but people of faith have not been without checks and balances. An informal kind of peer review came into play in selection of the canon of scripture and still functions in formulating church teachings (aka doctrine).

Science and religion are both community enterprises. The clear-cut purpose of belonging to the scientific community is to add something new to that community's accepted body of knowledge. In a less direct way, each believer's experience likewise adds to a religious community's collective knowledge. Yet religious people often seem more focused on what is already accepted than on what is new. That difference probably causes some misunderstanding. Is what is new intrinsically more valuable than what is old? Or could it be the other way around? Most people would agree that what is true will stand the test of time.

Despite a number of parallels I see between my practice of faith and my experience in science, I admit that the Bible, which holds a central place in Christian belief, has no parallel in the scientific community. And the Bible is the Christian's primary resource for knowing God.

The Bible as a Source of Truth

The fundamentals of the biblical doctrine of creation are that God exists, and has created the physical universe and all that is in it. "In the beginning," the book of Genesis pictures the primitive earth as it is increasingly populated by living creatures, culminating in human beings. We humans are said to be created "in God's image" to the extent, at least, that something of God's nature has been communicated to us. It's fair to say that all theists agree on this point. It is, after all, what defines us as theists.

Of course, if God does not exist, it's fair to say that the Bible must be a fraud or a fantasy, no matter how much reverence has been attached to it for so many centuries. Our focus here is not on God's existence, but on how theists who agree on the essentials of the creation story may disagree strongly on what to make of it—and, for that matter, on many other issues in the Bible.

An intelligent atheist can give a purely natural explanation for how the Bible came to be, for why people are so easily deceived into believing in a supernatural being, and for why we would be better off without any religion beyond scientism. All the intelligence is not on that side of the argument, however. Competent scholars who have delved into the biblical texts and studied the circumstances under which they were written have accepted the Bible at its face value.

To take the Bible seriously as God's revelation is not the same thing as taking it literally. The Bible is actually a library; a reader does not have to be a literary scholar to recognize that its books contain various types of writing. There are historical accounts, wise sayings, parables, prophecies, and even personal correspondence. About a fourth of the Bible was written in the form of poetry and was obviously intended to be read that way. Some of the prophetic books and especially the book of Revelation contain a strange kind of "apocalyptic" writing that incorporates symbolism perhaps intended to be obscure. The nearest modern equivalent may be political cartoons: Picture an elephant and a donkey drawn the same size, wearing funny hats and hurling epithets in American slang at each other. What could that possibly mean?

Speaking of politics, the Bible resembles the U.S. Constitution in several respects. First, it serves as a basis for doctrines not laid out in its pages, just as all U.S. laws are derived from our Constitution. Second, interpretations change, but the text itself remains fixed. The original Constitution is still on display, but the books of the Bible exist only as copies. Nevertheless, from linguistic studies and such archaeological findings as the Dead Sea Scrolls, scholars estimate that up to 98 percent of our present Old Testament is identical to the original documents. Because the texts were regarded as sacred, they were hand-copied with meticulous care from older copies by a class of people dedicated to that work (called "scribes" in the New Testament).

Recognition of the ancient text of Holy Scripture as the sacred Word of God was important in its preservation, but intensifies questions of interpretation. Is it the letter of the law that best conveys God's message, or its spirit? That question, which was paramount in translating the Bible from the original languages (classical Hebrew for most of the Old Testament, *Koiné*, Greek for all but a few words of the New), still comes up for readers of the Bible. Theological "conservatives" are tempted to stick too literally to the text as written or translated. "Liberals" are tempted to stray too far from it. With such a variety of literary genres in the Bible, it is not surprising that people can find passages to reinforce many conflicting positions. It is easy to caricature people who hurl verses at each other as Bible-thumpers. Actually, serious readers first try to discern what a passage meant to its writer and to its original readers, then how it should affect them as modern believers living in a different culture and speaking a different language. Crediting God as its ultimate author in some sense, believers consider the whole Bible authoritative. Many conservative Christians insist on a more restrictive term. To some, its words are infallible, meaning that they have the unfailing power to communicate what God wants us to know. To others, they are inerrant, meaning that they contain nothing untrue or misleading to believers who stick as closely as possible to the original text. Each position, while affirming the spiritual unity of the Bible as a whole, acknowledges that its different books were written under different conditions and for human as well as for divine purposes. Even those who defend the most literal position of inerrancy cannot avoid making choices between what is instructive for believers today and what may not apply because certain circumstances no longer exist. Execution by stoning may have been a harsh but necessary punishment for nomads living precariously in the desert thousands of years ago, but very few biblical literalists would consider it appropriate for Western societies today. The biblical claim that God's will has been revealed for all people includes the stipulation that the revelation came at a particular time in a particular language spoken by a particular people.

Much misreading of the Bible (in my opinion) stems from trying to read certain sections of it the way one would read modern science or modern history. Neither category could have been in the mind of the writer (or writers) of Genesis, who passed on to us the creator's account of our origins in a revelation of creative power and of God's love toward his creatures. Genesis also depicted how things went awry when the first humans rejected God's authority. That memorable account served as a preface to many subsequent stories in the Bible, of how God dealt with a disloyal "chosen people" in order to redeem them.

I think it was a misreading to take the "days of creation" as twenty-four-hour periods, another mistake to use familial genealogies in the Bible to calculate back to a date for the beginning. Those mistakes were compounded by taking certain New Testament passages to mean that no physical death of any kind occurred in the Garden of Eden before human rebellion brought death into human experience. It makes more sense to me that the consequence of such sin would be the "spiritual death" of which Jesus spoke, an enduring separation from God's presence. A certain logic exists behind the most literal ways of reading Genesis, but biblical interpretations should not ignore other sources of truth.

Geologists have firmly established that the earth must have existed for many millions of years before humans inhabited it. One way of reconciling Genesis with geology was to assign those missing eons to a supposed "gap" between Genesis 1:1 and the rest of the text. Generations of evangelicals encountered that idea in a footnote in C. I. Scofield's widely used *Reference Bible* (1909). That and other "stop-gap" interpretations were challenged by Bernard Ramm in his influential *The Christian View of Science and Scripture* (1954). Ramm was respectful of "hyper-orthodox" Christian writers, but infuriated some of them by labeling their books as of ordinary worth or limited orientation in his classified bibliography. Although as a progressive creationist he had come a long way from fundamentalism, Ramm later became a chief target of Oxford scholar James Barr in his *Fundamentalism* (1977). Most attempts at reconciliation of Genesis with modern science seem to me to distort the biblical creation story as it was written. Of course, modern science has its own "creation story" to tell. That story begins with a cosmic explosion, followed by billions of years of changes in lifeless space until earth appears as a stage on which it may take another billion years to get to any kind of living thing. At the last second, as it were, human beings come on stage to strut our stuff, including religion and science.

Judged simply as a human story, it can hardly be expected to hold the interest of ordinary readers as well as the biblical story. In contrast, Genesis sweeps past all those lifeless preliminaries to get to the point, assuming that the point is to answer our questions, and our children's questions, about how we got here.

The scientific story compresses all the human interest into a tiny fraction at the very end. The biblical story compresses eons into a single phrase, though it also indicates a stepwise progression in arriving at humanity from ground zero. Its truncated wording highlights a few breakthroughs at critical points, such as the first life and the first human beings. Science seems to agree that those were major steps.

A scientist might say that the long-drawn-out story must be the true one because, well, it's the scientific one. A Christian might contend that the shorter one is true because it's in the Bible as a revelation from the creator, who is indeed the story's main character. Why not value the truth in both stories? If we accept them both as true, we can still ask ourselves which story is better for any particular purpose. Do we need a lengthy story so full of detail that all human activity amounts to only an infinitesimal part of it? For some purposes, we probably do. Do we also need a brief story that introduces us as God's creatures, tells us whom to thank for the life that has been generously given to us in this "garden," and obliges us to care for all of God's creatures?

To those who think primarily in modern scientific categories, say, matter and energy, it may seem bizarre to hang on to a prescientific story, crediting "what makes the world go around" to an ineffable spiritual quality such as the love of God. A scientific story that unfolds without purpose or meaning may be unsatisfying to some, but it could nevertheless be true.

To equally modern people whose thinking has been shaped by the Bible, it is quite natural to attribute purpose and meaning to what has been created, and ultimate worth to its creator. A biblical story that raises many questions in our minds because it doesn't seem to make scientific sense may be unsatisfying to some, but it could nevertheless be true. Why do people feel a need for a creation story, anyway? Because they want to know who we are and where we come from. That's why, in my opinion, creation matters.

CHAPTER 4

The Science of Evolution and the Theology of Creation

by Martinez Hewlett and Ted Peters

Marty Hewlett (a molecular biologist) and Ted Peters (a professor of theology) are working together to define the appropriate relationship between science (and evolution) and religious faith. Each believes in both, and both see religion and science as complementary and potentially cooperative approaches to knowledge. They question how science and faith are to be defined, how to distinguish science as a legitimate source of knowledge, and attempts to turn science into a materialist philosophy. They are concerned with the difference between evolution as science and as ideology, into which it is too easily transformed. They describe four layers of meaning that they believe fall between the science of evolution and inappropriate ideologies built thereon: progress, social Darwinism, eugenics, and atheistic materialism. They also point to differences among types of creationists: scientific creationists, biblical creationists (both including young-earth creationists), and advocates of intelligent design. Both authors reject the pretensions of all these approaches to be science. Readers should note that they use uniformitarianism to mean "gradualism," a meaning slightly different from the way the term is used by others in the book. In accordance with others of us, they describe Darwinian evolution not as fact, but as the best approximation of fact that we now have. The authors also look at the approaches other religions take on the issues.

Are science and faith at war with one another? Should scientists think of themselves as modern and think of religious people as old fashioned, quaint, out of date, even as throwbacks to an era of magic and superstition? Should we make fun of religious people for holding to unenlightened prejudices and bigoted narrow-mindedness? Should modern people discard ancient religious traditions and replace them with up-to-date science?

Are religious people necessarily opposed to scientific advance? Should people of faith join forces to keep Charles Darwin's theory of evolution from poisoning the minds of our young people in school? Should we hiss and boo when scientists walk into the room wearing their lab coats?

It would be a big mistake to answer "yes" to all of these questions. It is a mistake to think that good, healthy science needs to replace religion like growing up replaces childhood. And it is an even bigger mistake to think that religion in general or Christianity in particular must define itself as antiscience.

Yes, there is a culture war going on, and in this chapter we would like to identify the armies in combat. A lot of smoke clouds the battlefield, so it is difficult to get a clear picture. It may appear that the battle is between science and religion. But, this is not the case. No army in this fight is opposed to science. All combatants affirm science, even celebrate science. Rather, the battle is over what constitutes good science and perhaps even the definition of *science* itself.

We will point out the following in our discussion: the difference between research scientists, on one hand, and those who would like to turn evolution into a materialist ideology, on the other hand; that among the Christians, we need to distinguish between creationists, intelligent design advocates, and theistic evolutionists; and that Jews and Muslims come at the study of evolution from quite different perspectives.

A word about us: We make up a team of scientist and theologian. Marty is a molecular biologist who teaches both university students and medical students. As a specialist in research on viruses, he uses the theory of evolution to understand how genes mutate. His research contributes to medical research for making medicines. He believes Darwin's model of evolution is indispensable for what he does. Furthermore, he is a devout Roman Catholic. He sees his science as his Christian vocation. His faith calls him to be the best scientist he can be.

Ted is a Lutheran pastor. He teaches theology to students preparing to become pastors as well as preparing to become professors of religion. Ted is concerned that we articulate the ancient Christian faith in our modern world in an intellectually credible fashion. We need to understand how God is present to persons of faith and how God works in the entire cosmos. For the last decade and a half Ted has been specializing in the relationship of genetic science to bioethics. He believes pastors and teachers should develop a healthy appreciation for science, because through the eyes of science we can better view the wonder and majesty of God's creation.

Evolution as Science

As we mentioned, Marty is a scientist. When he goes into his laboratory to study viruses, he wants nothing to do with a public controversy over Darwinism. He does not suddenly cease being a Christian and become an atheist. He finds studying nature exciting, and he wants to enjoy this excitement right along with the excitement of believing in Jesus Christ. He finds his faith can be reconciled with what Charles Darwin, as a scientist, said.

Let's pause for a moment to ask: Just what did Charles Darwin say in his influential book, *The Origin of Species by Means of Natural Selection* (1859/1964)? First, what did he *not* say? He did not say he would explain the origin of life. Rather, Darwin tells us what he thinks accounts for the variety of species of different life-forms. The theory of evolution is not a theory about origins of the world or even about the origin of life. It is not a theory of creation.

The realm of nature is replete with numerous different species, a wondrous rainbow of living creatures with curious variety and stunning beauty. Where do these differences come from? Why are they changing over time? Darwin's proposed answer is that individuals within a species are born different; they inherit slightly different traits. When a crisis in the environment confronts the group, some die before they can reproduce. Others live on. Those who survive carry a selected set of inherited traits. Those who produce offspring to carry on their traits are reproductively more fit. Over long periods of time, the list of inherited traits in a population changes. New species emerge. The change in inherited traits is known as random variation, and the alteration of the population is known as natural selection. Evolution means descent with modification over deep time, over long periods of time with a slow rate of change. The rate of change is so slow some call it uniformitarian or gradualist.

Darwin suspected that something was happening to cause variety in our inherited traits. But, he was not yet aware of the science of genetics or how DNA works. That would come much later. What Darwin saw as random variation in inheritance would later be explained as randomness in genetic mutations. By the middle of the twentieth century, scientists could combine random variation in genetic inheritance with Darwin's concept of natural selection. This produced a comprehensive theory called the neo-Darwinian synthesis. The entire scientific tradition beginning with *The Origin of Species* and including the neo-Darwinian synthesis combined with even newer discoveries we refer to as Darwinism or the Darwinian model of evolution. Practicing scientists think of this field as simply evolutionary biology.

Notice that we refer to the theory of evolution as a model, the Darwinian model. This is the way scientists talk to each other. The Darwinian model is a scientific picture of reality—a theory—that has inspired research into retrieving fossils, digging up skeletal remains, investigating DNA to compare one species with another, and the reconstruction of biological history. It also provides the framework for studying cellular processes, and this leads to medical research and the development of new therapies. Darwinism has proven itself to be an incredibly fertile theory, generating new knowledge at a rapid rate.

Understanding this is important, because the word *theory* is often flung around on the battlefield and abused to no end. In common usage, something that is theoretical is considered to be unproven or speculative. However, in science, the word *theory* is very different. A scientific theory is a model that has withstood a number of experimental challenges. Of course it can be falsified as new observations are made. But, to date, the theory of evolution as a scientific model is supported by all of the data that have been gathered.

Should we think of Darwin's theory as absolute truth? No. It is a model that gives directions for scientists to pursue research. That is its value. Because science changes rapidly, we can almost forecast that the theory of evolution may be replaced by a still better one in the decades to come. To treat this theory as final would be like building a house on sand.

We want to say that the Darwinian theory of evolution constitutes the best science to date. Even if it gets replaced at some future time by a still better theory, today it offers a more progressive program of research than any of the proposed alternatives.

Darwinism as Ideology

It is difficult to distinguish Darwinism as science from Darwinism as ideology. The science is like an oil deposit, buried below layers of cultural ideology. We have to drill to get at it. Let's look at four layers of ideological covering (Figure 4.1).

The layer of topsoil is *progress*. The vague concept of progress had already appeared in Western Europe and North America due to advances in industrialization. But with Darwin it became a social doctrine with alleged biological justification. Belief in progress appeared to be a response to what nature itself was communicating to human civilization. To evolve came to mean to progress, to improve, and to advance. This continues to be the popular notion of evolution, even though today's laboratory scientists repudiate the idea that there is any progress at the biological level. Progress belongs to the cultural picture of evolution, not the scientific model. Like the scientists, most Christian theologians reject the notion of natural progress as well.

The second layer, like clay, is *social Darwinism*. Herbert Spencer, who coined the phrase "survival of the fittest" which Darwin saw as the equivalent of natural selection, used biological evolution to ground a social ethic. This was the ethic of laissez-faire capitalism. This form of social organization could disregard the needs

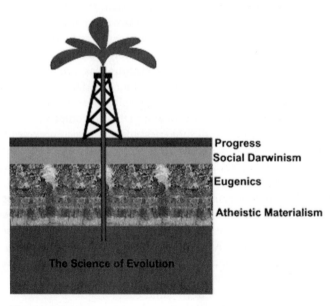

Figure 4.1
The Science of Evolution

of poor and socially unfit individuals in favor of wealthy and fitter people who would lead to an evolutionary advance for the human race. Social Darwinism fostered belief that progress is built right into nature; and it is ethical for us to speed up progress by socially supporting the fit over the unfit. This led to eugenics, which we treat next.

The third layer, like sedimentary rock, is *eugenics*. Eugenics grows out of social Darwinism. Francis Galton, Darwin's cousin, sought to take social control over human evolution through good breeding practices. He wanted to encourage the right kind of marriages, and his eugenics disciples promoted "fitter families." Castrating prisoners would help prevent unfit families from producing children in England and the United States. Eugenics included a heavy dose of racism, presuming that white English people were the most evolutionarily advanced. Adolph Hitler in Germany incorporated social Darwinism and eugenics in developing his doctrine of "racial hygiene," and used this science to support Nazi belief in Aryan superiority over the Jews. Darwinian eugenics served to justify putting children who were mentally and physically disabled into gas chambers before they could reproduce.

The fourth layer, like shale, is *atheistic materialism*. By "materialism" we mean the belief that the only reality that exists is material. Nothing like spirit exists. Neither does God. Because the only reality is material, science, which studies the material world, is the only source of knowledge. Religion becomes a form of false knowledge or fiction. Thomas Huxley and later his grandson Julian Huxley saw Darwin's biology as providing a scientific confirmation of their materialism and their atheism. So enthusiastic were the Huxleys that they hoped a materialist religion based on evolution would dump Christianity and replace it. It is belief in atheistic materialism in the late nineteenth century that led to the idea that science and religion are at war. Before that, no conflict existed. The model of warfare was proposed so that Darwinian atheists could fight Christianity, win, and replace childish Christianity with a mature science. Darwin's theory of evolution provided a form of science that seemed to justify withdrawal from church authority.

The result is that the essential science of evolutionary biology has become buried beneath layers of philosophical or cultural ideology. Serious theology needs to drill deeply to discover the scientifically valuable oil underneath, rather than judge the science by the surface ideologies.

Virtually no religious leader wants to settle for any of these four layers of ideological sediment, even though liberal Protestants have given considerable support to eugenics and progress. One of the reasons Christian groups such as the scientific creationists and intelligent design supporters bring such passion into the war over evolution is that they fear evolution endorses these anti-Christian and anticompassion ideologies. We believe that the science of Darwinism can and should be extricated from these layers of ideological covering.

Biblical Creationism and Scientific Creationism

The Christian religion walks hand in hand with natural science. Renaissance theologians affirmed the two-books idea: the book of nature tells us about God as creator while the Bible tells us about God the redeemer. Many of the modern world's pioneer scientists were devout Christians, some clergy: Copernicus, Kepler, Galileo, and Newton. Today the Vatican sponsors its own observatory that searches for extraterrestrial life, among other scientific enterprises.

With this history in mind, it seems odd that we should see a war break out over evolutionary biology. As we mentioned, the first shot was fired in the late nineteenth century by disciples of Darwin who deliberately sought to upset the church. By 1925 Christian fundamentalism was organizing against the teaching of Darwinian evolution in the public schools. Why? Because of the layers of ideology described previously. Because they do not like the ideologies, anti-Darwinists have organized against the science as well. The baby is getting thrown out with the bath water.

Christians today who oppose Darwinism come in two species, creationists and intelligent design advocates. Among the creationists two subspecies have evolved, the biblical creationists and the scientific creationists. The two are frequently seen with one another, to be sure, but their arguments against Darwinism take different forms. The first argues on the basis of the Bible's authority; the second provides scientific arguments for the inadequacy of the Darwinian model.

Answers in Genesis (AiG) provides a good example of biblical creationism. Headed by Australian Ken Ham, its website reminds us that all knowledge or wisdom begins with the fear of the Lord (Proverbs 1:7, www.answersingenesis.org/).

The scientific creationists are much more valiant on the cultural battlefield. The Institute for Creation Research (ICR) near San Diego is the most influential representative of this position: www.icr.org/.

The chief weapon of the scientific creationists is scientific argumentation. They identify themselves as *scientific* creationists, not biblical creationists. They argue against Darwinism because they believe the Darwinian model is inferior to their own model, creation science. They are aggressive because they are fighting for the soul of civilization, to prevent our culture's deterioration into atheistic materialism and social Darwinism that leads to a subhuman morality. Despite their complaint about Darwinian ideology, creationists attack the scientific theory of evolution by denying that the evolution of species has happened.

The young-earth creationists (YECs) have developed a sophisticated school of thought for studying their alternative to Darwinism. This group received the name "young-earth creationism" because of the belief that the earth is less than 10,000 years old. YECs try to refute the idea of deep time, that different species evolved gradually over long periods of time. The consensus among establishment scientists is that the earth is 4.5 billion years old, and the appearance of life first occurred about 3.8 billion years ago. YECs, in contrast, date the origin of earth at only 10,000 years ago.

YECs believe God created the world from nothing. Theologians use Latin to call this *creation ex nihilo*. This is not unusual. Virtually all Christians believe this. It does not contradict the theory of evolution, because evolution is not about the origin of the world or even life. Evolutionary theory tries to explain how one species developed out of another, what we have come to call "macroevolution."

YECs deny that any macroevolution occurred. One can witness microevolution occurring under a microscope, of course; so YECs affirm that evolution occurs *within* a species, but not *between* a previous species and a new species. What is so important to creationists is that species remain fixed. When reading Genesis, they see that God created ten different kinds of things. This word, *kind*, becomes the equivalent of *species*. So, YECs go to great lengths to repudiate the idea of macroevolution from one species to another.

This leads creationists to oppose the Darwinian model on the grounds that the ideas of *mutation and natural selection are insufficient to explain development of all living kinds from a single point of origin.* What creationists substitute for this natural explanation is the assertion that God created each species (each kind) as we see it today. No evolution from one species to another has occurred. This is the single most important scientific sense in which creationists are anti-Darwin.

What kind of evidence do creationists offer? One of the chief arguments against evolution from one kind or species to another is the alleged absence of transitional forms, what we popularly call the "missing links." If one species gradually gave way to a subsequent species and then died out, one would expect its fossil remains to chronicle the transition. Yet, claim the creationists, no such fossil record of transitional species has been found. Establishment scientists dispute this, to be sure, claiming to have found numerous transitional forms such as fossils of reptiles with wings that demonstrate evolution from sea creatures to flying creatures.

One of the implications of the creationist position is rejection of *common descent.* That is, creationists say, *apes and humans have separate ancestry.* Creationists affirm that the human race was especially created by God, as a distinct kind. They refute the standard Darwinian claim that humanity was selected from among a variety of prehuman higher primates. In addition, the entire human race is descended from a single pair of parents, Adam and Eve, say YECs.

Ethically as well as historically, creationists are adamant in affirming that all races and all ethnicities are united. No one race is allegedly more highly evolved than another, say creationists. There is only one human race. Creationists fear that social Darwinists could support racial discrimination if they say that separate races descended from separate species of monkeys. Even if social Darwinists on the eve of the twentieth century might have held such a view, evolutionary theorists in the twenty-first century do not appeal to common descent to justify racism.

How do we explain the fossil record that seems to support the Darwinian model? Creationists teach that *earth's geology is explained by catastrophism, including a worldwide flood.* Based on Genesis 6–8, flood geology provides an alternative explanation for the fossil record, an alternative to uniformitarianism, which holds that fossils were formed at a uniform rate over deep time. Creationist catastrophism ascribes to Noah's flood, dated three to five thousand years after Abraham, the reason we find so many fossils in sedimentary rock. If the Darwinian model were correct, argue the creationists, then we would see a geological ladder with simple fossils at the bottom and human fossils at the top; and such a stratification would support the idea of evolution over deep time. However, they say what we find are fossils of all life-forms at all levels. Therefore, the fossil record supports catastrophism, say creationists. On this point, Darwin's defenders contend that odd geological formations are due to shifting; and this explains why rock layers do not provide a nice neat ladder of time with all the fossils in their proper strata.

One important item for us to observe here is this: YECs offer scientific arguments against the Darwinian model. Whether appealing to lack of transitional forms or catastrophism, these are appeals to science and not appeals to the authority of the Bible. Whether this counts among establishment scientists as good science or not, scientific creationists see themselves as making scientific arguments against the Darwinian model.

Before leaving the creationists, let us turn from the science to the ideology. All creationists complain that Darwinism corrupts the morals of our civilization. What do they mean? Do they reject progress? No, not necessarily. Nearly everyone in Western culture affirms belief in progress. We would believe in progress with or without evolutionary theory. Charles Darwin presupposed progress, and his evolutionary theory reinforced the idea of progress. However, today's scientists agree that no such thing as progress can be seen in the biology, even if the idea of evolution is used to support progress ideologically.

What energizes and angers the creationists are social Darwinism, eugenics, and atheistic materialism. These are the poisons that could corrupt our youth in schools. In the early twentieth century the anti-Darwinists complained that these ideologies would lead to militarism, racial discrimination, and economic injustice. In recent decades, in contrast, they have complained about drug use, homosexuality, and promiscuity. In our judgment, the latter seem to have little relationship to the former. It would be hard to justify blaming the average high school science teacher for corrupting our youth on such matters.

Intelligent Design

Do fundamentalists, creationists, and intelligent design supporters all play on the same team? What kind of platoon system do we have here? Perhaps we can clarify by offering a brief chronicle of anti-Darwinian views in North America. The fundamentalists entered the game first by standing against the teaching of evolution in public schools from the 1920s into the 1960s; and remnants continue to spar under the label of biblical creationism. The scientific creationists starred in the game from the late 1960s through the mid-1990s. From the early 1990s to the present, intelligent design has rotated into the varsity spotlight. During this entire period, a reserve group of evolutionary theists has simply watched the contest from the bench, not actively in the game.

Just what is the intelligent design (ID) strategy? If we look at advanced life-forms, we see complexity. Living beings are complex—that is, we cannot take them apart and reduce them to their chemicals and have them remain alive. This reduction would kill them. Complex living beings and biological systems within living beings are not like wooden walls; we cannot construct them with component elements like nailing boards on one another. They are irreducibly complex. So, how did they develop? How did they evolve? They could not have evolved gradually step-by-step through random genetic variation and natural selection. Complex systems in nature must be the result of a designer, an intelligent designer who is transcendent and who intervenes in natural evolution to scoot it along. This in a nutshell is the ID argument.

Look at the animal eye or human eye, for example. The component cells that make up the eye each have a different function. No cell individually sees; only the system of cells provides sight for the organism. The eye is designed for sight and could not have evolved gradually through uniform small increments of change resulting from random mutations and environmental selection. The entire complex system for seeing must have appeared at once. A designer who wanted creatures to see must have intervened to make this happen.

As stated previously, the purpose of an eye is to see. Is it designed to make seeing possible? St. Thomas Aquinas, who lived in the twelfth century, noticed that some things that we observe in the world behave as though they had a purpose. He argued that the idea of purpose for nature is an example of God's governance of the universe. He said that when you see things acting for a specific end, you might infer the governing action of God. Notice that he did not use the word *design*. Nonetheless, later generations of scholars called his statement "the argument from design."

Today's ID advocates speak of design rather than governance and refrain from applying the word *God* because they want to be scientific and not religious. So, within the framework of science, the ID position supports macroevolution understood as change over time. Yet, ID denies that random variation and natural selection can provide an adequate explanation for the appearance of complexity in the natural world. Appeal to an intelligent designer provides a superior scientific explanation.

In addition to scholars such as these, ID is promoted in the public square by the Discovery Institute of Seattle, Washington, www.discoveryinstitute.org. A motto of the institute is "teach the controversy." The goal is to present ID as a scientific theory that provides an alternative to the Darwinian model; the institute advocates offering this alternative to children in the public school system.

At this point a controversy erupts. Defenders of Darwinism who take a strong stand against intelligent design accuse the ideology of being religious. Further, they accuse ID of being creationism in disguise. Actually, the logic proceeds this way: If pro-Darwinists can persuade the public that ID is creationism, then it follows that ID is religious. If they can persuade the public that ID is religious, then it follows that ID is not science. If ID is religion in disguise, then it can be excluded from public school science classes on the grounds that it violates the First Amendment to the U.S. Constitution which says the government cannot favor one religious sect over another. Some enemies use the term *intelligent design creationism* in an attempt to force the two into the same category. ID supporters vociferously deny that they are creationists; and they deny they are presenting a religious perspective. Rather, they claim to be providing a scientific model for the origin of species.

Theologically, the ID position differs from that of scientific creationism. The creationists, as their name indicates, are concerned about creation—that is, they assert that God created all species in their respective "kinds" at the beginning. No macroevolution has taken place since. ID, in contrast, is not concerned about creation but rather about change within the created order. ID finds it can accept something like macroevolution, but it adds that intelligent design rather than natural selection better explains macroevolution. Creationism denies that evolution takes place, whereas ID affirms evolution by offering an alternative to natural selection to explain evolution. This is quite a big difference. Both scientific creationists and ID supporters claim to be making scientific arguments, even if on Sundays they find themselves sitting next to one another in evangelical churches.

We (the authors) raise both scientific and theological objections to ID. Scientifically, the appeal to a transcendent designer to explain marvels of complexity such as the design of the eye avoids what the evidence says, namely, scientists have gathered many primitive and partially developed forms of the eye that demonstrate its gradual evolution over time. Theologically, ID trivializes God's work. If God intervenes in evolution to develop the eye, why do we still have to wear glasses? Is God less than a fully intelligent designer? What appears on the ID list of designs fails to include what is important to New Testament Christians, namely, God the redeemer heals. If God the redeemer had actually designed the eye, we would all have twenty-twenty vision.

Finally, we want to say this: Intelligent design is not science, nor should it be treated as science on a par with the Darwinian model of evolution. ID does not provide us with a fertile research program. It does not stimulate the development of new knowledge. ID is not going to predict what will happen in nature, nor does it provide the kind of knowledge we need to develop new medicines based on those predictions. Neither creationism nor ID passes the test for what counts as the best science. The Christian faith demands the best science, and neither creationism nor intelligent design measure up to this standard.

Jewish Interests in the Evolution Controversy

Is the war between evolution and creation strictly a war for Christian combatants? What about Jews and Muslims?

From the perspective of most of Judaism, the battle over evolution is somebody else's war. It is not a Jewish problem. The Jewish understanding is that God's creation at the beginning was unfinished; so it is no surprise that a scientific theory such as evolution might arise that shows ongoing creation. In addition, the Hebrew concept of *Tikkun Olam*, according to which we in the human race are mandated by God to fix what is broken in creation, leads to the strong emphasis in Jewish culture on healing, including the scientific pursuit of medicine.

Jewish interpreters of the Bible have a rich tradition. The tradition of *halakhah* permits and even encourages expansion from the literal character of God's revelation to the chosen people toward universal wisdom and shared knowledge. It permits and even encourages healthy hospitality to science. When modern science offers new understandings of the natural world, Jewish interpreters quickly incorporate this into their interpretation of God's work in creation. A conflict with the Darwinian model of evolution is less likely to arise in Judaism than in other religions of the book.

Even so, some Orthodox Jews see a conflict between the Darwinian model and allegiance to the biblical account of creation in the book of Genesis. Some Orthodox Jews find themselves in sympathy with Christian creationists and borrow Christian arguments. On balance, however, the dominant view of contemporary Judaism is to treat Genesis symbolically or figuratively, not literally; hence, relatively little difficulty with Darwinian evolution has arisen.

Muslim Interests in the Evolution Controversy

The religion of Islam, somewhat like Christianity, was born in an ancient culture now long past. We all have to mature in a world permeated with modern science. "God is the Creator of everything," says the Qur'an (13:16). Now, did God create once and for all, only at the beginning? Elsewhere we read: "Were we worn out by the first creation?" (50:15). Could this indicate a second creation or, better, continuous creation? Some Muslims, especially those educated in the West, think so. Westernized Muslims want to interpret the Qur'an in such a way that the road can be paved for evolutionary theory to travel right into the heart of Islamic theology.

Not every Muslim would concur that Islam can easily open its gates to evolutionary science, because that science seems to be connected to materialist ideology. The atheistic materialism that so frequently accompanies evolutionary science denies the existence of the human mind, of spiritual reality, and even God. The Islamic religious vision retains the independent existence of mind and spirit, as well as God. It is a perversion to say that mind simply evolved from a material base; and it is an even bigger perversion to deny that the creator God has a design operative in natural processes.

Some Muslims, especially in Turkey, go still further down the anti-Darwinian road. Like America, a culture war between religion and secularism remains hot. The Turkish public school system insists on teaching a Darwinian model of evolution as the only approach to biology. Many Muslims feel this constitutes a secular intrusion into their religious beliefs. They borrow many of the arguments raised by scientific creationists and intelligent design advocates to use in the Turkish culture war.

In summary, among today's Muslims we can find a spectrum. On one end, we can find full acceptance of Darwinian evolution complete with precedents identified in the Qur'an. In the middle we can find toleration for the science with rejection of the materialist ideology. At the other end we find rejection of Darwinian evolution parallel to what we find in creationism and ID.

Christian Theistic Evolution

Should Christians take a stand against Darwinism? One would think so if we listen only to what the scientific creationists and intelligent design advocates say. The problem is that both suggest that to be Christian is to be opposed to Darwinism. The so-called Christian view is placed over against the Darwinian view. This is misleading, we believe. Why? Because for more than a century many Christians have

	Science in General	Evolutionary Science	Evolutionary Ideology
Darwinian science	Yes	Yes	Not necessarily
Darwinian ideology	Yes	Yes	Yes
Creationism	Yes	No	No
Intelligent design	Yes	No	No
Judaism	Yes	Yes	Not necessarily
Westernized Islam	Yes	Yes	No
Theistic evolution	Yes	Yes	No

made their peace with Darwinian evolution. Those who both affirm their Christian faith and accept natural selection as a scientific explanation for macroevolution play on a team we will call *theistic evolution*.

Playing forward on the team of theistic evolutionists we can find conservatives such as B. B. Warfield, the famous Princeton theologian at the end of the nineteenth century. Warfield provided the American fundamentalists with their doctrine of scriptural inspiration. What is widely overlooked is that Warfield was also a supporter of Darwinism. He saw God's work in bringing the human race into existence through evolution as a parallel to the way the Holy Spirit inspired the writers of the New Testament. In fact, a significant minority of the early fundamentalists prior to the 1920s were theistic evolutionists. What historians frequently forget is that the original Christian fundamentalism did not find itself opposed to science in general or to evolution in particular; the enemy of fundamentalism was liberal Protestantism. In the first decades, fundamentalists could also be Darwinists.

Warfield was a Protestant. Catholics could be theistic evolutionists, too. Pierre Teilhard de Chardin, a Jesuit priest and paleontologist, is known for discovering Peking Man in 1929. Teilhard combined Darwinian evolution with the Christian doctrines of creation and redemption, creating a model of world history over deep time that traces the development of life from inanimate matter up through sentient beings into intellectual and spiritual achievements. Teilhard projects a future in which independent human intelligences will unite with one another in a grand mystical union. Our minds will become attuned to one another's minds, and with God. Teilhard, who died in 1955, may have been the most comprehensive of the theistic evolutionists to date.

We (the authors) place ourselves in the theistic evolution camp somewhere between Warfield and Teilhard. In what follows we would like to share with you some key strategies for an aggressive game plan for uniting evolutionary science with the Christian vision of creation and redemption.

We offer seven principles of theistic evolution. They provide modest illumination, not the brightness of final truth. Borrowing from science, they make up a "theological model" that we hope will shed light on further reflection and provide spiritual guidance. First, we believe that *the Darwinian model of evolution should be conditionally accepted*. We accept and work with the Darwinian model as we would any other scientific theory—that is, if it's fertile for the growth of new knowledge, then it is worth embracing for the time being. No scientific theory is eternal. Eventually, all theories get replaced with better ones. The Darwinian model is today's best science. Scientific creationism and intelligent design provide only inferior science, perhaps not even science at all.

Second, *God is the primary cause while nature operates according to secondary causes*. As the primary cause, God is the creator of all things. God brought the world into existence from nothing. And God continues to sustain the world in its existence. Within the created order, the world operates according to laws and principles. Events are contingent and sometimes free—that is, what happens in nature and in human life is unpredictable. Yet, all that happens is the result of secondary causes, the result of one natural creature relating to another natural creature. Science studies the realm of secondary causation, not primary causation. Science can discern the laws that govern natural processes; but it cannot perceive the source of those laws and processes.

Third, *God has a purpose for nature that scientists cannot see within nature.* We do not expect a research scientist looking through the lenses of random variation and natural selection to perceive a grand design in nature or an inherent purpose toward which all things are moving. As both ID supporters and evolutionary biologists acknowledge, some systems in nature exhibit characteristics of design. The eye, for example, is designed for seeing. Yet, local design in complex systems does not in itself give evidence of a single grand design for the totality of the created universe. As Christians, we believe the entire created universe has a purpose, a divinely appointed purpose. To discern that purpose we will need to rely on a special revelation from God.

Fourth, *God's promised new creation provides the purpose for the present creation.* We rely on three important passages from scripture. First, Genesis 1:31: "God saw everything he had made, and indeed, it was very good." Second, Revelation 21:1: "Then I saw a new heaven and a new earth." Third, between these two, we live with St. Paul who wrote in 1 Corinthians 13:12: "now we see in a mirror dimly." We are cautious, because we can only see dimly in a mirror that reflects back what we project into it. Because science cannot shine light on the new creation promised by the Bible, we can apprehend it only in faith and trust.

Fifth, *God creates from the future, not from the past.* We believe that God creates the world by giving it a future. This is what God did at the beginning, in Genesis 1:1–2:4a. For God to say that this world is "very good," God must already have had in mind the anticipated new creation prophesied in Revelation 21 and 22. This will be the redeemed creation. It will be the creation where all illnesses will be healed, where there will be no crying nor pain, and where death shall be no more. Further, it will be the creation where the lion will lie down with the lamb, and we the human race will live in harmony with all of nature. Only when the created world has attained this redeemed state will it finally be created and dubbed "very good."

Sixth, *the book of Genesis does not describe a finished event in the past; rather it describes the full sweep of God's creative activities that includes us today.* The account of creation in Genesis 1:1–2:4a, we believe, applies to the entire history of the cosmos, beginning perhaps with the Big Bang 13.7 billion years ago and extending into the future far enough to take into account the advent of the new creation the Bible promises. Right now, God is at work. God is working as primary cause with all of nature's secondary causes—natural causes as understood by physicists, chemists, biologists, geneticists, and neuroscientists—to bring into existence an ever more complex realm of interaction between ourselves, our world, and our God. Today we find ourselves somewhere between day one and day six. Day seven, the Sabbath, is scheduled for the day after the arrival of the prophesied New Jerusalem of the closing chapters of the Bible. Then God can declare that all of creation is "very good" and take that well-deserved divine rest.

Seventh, *redemption coincides with creation.* One of the mistakes of both the creationists and the ID supporters is to limit the theological questions posed to science to the domain of creation. We believe creation cannot be understood from the perspective of faith unless it is viewed in light of redemption. So, even if creationism or ID should be successful at unseating the Darwinian model, it would not follow that the distinctively Christian viewpoint will have prevailed. What is distinctively Christian is not an explanation for a biological world replete with extinctions, predator–prey violence, suffering from disease, and falling by the wayside while only the reproductively fit survive; rather, what is distinctively Christian is reliance on Isaiah's prophecy that in God's kingdom the lion will lie down with the lamb and all of the creation will live in harmony. Without this transformative vision, we cannot deal adequately with God's relation to the creation; and we cannot understand clearly where science can be helpful or not helpful in articulating our faith in God.

Note that we do not conflate evolution with progress. We do not buy this ideology, or any of the other Darwinian ideologies. We do not want to Christianize Darwinism. Rather, we assess the Darwinian model from the standpoint of the divine promise of a new creation. We believe that God's creative work is not done yet. We anticipate its furtherance and its consummate fulfillment.

What Should Our Schools Teach?

One of our chief concerns is that young people in our schools—whether public schools, Christian day schools, Roman Catholic parochial schools, or even home schooling situations—receive the best science. Creationism and intelligent design are not the best science. Even if we agree to "teach the controversy," we should proceed to teach the Darwinian model as the science that has proven itself for more than a century to be a fertile theory, which generates new knowledge.

In conclusion, a strong faith in God the creator and redeemer need not fear good science; rather, science should be seen as a window looking out on the magnificent complexity that inheres in the natural world. When it comes to competing models in the evolution controversy, we should allow the better theory or model to win out. Victory will be measured by fertility. As of this point in time, the Darwinian model should be declared the winner. Without baptizing evolutionary biology as absolute, we believe Christians along with Jews and Muslims should encourage young people in schools to benefit from its teaching.

CHAPTER 5

The Intelligent Design Controversy Summarized

by Phillip E. Johnson

In an argument cut short by ill health, Phillip Johnson argues for the importance of intelligent design in explaining the evolution of modern life-forms. He agrees to the methods of science, and that conclusions need to be pursued scientifically; and he agrees to the existence of microevolution (within kinds) by principles of natural selection, but denies the validity of extrapolating from micro- to macroevolution (long-term branching of the family tree). He argues particularly that evolutionary theory has not explained the origin of life. He suggests that the doctrine of evolution is as much grounded in ideology as other faiths. He argues that science will in the end demonstrate that ID must be used to explain life-forms because of the inadequacies and inadequate evidence for Darwinian evolution. He argues further that his intent has never been to affect teaching in public school, but to open universities and the scientific community to plausible alternatives to Darwinian theory.

Every newspaper reader knows the state of the legal controversy surrounding mention of intelligent design or even skepticism about the Darwinian mechanism in the public schools. The scientific organizations and secularist legal advocacy groups have mounted a powerful counterattack, and have convinced many journalists and some judges that attempts to reduce the dogmatism with which the Darwinian story is presented in public schools are inherently unconstitutional because of the presumed motivation behind the attempts.

For those who accept the official story—that the only purpose of the intelligent design movement was to find a way around constitutional rulings to allow the insertion of a religious doctrine into the public schools—it seems that the controversy has been resolved in favor of Darwinism. However, the official story is false. Scientific critics of Darwinism, like William Dembski and myself, were never interested primarily in changing public school teaching. Our ambition has been to legitimate an alternative to strict Darwinism in the universities and in the science community itself, by showing that evidence considered without philosophical bias points to the probable participation of an intelligent cause in the major innovations in the history of life, including the so far unexplained appearance of the baffling complexity of the cell. This possibility should not be anathema to scientists, because it merely involves employing in biology the same methods for detecting intelligence that are routinely employed in other contexts, such as the interpretation of suspected radio signals from outer space. If the evidence of intelligence is there but is disregarded because Darwinist biologists fear that the intelligence might be taken to be something unacceptable—such as God—then it is the Darwinists, rather than their critics, who are acting from a religious prejudice.

The first element to keep in mind in evaluating the claims of Darwinian evolution in its confrontation with intelligent design theory is the necessary extrapolation—or leap—Darwinists rely on to go from microevolution, which is the only kind of evolution that can be demonstrated, to the grand story of molecule-to-man macroevolution. Microevolution is merely the gradual modification of a population in any degree, however slight. Macroevolution in the relevant sense involves the introduction of new genetic information, and the consequent appearance of new complex functional organs.

Modification of a species by natural selection goes on all the time, because some individual organisms are likely to be more successful at leaving viable offspring than others. Only the successful reproducers pass their genes on to the next generation, so, over many generations, the population inevitably becomes composed of individuals who inherited their genes from the most successful reproducers.

This process explains how a fundamentally stable species of bacteria or viruses can become temporarily resistant to an antibiotic drug while the drug pervades their environment. Only the individuals who happen to be relatively resistant survive to leave offspring, and so their genes come to dominate the population. When the drug is removed for a time, the population tends to lose its resistance because the susceptible organisms are once again able to leave offspring, and may be more fit than those who are specialized to resist a drug no longer present.

There is no doubt that microevolution occurs, and that populations are continually modified by it without being transformed in any fundamental sense. It is doubtful that microevolution tells us anything significant about the interesting and controversial aspects of evolutionary theory—like how a single-celled organism like a bacterium becomes a complex, multicellular animal, or how an ape becomes a human being. Observed microevolution is a conservative process that shows how a species can remain in existence through severe environmental stress by adapting to local conditions.

Convinced Darwinists find the extrapolation from micro to macro to be entirely reasonable and require no proof for it beyond the availability of vast amounts of time. The crucial equation, then, is that microevolution plus deep time equals all the macroevolution necessary to produce whatever species now exist. This equation might be justifiable if microevolution was the same sort of thing as macroevolution, only less of it. On the contrary, microevolution—which is the only form of evolution that can be demonstrated—is a conservative force that merely involves a re-sorting of the gene pool in a population to enable an existing species to adapt to changing environmental circumstances without fundamental change. It does not produce new biological information or the kind of change that would require the species to be put into a different place in the taxonomic hierarchy.

Intelligent design theorists do not necessarily deny that macroevolutionary changes have somehow occurred, but we do deny that the unintelligent causes at work in microevolution are sufficient to account for the appearance of new genetic information or new body plans. That being the case, it is legitimate and even necessary to consider that some intelligent cause may have been needed to produce the marvels of integrated functional complexity that we find all around us in living creatures.

Another reason for considering the possible role of intelligent causes in biology is the deep mystery that surrounds the question of how the first living cell came into existence. Research into this subject is so discouraging that Darwinists sometimes disavow the subject entirely, saying that biological evolution begins with a cell already in existence. Nonetheless, a naturalistic explanation for the first crucial step is needed if the theory is not to be left incomplete, and both textbooks and museum exhibits generally state or imply incorrectly that a solution to the origin-of-life question is either already in hand or about to be discovered.

Any argument about the validity of evolutionary theory is in large part a bet about what future scientists will discover. Our scientists are very smart, and very industrious. They may follow a false path for a while, or even a long while, but in the end, their methods will almost certainly find truth. If it is true that life originated by an unguided series of chemical combinations, and then proceeded to its present state of complexity and diversity by the Darwinian mechanism of random genetic variation and differential reproduction, then our scientists will eventually put an end to present controversies by employing the tried-and-true methods of experimental science, rather than by intimidating skeptics and attacking their motives. On the other hand, if the truth is something more mysterious and less welcome to today's scientific culture, then a more impartial scientific community of the future will eventually discover that truth also. In the long run, it is always science—by which I mean careful, impartial investigation—on which we must rely.

For now, it is both reasonable and necessary that there should be robust criticism of claims that go beyond the available evidence, especially when those claims have great cultural importance.

PART II

Historical Markers and the Global Impact of the Debate

Intelligent Design and the Native's Point of View (Assuming the Native Is an Educated Eighteenth-Century European)

by Jonathan Marks

Jonathan Marks traces the roots of evolutionary theory back before Darwin to a series of intellectual ideas and movements extending back to the seventeenth century. Historical questions include whether there could have been people before Adam; to what degree human beings are different from other animals; is human nature "degraded"; whether life can be aligned on a great chain or hierarchy of being or is to be seen as a branching into diverse forms not arrangeable in hierarchical terms; how the relationship between cause and effect is to be understood; whether human variants or "races" derive from a single creation or many. Marks provides a description of "natural theology," beginning in the seventeenth century and ultimately offers a rebuttal of creationism and intelligent design.

Anthropology and the History of Ideas

Let's try to put ourselves ethnographically in the place of someone trying to make sense of the human species around the year 1750. We assume that new knowledge is valuable; that demonstration, experiment, and reason are the most likely ways of producing reliable knowledge; and that we limit our scope of interests to the natural world. What data and issues would be the most deserving of our attention?

1. *Could there have been people before Adam?* The first to make this suggestion was a Frenchman named Isaac de la Peyrère, in a 1655 book called *Pre-Adamites*. Perhaps, argued Peyrère, the biblical text of human origin describes only a single, local creation, the ancestors of the peoples of the Middle East. With so many diverse peoples now known, is it more reasonable to think they all descended from a common source, or that, rather, they may be the products of separate, unrecorded creative acts? Peyrère becomes a patriarch not only of biblical criticism, but of polygenism, the theory of multiple human origins (see the following text).

2. *Are humans really so different from other animals?* Edward Tyson's 1699 study of the anatomy of a chimpanzee made it abundantly clear that we are linked corporeally with the beasts. Tyson interpreted his results as the popular philosophy of his day would have it—based on the work of Descartes that our bodies connect us materially to the rest of the living world, but that our minds and souls are the portals through which we partake of the divine. The ape could not speak, much less reason, in spite of his physical similarity to a young boy—a fact rendered sensible through Cartesian dualism, but which nevertheless bridged an important gap between people and nature.

3. *Is human nature really so degraded?* The idea that people fell from grace in a primordial Eden, and are doomed to live in misery on account of it, was certainly a self-serving philosophy for the medieval clergy and aristocracy to preach. It helped ensure that people would not even bother to try to improve their lot in this world: (a good Christian should be focusing on the *next* world, in any event). And yet the economics of colonialism and the beginnings of the industrial evolution made upward mobility more possible than ever, and you could reasonably dream of making a better life for yourself—perhaps even to envision a world in which all citizens might be entitled to the same rights. The doctrine of progress, although ultimately flawed, nevertheless helped turn minds away from the static social world of feudalism and toward the interpretation of history in terms of social and political ferment, mobility, and mutability.

4. *Is life really one-dimensional?* The Great Chain of Being—that all species could be ranked along a single scale of increasing perfection, with us at the top—had dominated scholarly thought about nature for many centuries. In 1735 the Swedish physician–botanist Carl Linnaeus (who published under the Latin name Carolus) published a small pamphlet that undermined the idea of a "great chain." In his *System of Nature*, Linnaeus organized species not in terms of how similar they are to us, but by how similar they are to one another. By the turn of the nineteenth century, the naturalist Georges Cuvier could argue that a great chain was impossible, for there were four kinds of animals—segmented (i.e., arthropods), shelled (i.e., mollusks), radial (i.e., those with other than a bilateral symmetry), and vertebrate—and they were so different in body plan as to be incomparable to one another, and

thus not rankable. In such a system, however, we fell in among a group of animals Linnaeus called "Mammals" in 1758, and more tightly within a group he called "Primates," comprised of apes, monkeys, lemurs, and bats. The meaning of this arrangement was obscure, even considering the mistaken inclusion of bats into primates.

5. *How does causality work?* The experience of the physical sciences was that causes precede effects. Something in the future, generally speaking, cannot cause something in the past. In 1776, Edward Gibbon began publishing his monumental analytic work on the history of the Roman Empire, explaining the present (at any point in time) in terms of the past. With physics and society becoming more rigorously historicized, philosopher David Hume launched a vigorous critique against the sloppy inference of causal relations. And yet, biology was not historical at all. On the mountains of Ararat, where Noah's ark landed, the animals getting off the boat appeared to be adapted *not* to where they were (Turkey or Armenia, presumably), but rather to where they were going *to end up* (polar bears to the arctic; bison to the Great Plains; pandas to bamboo forests). This posed a problem, however: How could their adaptations exist for future use? It would seem as though history was working in reverse here—the future (where they will end up being adapted) is causing their present state. And more practically, how could the animals even get from Ararat to where they were adapted without dying first? Just imagine being a polar bear in the Near East.

6. *Aren't we all one species?* One odd implication of Isaac de la Peyrère's work on pre-Adamites was the suggestion that different groups of people might be the products of separate creative acts. The obvious interfertility of all people (demonstrated by sailors over the centuries) suggested monogenism, that all people are the products of a single creative act and thus share a common ancestry. This was most compatible with a literal reading of the Bible, but also carried with it an important biological implication: that somehow the human form must be to some extent mutable, for different-looking peoples would all be descended from Adam and Eve, regardless of what they looked like today. Alternatively, the institution of slavery was widely rationalized by the proposition that enslaved peoples were beastly and were unconnected genealogically to the slavers. Polygenism required a looser reading of scripture and a strictly creationist view of human prehistory—that the differences among peoples are today as they have always been. Polygenism reached the height of its popularity around the time of the Civil War, perhaps unsurprisingly, but faded in the aftermath of the war. What remained was the position that because humans are all one species, the human form must have changed somewhat over time.

The Logic of Natural Theology

Back in the 1600s a radical way of thinking about the world had emerged in Europe. In the first place, it was represented by a privileged new form of knowledge, comprised of experiment, demonstration, and reason—as opposed to other forms of knowledge, such as revelation and tradition. This "new philosophy" (a label applied by the poet John Donne) specialized in falsifying received wisdom: When Galileo showed that there are things going around the planet Jupiter, for example, it could no longer be maintained that everything goes around the earth.

By privileging reason over other forms of thought, philosophers of the seventeenth century quickly proved threatening to established knowledge. If we know that dead people cannot write, and the book of Deuteronomy describes the death and burial of Moses—argued the philosopher Spinoza—then how can we believe he wrote that book, as we have traditionally been told? Spinoza was excommunicated by the Amsterdam Jewish community for such thoughts, but the names of excommunicators are lost to history, whereas Spinoza himself is widely acknowledged as one of the founders of modern rationalist philosophy. Miracles became sidelined, interesting only to the credulous and childlike; and what the ancients ascribed to miracle was reinterpreted as simply primitive ignorance. The new philosophy—or science, as it came to be known—soon developed its own social organizations (such as the Royal Society), and specialized forums for dissemination or documenting claims (the scientific paper).

Its most radical intellectual practice was to construct a barrier between the natural realm and the supernatural realm. Anthropologists since Bronislaw Malinowski in the 1920s have appreciated the extent to which most people do *not* make such a distinction; spiritual forces suffuse human existence, and it makes no more sense to separate those forces from daily life than it does to separate the eggs from the rest of a cake. As late as the 1890s, in England, Thomas Huxley was waging a social war to professionalize science education and take it out of the hands of country parsons—because it was still so widely assumed that nature and religion somehow go together.

Nevertheless, what united these seventeenth-century scholars was the goal of understanding the regularities that govern the physical world, independently of the spiritual world. Indeed, Isaac Newton's 1687 work, the *Principia*, showed that something as mysterious and arcane as gravity could be reduced to mathematics. Moreover, it showed that the same regularities existed in the heavens (in the motion of planets) as on earth (in the falling of apples). Wherever God was—and you could hardly find a person more "spiritual" than Newton—it did not seem as though his domain was in outer space, if earthly rules of physics could be seen to apply there.

And yet, as creator of the universe, he left his imprint on it. Discovering the regularities that govern the workings of the universe could be seen as glimpsing into God's mind. This would have been the height of blasphemy a few hundred years earlier, but now could be taken as a respectable—indeed, as a reverential—goal. Newton was hailed as one who had decoded some of God's deepest secrets, and the merits of continuing in that vein were taken as self-evident. Consider this: In describing the achievement of sequencing the human genome with millennial technology, geneticist Francis Collins (Wode, 2000) invoked a metaphor from centuries earlier: "We have caught the first glimpse of our own instruction book, previously known only to God." British scholars were more eager to discover God's hidden secrets in earthly biological facts than were their counterparts on the Continent. From John Ray's *The Wisdom of God Manifested in the Works of Creation* (1691) through William Paley's *Natural Theology* (1802) and the diverse Bridgewater Treatises of the 1830s, these scholars believed that the greatest goal of the study of life was to testify to the power, beneficence, and bounty of God.

This was in fact the biology that Charles Darwin studied while a student at Cambridge and Edinburgh. But for all its piety, natural theology was increasingly difficult to sustain, as the meaning of biological patterns in nature became more obscure. John Ray had understood God's wisdom to reach expression in the Great Chain of Being, which connected all living forms to each other; consequently he had pronounced extinction impossible, as it would represent the destruction of God's plan. And yet by the 1700s, two things were clear: species in historical times had been driven to extinction (notably the dodo), and prehistoric times were positively rife with now-extinct animals. Clearly if God's plan really were manifested in the works of creation, it was a somewhat different plan than the one that Ray saw.

A second problem was that of the Linnaean hierarchy, which had superseded the great chain as an organizing principle for species in the eighteenth century, but whose meaning was quite unfathomable. Linnaeus himself didn't speculate on it, but the nested hierarchy seemed to suggest that God had two concurrent plans: one that showed common themes in the underlying structures of diverse species, and one that showed the ways in which particular animal species fit in perfectly with their environments. The first was hard to explain, seemingly a lapse of creativity on his part, or else simple laziness. The second was also hard to explain, except teleologically—with God fashioning animals for environments that existed not on Mt. Ararat, where they were starting from, but for those elsewhere on earth, which they would most likely go extinct before reaching. The most basic facts of modern biology in 1780 posed very difficult theological problems for biologists trying to make sense of God's handiwork.

Third, by the 1790s the field of philology, or the study of language, was developing. Early philologists could show that very different languages seemed to share basic similarities, and could be grouped into clusters of similarity, rather like what Linnaeus had accomplished with species. In this case, however, the clusters had been produced only in the last few thousand years, as written records documented the diversification of, say, European languages from medieval Germanic and Latin ancestors. Not only was language diversification a documented historical process, but this contradicted the static view of language given in the Bible—in which God makes languages different from one another at the Tower of Babel, and they presumably stay that way. Clearly, there was a lot more to understanding linguistic changes over time than the Bible gives us. Moreover, if philologists were right, then languages from India to Ireland were descended from a very remote common ancestral language—Indo-European—which was probably spoken long before the Tower of Babel was supposed to have been built, and which presumably rendered the Tower of Babel as an explanation for language diversity merely a pleasant fiction.

Fourth, by the early nineteenth century it was clear that there had existed in remote times an extraordinary array of living beings, sharing some similarities with known living forms, but often wildly unfamiliar in themselves. Not only was widespread extinction an obvious fact, but it was also clear that the extinct species had not all lived and died at the same time; rather, they had died in particular geological formations, which implied specific periods in earth history. Forget Noah's flood—the history of life on earth incorporated repeated successions of fauna, as older species continually died out and were replaced in the fossil record by different kinds of animals. Once again, it was difficult to make theological sense of such data: it implied many false steps, indeed design flaws, in the history of life. And to muddy the picture even more, death and sin are theologically connected: St. Paul's Epistle to the Romans (6:23) says, "For the wages of sin is death; but the gift of God is eternal life through Jesus Christ our Lord." And yet there was surely an awful lot of death, apparently unconnected to sin, evident in the history of life.

Fifth, by the 1830s it was clear that the geographic distribution of species could not sustain a simple biblical interpretation. If God made animals to be adapted to their environment, and clearly enjoyed recycling body plans, we might expect that the species from a rain forest in South America might appear as well in the rain forest of Africa. And yet they did not. Further, extinct animals in one area seemed to be similar to the ones there presently, and rather less so to other living or extinct species. As a young naturalist wrote in 1839, "This wonderful relationship in the same continent between the dead and the living will, I do not doubt, hereafter throw more light on the appearance of organic beings on our earth, and their disappearance from it, than any other class of facts" (p. 187). Moreover, there would also be no reason to expect species on different islands in an archipelago to be slightly different from one another, and yet they indeed seemed to be, as Darwin also acknowledged in *The Voyage of the Beagle* (1839).

Sixth, the antiquity of the human species was under relentless assault. Crude stone tools were turning up in ancient geological deposits all over Europe, and they clearly implied the existence of crude ancient people. Were they from before Adam and Eve, or after? Although this may seem like a silly question, it actually had important theological implications. It seemed by the 1850s that the best way to rescue scripture and reconcile it with science was to see the Garden of Eden as the beginning of the modern earth, but preceded by untold eons of premodern life. Adam and Eve, created in the Garden of Eden, were given a world prepared for them, with essentially modern species. The stone tools were obviously fashioned by human hands, and were thus post-Adam.

All of which yielded a satisfyingly pious interpretation of the data—unless one could produce solid evidence of stone tools along with extinct animals. That would put Adam and Eve in a premodern world; indeed it would effectively make them premodern, and essentially destroy what was left of the Garden of Eden story. The idea that Adam and Eve would have lived with dinosaurs was far more theologically problematic: at very least, it rendered the Garden of Eden itself an entirely unfamiliar spot, and suddenly expanded by orders of magnitude the number of species Noah would have to get on board the ark. And at worst, it could render the divine origin of humankind a pleasant biblical fable, like Noah's ark and the Tower of Babel.

The great antiquity of the earth, and of life, had been the centerpiece of Charles Lyell's *Principles of Geology* in the early 1830s. But even Lyell held out against the idea of people actually coexisting with extinct animals—for the natural theologian, a lot hung on that association, and it would have to stand up to especially rigorous standards. Finally, in 1858, careful excavations at Brixham Cave in England made the association impossible to deny. Darwin's *The Origin of Species* was published the following year. Lyell himself published *The Antiquity of Man* a few years later.

Natural theology was what Darwin destroyed, the idea that the history of life—that is, the origin of species—can best be understood as a series of miracles and that God created things for a purpose, which can be revealed by appropriate study and meditation. The origin of life itself might still be a miracle, but the number of such miracles shrank to "one or a few" in the last paragraph of *The Origin of Species*. Darwin showed that the history of life could be explained by understandable natural forces, and probably ought to be. The glory and wisdom of God were nice, but could be safely isolated from a discussion of the diversity of life, whose patterns were more satisfactorily explained by common ancestry.

None of which is to say that the history of life, and the ultimate emergence of our own species, were not part of a great plan unfolding. Rather, we simply have no access to the plan, and we don't seem to need to refer to it to figure out what happened. Darwinism explained homology (the correspondence of parts in very different animals) as relics of ancient common ancestry, and explained adaptation as a consequence of the unique historical trajectory taken by each species. It also explained the mysterious, yet obvious, Linnaean pattern of groups-within-groups as a first approximation of the patterns of ancestry among the species.

The Challenge to Intelligent Design

Clearly it is difficult to infer the hand of God from his ostensible work on earth. His handiwork could be interpreted as a great chain or as a nested hierarchy. His wisdom is demonstrated by both the impossibility of extinction and by the prevalence of extinction. Genetics and paleontology now show that the diversity of life can be accounted for by a small number of natural processes, and so scientifically it probably ought to be. Whatever his plan is, it is not accessible to science; that is, it is not knowable by the conventions of reliability established since the seventeenth century.

We pay a high price for extending the barrier between nature and "supernature," constructed during the 1600s, to human origins. It becomes difficult to maintain, for example, that humans alone are endowed with a divine soul. Either all living creatures have divine souls (a position compatible with Hinduism, for example), or none does. If humans have them, how can chimpanzees and gorillas and the extinct *Paranthropus boisei* not? One recourse would be to mark out a spiritual origin of the human species at some point, based on arbitrary criteria. True or not, it lies outside the domain of scientific competence and interest.

Creationism was an unmarked category prior to Darwin—it was normative, or taken for granted so pervasively that it did not require a name. As a political movement, it arose in opposition to Darwinism, particularly motivated by religious issues; for Darwinism had sucked the theology right out of natural theology.

But just what was Darwinism? Darwin quickly became such an intellectual icon that all sorts of intellectual positions, often quite loosely affiliated with the dual propositions of Darwinism—that life is genealogically connected, and adaptation is the result of natural selection—claimed him as their namesake or godfather. A late-nineteenth-century scientific movement preached exploitation, colonialism, war, and genocide in the name of Darwin; likewise, various forms of scientific racism and genetic determinism in the twentieth century also linked themselves to Darwin.

It would be nice to keep Darwin's name unsullied, and an argument could be made that scientists have a responsibility to do so. At very least, associating Darwin's name with social and political positions makes it more difficult to discuss the basic biology of Darwinism. And yet, we acknowledge that science in the modern world is a social discourse, in which legitimacy is conferred on ideas perceived to be scientific. As a result, it is not surprising that the voice of authority that comes with science might be usurped by both the nonscientific ideas held by scientists, and by ideas that are themselves not scientific at all, or even antiscientific. As an example of the former, there is the Charles Darwin Institute, maintained today by psychologist J. P. Rushton, who believes that human races have evolved to be different intellectually and sexually, and whose work is repudiated in anthropology and biology. As examples of the latter are religious sects such as Christian Science and Scientology.

The Scopes trial in 1925 showed that, however distasteful Darwinism may seem, banning the teaching of evolution would be unsuccessful; and half a century later, creationists developed a new strategy: scientific creationism. Here, with the literal truth of the Bible as axiomatic, creationists attempted to bend nature to conform to it. The geological column, and the apparent evidence of untold ages of earth history, such as the Grand Canyon, would all be explained by recourse to Noah's flood. Genetics would be dismissed, fossils connecting living groups of animals would be explained as lies, and bogus footprints of humans and dinosaurs in Texas would be brandished as evidence for the coexistence of those species, and by a bizarre extension, for the truth of the Bible. Scientific creationism was unable to convince a federal court of its sincerity or competency as science in 1981.

In the 1990s, creationists adopted a new legal strategy. Rather than challenge science on its own turf—that is, rather than trying to show that creationism really is science—creationists now tried to wrest science from the scientists. Intelligent design (ID) was consciously formulated to oppose the assumption of naturalism central to the methods of modern science, and sought to expand what counts as "science" to include supernatural agency. In other words, intelligent design seeks to breach the wall constructed between nature and supernature in the seventeenth century, on which modern scientific reasoning is to a large extent founded.

The problem is that supernatural forces are by definition capricious. They constitute the very opposite of the physical regularities that science tries to analyze. If you believe in angular momentum and inertia, then you cannot believe that the earth stopped rotating while the Hebrews were laying siege to Gibeon, and started up again a day later (Joshua 10:12–13), without engendering globally cataclysmic consequences.

Intelligent design itself calls attention to the methodological assumptions of science, and tries to cast a wide net. Arguing ostensibly on behalf of the imminent presence of a benevolent deity, ID has successfully extended its appeal beyond the evangelical Protestants and biblical literalists who see it as a "wedge" by which to topple Darwinism in science class.

It's not that ID is demonstrably wrong—it is just anachronistic. The issues it engages are not those of Darwinism, but of rationalism, in the decades that preceded Darwin. In some sense Darwinism is an automatic outgrowth of rationalism: Given a set of methods for thinking about the world, it stands to reason that sooner or later the idea of common descent will arise (as in fact it did with several other scholars in Victorian England, such as Alfred Russel Wallace and Herbert Spencer). It is simply the theory that best explains the data, which is what science aims to produce.

ID's confrontation, then, is not so much with the specific interpretation of the data on the history of life, but with the intellectual methods by which data are interpreted. This is not about whether we came from apes, but about how we draw scientific inferences. It is about what counts as reliable and useful knowledge: Is the naturalistic explanation the best, or should supernatural explanations be admitted into the arsenal of scientific tools as well? (I sense parapsychologists and cryptozoologists drooling in anticipation of legitimacy!) Let's pose four questions of intelligent design to show how difficult it is as a source of reliable knowledge.

First, can we identify "design" in the world without a designer? I live in the state of North Carolina, which has a very distinctive and easily recognizable form (see Figure 6.1).

It is quite complex; I could not approximate it very well freehand. Why does it look the way it does? As the creationists commonly do, let me suggest two alternatives. One, the form of the state of North Carolina came into existence incrementally via a set of processes and events ranging from the geology of the Atlantic coastline and the shape of the Catawba River, to treaties and agreements made with various Indian tribes, and with the states of Virginia, Georgia, Tennessee, and South Carolina—complex processes and events, but ultimately studiable and knowable. And two, the state of North Carolina was zapped into existence by the hand of a divine state-maker.

Alternatively, is it more persuasive to regard the intricate structure of a snowflake as the result of complex, but knowable, processes of crystal growth; or as the result of the intervention of a divine snowflake-etcher?

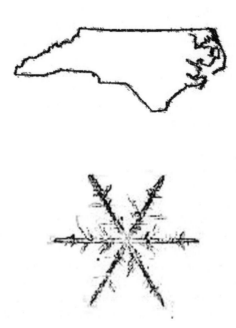

Figure 6.1
Top, North Carolina. Bottom, a snowflake. Illustrations not to scale

Yes, intricacies and complexities can indeed be found in nature without requiring the active and immediate intervention of a supernatural power. Certainly a naturalistic, historical explanation is compatible with the idea of a master plan behind it—except that the plan, if it exists at all, can be detected only in retrospect, and thus can't really play a part in scientific investigations. An intelligent designer is a necessary hypothesis neither scientifically nor theologically.

Second, in order to make ID operational scientifically, we must know when and how to invoke it. If the hallmarks of design can be seen in anything from a snowflake to an eyeball, what are its limits? In other words, what would the *absence* of design look like?

One of the least designed things I can imagine would be a sidewalk crack. Of course it is subject to structural features of the concrete, but a sidewalk crack is also a highly random series of directional changes. And cracks just seem to happen "naturally." Yet, to try and reproduce a sidewalk crack precisely is most difficult, for, like the snowflake, it is very intricate. In other words, there is as much evidence of design in a sidewalk crack as there is in anything else. So what does the designer add to an analysis of the world? Is a sidewalk crack different for being designed or for not being designed?

Third, let's say that I could recreate that sidewalk crack using a jigsaw. I now have the original, very random, sidewalk crack and the precisely designed (by me) copy. What criteria are at your disposal for telling them apart? If you cannot tell something designed from something not designed, then you can effectively treat everything as if it were not designed. Alternatively, you could treat everything as if it were designed, but why would you bother? You would be adding a complication without helping the analysis.

Finally, to return to the question that originally animated the natural theologians: What attributes can we discern about the designer from his work on earth? The people who have traditionally been interested in doing this have sought to glorify God, not to understand his workings—they had a vested interest in making God look good. And yet the *imperfections* of nature show that he did not design things optimally—acne, impacted wisdom teeth, and cancer could all be considered rather severe design flaws of ordinary bodies. The *biases* of nature show that, for example, considered in terms of taxonomic diversity, biomass, and sheer numbers, the designer has "an inordinate fondness for beetles" (as a famous wisecrack put it). The *failures* of nature show that, in a nutshell, nearly every species that has ever come to exist has gone to extinction—hardly a track record worthy of admiration, much less of awe. The *patterns* of nature, the Linnaean nested hierarchy, show that he surely wanted to make it look as if life were genealogically connected—for if that pattern does not reflect common descent, then what might it instead reflect?

The association of the Linnaean nested hierarchy with a common ancestry for animal species was evident from the beginning. Linnaeus's eighteenth-century rival, the naturalist Count de Buffon, objected to the whole system Linnaeus was proposing, and which was rapidly accepted in academic circles for its obviousness, on the grounds that the Linnaean system had no reason to exist. Because Linnaeus chose not to speculate on why the pattern exists, or what it might mean, Buffon found the exercise of classifying species within this framework silly. The meaning of such a pattern was clear, and it was more or less blasphemous: It may be pondered whether . . . this constant conformity of design followed from man to quadrupeds, from quadrupeds to cetaceans, from cetaceans to birds, from birds to reptiles, from reptiles to fish, etc., seem not to indicate that in creating these animals, the supreme Being has wished to use an idea, and yet to vary it in all possible ways, so that man could admire equally the simplicity and magnificence of execution of this design.

> From this point of view, not only the donkey and horse, but as well man, apes, quadrupeds, and all the animals could be regarded as constituting the same family. . . . And if it is once admitted that there are families of plants and animals, that the donkey is of the horse family, and that it differs only because it has degenerated, then one could equally say that man and ape have had a common origin like the horse and donkey—that each family among the animals and vegetables have had but a single stem, and that all animals have emerged from but a single animal which, through the succession of time, has produced by improvement and degeneration all the races of animals.
>
> The naturalists who establish so casually the families of plants and animals do not seem to have grasped sufficiently the full scope of these consequences, which would reduce the immediate products of creation to a number of individuals as small as one might wish. For if it were once proved that these families could be established rationally—if it were true that the donkey were but a degenerated horse—then there would be no limits to the power of nature. One would then not be wrong to suppose that she could have drawn with time, all other organized beings from a single being.
>
> But no: it is certain, from revelation, that all animals have participated equally in the grace of creation, that the pair of each species and of all species emerged fully formed from the hands of the Creator.

Buffon grasped the problem with crystal clarity a century before Darwin. The nested hierarchy is most plausibly explained as the trail of a common ancestry, which is precisely why he rejected it. As with languages, the pattern is that of a family tree. Nowadays, it is precisely why we find that hierarchy so useful. The challenge lies for the creationist, who rejects the common ancestry of animals: If the features that make us similar to apes as Hominoidea—that make Hominoidea and Old World monkeys similar as Catarrhini, that make Catarrhini and other creatures similar as primates, that make primates and other creatures similar as mammals, that make mammals and other creatures similar as vertebrates, and that make vertebrates and other creatures similar as animals—if this distribution of characteristics does *not* indicate something about relative proximity of descent, then just what *does* it indicate?

The simple fact is that there is no scientific theory of intelligent design. It is a legal strategy, not a scientific theory; it was developed by a legal scholar—Phillip Johnson of University of California–Berkeley. It draws its support from evangelical Christians, many of whom do take the Bible as literally true, and draw on the same materials as the discredited scientific creationists from a generation ago. At the same time, however, ID reaches out to deists, Jews, Hindus—to anyone who wants to find meaning in life and feels that science is robbing them of that meaning. It even drew a favorable comment from a high-ranking Catholic cardinal, in spite of the Church's formally pro-Darwinian position.

This outreach has prompted a backlash among some hard-line Protestant evangelicals, who see ID as being "soft" on the real issue of biblical inerrancy. And they are right—for there is nothing particularly biblical about ID. It is, for example, just as compatible with polytheism as it is with monotheism. If a Timex watch implies a designer and a Rolex watch implies a designer, why should they necessarily imply the same one? And if, by analogy, *Homo sapiens* implies a designer, what is implied by *Paranthropus boisei*? The same designer, in a restless moment? A different, somewhat less-competent, designer?

And if you can't tell those basic alternatives apart, then what really is the value of invoking an intelligent designer for understanding the diversity of life?

Conclusion

History is very much a key for making sense of intelligent design. Much of its appeal lies in the adoption of a seventeenth-century metaphor—that the universe is like a giant machine, the mechanical philosophy. It is certainly true that, by treating nature as if it were a machine that you can analyze part-by-part, you can gain certain insights—for example, William Harvey's discovery that the heart is like a pump. That, however, is a valuable simile: The heart is *like* a pump, the universe is *like* a machine.

Intelligent design takes this three-hundred-year-old idea and argues that because the universe is indeed like a machine, then it must have a builder, as machines do. But that is to fail to appreciate that the mechanical philosophy was a literary device, not a literal truth, in the first place. The universe does not have to have a builder, because it is merely *like* a machine in some ways—it is not actually a machine and therefore is not automatically entitled to all the properties of machines.

As Robert Hooke, an early advocate and practitioner of science, pointed out, this is not about what God can do—it's about what nature can do.

CHAPTER 7

William Jennings Bryan and the Trial of John T. Scopes

by Richard H. Robbins

The trial of John Scopes for violating a Tennessee law against the teaching of evolution ranks as the seminal moment in the debate over Darwin and the Bible. Had not William Jennings Bryan joined the prosecution team, it is unlikely that the trial would have ever gained the notoriety that it did. Most people know the Scopes trial from the dramatization Inherit the Wind. *First a play on Broadway in 1955 and, in 1960, a major Hollywood film, it portrays Bryan as a windbag and religious zealot.* Inherit the Wind, *however, was intended as a critique of the McCarthy "witch hunt," not of the Scopes trial, and took considerable liberties with the actual history of the event, and with Bryan's performance and views. Numerous authors, including Ronald Numbers (1982, 1992), Stephen Jay Gould (1991c), Christopher Toumey (1994), Edward Larson (1997), and Michael Kazin (2006) have, to various degrees, defended Bryan, demonstrating the extent to which Bryan's position on evolution was perfectly consistent with his progressive political agenda. In the following article Richard Robbins provides a history of the Scopes trial and argues that Bryan's position was not only consistent with his political beliefs, but that, given the way that Darwin's theories were being used, was entirely reasonable.*

The trial of John T. Scopes ranks as one of the most familiar events of American scientific history, right there with Benjamin Franklin's kite and the atomic bomb (Numbers, 1998, p. 7). It is typically used to illustrate the conflict between science and religion or between urban and rural values. But, as Ronald Numbers (1998) points out, in spite of hundreds of scholarly studies of the antievolution movement, Christian fundamentalism, and, most of all, the role of William Jennings Bryan, the Scopes trial remains, as he put it, "a grotesquely misunderstood event" (p. 76).

Any discussion of the trial must focus on the role of Bryan. He led the campaign against Darwinism, and, although he didn't demand that evolution not be taught, he stipulated that it should be as theory only, and that the story of creation in Genesis be taught with it. Yet if the Scopes trial remains grotesquely misunderstood, Bryan's views have been even more greatly distorted (see Kazin, 2006). As I'll try to demonstrate, Bryan not only had some sound arguments to make, but his views on politics, religion, and science still have relevance today.

The facts of what led up to the Scopes trial are relatively straightforward. In January of 1925, the Tennessee legislature voted 71 to 5 to make it unlawful for public schools "to teach any theory that denies the story of the Divine Creation of man as taught in the Bible, and to teach instead that man has descended from a lower order of animals." Violation of the law carried a fine of $100 to $500. The Tennessee legislature was not the first to take up the issue; Oklahoma had already adopted a law prohibiting textbooks that promoted evolution, and Florida had condemned the teaching of Darwinism as "improper and subversive" (Numbers, 1998, pp. 77–78).

The American Civil Liberties Union (ACLU), alarmed over government restrictions placed on individual freedoms during and after World War I, wanted to use the Tennessee law to highlight the constitutional right to freedom of speech. It advertised for someone to violate the Tennessee law, promising to defend him or her in court and pay the expenses of the prosecution. In Dayton, Tennessee, citizens of the town, concerned about the economic decline of their community, convinced John Scopes to be a test case, hoping that the publicity of the trial would help

William Jennings Bryan enjoyed a meteoric rise from congressman to Democratic presidential candidate and remained a leading figure in the Democratic party until his death in 1925.

revitalize the town's economy. In one of the many ironies of the case, Scopes was not a biology teacher; he had been hired to coach the football and basketball team and teach algebra and physics. He substituted in a biology class, but, in fact, couldn't actually remember whether or not he had mentioned evolution, although students testified that he had (see Larson, 1997, pp. 89–91).

If the citizens wanted public recognition, they got everything that they desired. Hundreds of journalists flocked to Dayton, including H. L. Mencken, one of the best-known journalists in the country. Shortly after the trial, North Carolina sociologist Howard W. Odum estimated that the trial was discussed by "some 2310 daily newspapers in this country, some 13,267 weeklies, about 3613 monthlies, no less than 392 quarterlies with perhaps another five hundred including bi-monthlies and semi-monthlies, tri-weeklies and odd types." His search had turned up "no periodical of any sort, agricultural or trade as well, which has ignored the subject." "For the first time in the history of American jurisprudence," noted the *Chicago Daily Tribune*, "radio went into a court of law and broadcast to the earphones and loudspeakers of all radio set owners who cared to listen to the entire proceedings of a criminal trial." It was, said some people, "the world's most famous court trial." (Numbers, 1998, pp. 78–79).

The participants in the trial demanded national attention. There was, first of all, William Jennings Bryan, perhaps the most famous politician in the country, and the central character in the drama. Then there was Clarence Darrow, probably the most famous trial lawyer of his time. Darrow had been involved in most of the high-profile cases of the decade, including the defense the previous year of Leopold and Loeb for their thrill killing of fourteen-year-old Bobby Franks. Darrow campaigned for Bryan during one of his presidential runs, generally shared his political philosophy, and his law partner, attorney and writer, Edgar Lee Masters, had been one of Bryan's closest friends and political supporters (Kazin, 2006, p. 211). But Darrow had come to despise Bryan, largely because of Bryan's religiousity. Darrow was a notorious atheist. He sincerely believed, as Edward J. Larson put it in his Pulitzer Prize–winning book *Summer for the Gods*, that the biblical concept of original sin for all and salvation for some through divine grace was, as he described it, "a very dangerous doctrine, silly, impossible, and wicked" (Larson, 1997, p. 71).

None of the participants expected anything to be decided in Dayton. The law said that a teacher could not teach evolution, and Scopes claimed that he had. The ACLU, and Darrow, assumed that after Scopes was found guilty, they would appeal the case, if necessary, to the Supreme Court of the United States.

To get a more accurate picture of the trial, and to get a better understanding of the intersection of religion, politics, and science in the United States, we need to first examine the personal and political history of Bryan. It was, after all, his crusade to get legislatures to regulate the teaching of evolution that started the whole thing. The question is, why did Bryan, perhaps one of the most popular and influential politicians in American history, get involved in the debate over Darwin and the Bible?

The Life and Politics of William Jennings Bryan

Bryan enjoyed a meteoric political career that began with his election to the House of Representatives as a thirty-year-old Democratic populist from Nebraska in 1890 and progressed to his campaign for president in 1896, which he narrowly lost, in spite of being greatly outspent by William McKinley. Bryan ran twice more for president, in 1900 and in 1908, and later served as secretary of state under Woodrow Wilson. For over thirty years he was one of, if not the most, influential member of the Democratic Party, and, other than Woodrow Wilson and Theodore Roosevelt, probably the most influential politician of the Progressive era from the mid-1890s to the early 1920s.

Bryan was an ardent admirer of Thomas Jefferson. His favorite gift to other public figures was *The Jeffersonian Cyclopedia*, a compilation of Jefferson's opinions. When he listed the ten books that most affected his life, he put only the Bible ahead of it. He wrote to one admirer that Jefferson's motto of equal rights to all and privileges to none is the fundamental law that governs legislation and the administration of government (Kazin, 2006, p. xv).

Among the issues that Bryan proposed and campaigned for (most of which were enacted either during his lifetime or after), were:

- A progressive income tax
- Women's suffrage
- The issuance of paper money by the government through a national bank
- Federal deposit insurance
- Government control of corporate monopolies
- Protest of imperialism, arguing against the invasion of Cuba and against the U.S. colonization of the Philippines
- Avoidance of military confrontation through negotiation
- Direct election of U.S. senators
- Campaign assistance to candidates to ensure that their positions got a fair hearing
- Imposition of a limit on corporate donations to political candidates
- An eight-hour workday for public employees and the recognition of workers' right to organize
- Call to Congress to enact pure food and drug laws
- Municipal ownership of utilities and streetcars

"With the exception of the men who have occupied the White House," wrote past head of the Federal Reserve and senator from California William Gibbs McAdoo in 1931, "Bryan . . . had more to do with the shaping of the public policies of the last forty years than any other American citizen" (Kazin, 2006, p. 304).

His support of racial segregation in the South was one of the major flaws in Bryan's Progressive agenda. He believed that people of color around the world were fully capable of self-government and protested vehemently against colonialism and imperialism. But he felt that blacks in the United States, because of centuries of slavery, were not yet politically competent until they were given full educational opportunities (Cherny, 1985, p. 199). Because much of his political support came from the South, his support of segregation may have also been a case of political expediency.

In brief, Bryan set the agenda for the Democratic Party, served as its spokesperson for almost thirty years, and earned the nickname "The Great Commoner" for his efforts to improve the lives of the American middle and underclass. But central and perhaps indispensable to Bryan's political agenda were his religious convictions.

The Role of Religion in Bryan's Life and Politics

During an era without radio or television, when Americans flocked to hear famous orators such as Henry Ward Beecher, Frederick Douglass, and Anna Howard Shaw, millions came to hear Bryan lecture. Beginning in 1904, Bryan traveled the country every summer for twenty years expounding his ideas on politics, religion, and morality on the so-called Chautauqua circuit—weeklong summer programs that drew millions of Americans. Bryan, said one program organizer, was good for "forty acres of parked Fords, anywhere, at any time of the day or night" (Kazin, 2006, p. 131). In another of the many ironies of the Scopes trial, in 1919 Bryan had been the commencement speaker at John T. Scopes's high school graduation (p. 287).

Bryan was a devoutly religious man. Nominally he was a Presbyterian, holding Bible readings for his family each evening; yet he was also tolerant of other beliefs. He fought against anti-Catholicism and anti-Semitism, although he was less tolerant of non-Judeo-Christian religions (e.g., Hinduism, Buddhism), seeing them as "heathen" and "misguided." But Bryan, contrary to popular portrayals, was not a fundamentalist and never advocated a literal reading of the Bible. He spent the last portion of his life as an evangelist, giving talks and Bible readings around the country and each Sunday at Royal Palm Park in Miami, where he had gone to live in hopes of finding a place to relieve his wife's crippling arthritis.

For Bryan, religion was an essential element in politics and morality. Any sort of social or political reform required two things: individual religious faith and majoritarian governmental action, both of which played a role in his campaign against evolution. "My father taught me," he said, "to believe in democracy as well as Christianity" (Larson, 1997, p. 37).

Bryan was allied with leading Protestant reformers who held that authentic Christianity was "applied Christianity." He was a believer in the "Social Gospel," a movement that sought to apply, as one advocate put it, "the teaching of Jesus and the total message of the Christian salvation to society, the economic life, and social institutions . . . as well as to individuals." "Christ is not the only guide and friend in all the work that man undertakes," Bryan told an audience in 1912, "but his name can be invoked for the correction of every abuse and the eradication of every evil, in private and public life" (Kazin, 2006, p. 124).

Bryan's beliefs about the role of religion in politics and social activism were probably most systematically argued in one of his standard public talks, "The Prince of Peace." "Religion is the foundation of morality" in individuals and in society, he said. By trying to live up to a standard of personal responsibility to God, "men and women learn to restrain their selfish appetites and to serve the common welfare" (Kazin, 2006, p. 140). He sincerely believed that without religion, there could be no sense of responsibility to others. In many ways, Bryan's position was similar to

Jefferson's, who believed that the Bible stood as one of the most perfect systems of morality ever written. "What greater miracle than this," he exclaimed, "that converts a selfish, self-centered human being into a center from which good influences flow out in every direction" (p. 140).

It is probably no coincidence that another of Bryan's heroes was the Russian novelist and philosopher Count Leo Tolstoy, who, like Jefferson, had extracted from the Bible its ethical teachings divorced from the spiritual message. Bryan described Tolstoy as "the intellectual giant of Russia, the moral Titan of Europe, and the world's most conspicuous exponent of the doctrine of love" (Cherny, 1985, p. 98). Like Tolstoy, Bryan believed that religion was a practical faith that taught people how to live in harmony with others. They met in December of 1903 during Bryan's tour of Europe and spent twelve hours in conversation, Bryan coming away feeling that he had met a "kindred spirit" (Kazin, 2006, p. 126).

For Bryan, morality comprised a set of rules made by God, rules that people obeyed because of their desire for immortality. This view influenced even his economic beliefs. He said, for example, that corporations, because they had no soul, were under no obligation to follow moral rules, hence, needed to be closely regulated. If a corporation "can avoid punishment here," Bryan concluded, "it need not worry about the hereafter" (Cherny, 1985, p. 188).

The Campaign against Evolution

Darwin's theory of evolution, as understood by Bryan, presented him with a dilemma: Here was a theory of the origin of humanity, that not only contradicted the account of creation in Genesis, but that was used also by Rockefeller and Carnegie to justify their accumulation of great wealth and destroy others, was used by the Germans to justify their militancy and attempt to destroy Great Britain, and resulted in the creation of the field of eugenics that morphed into the Third Reich's killing machine and the "elimination" of over six million "defectives." In the United States, eugenic policy led to the involuntary sterilization of hundreds of thousands of people deemed "defective" by one government or court official or another. Bryan was not going after science, as his popular critics liked to portray it; he was going after a worldview that for him justified everything that he despised: bigotry, sexism, war, and hatred. In addition, the theory of evolution challenged the truth of what for Bryant was the antithesis of all of this—the Bible.

Bryan, contrary to popular opinion, did not totally reject the theory of evolution. He was perfectly willing to accept it as an explanation for the development of life *up to* the creation of human beings. That, he insisted, must be attributed to divine intervention.

Bryan's concern about evolution surfaced in 1904, when he gave his first public address about Darwin. Darwinism was "dangerous," he said, for both religious and social reasons. "I object to the Darwinian theory," he said, "because I fear that we shall lose the consciousness of God's presence in our daily life, if we accept the theory that through the ages no spiritual force has touched the life of man and shaped the destiny of nations." And then he added another objection: "The Darwinian theory represents man as reaching his present perfection by the operation of the law of hate—the merciless law by which the strong crowd out and kill off the weak" (Larson, 1997, p. 39).

Later, Bryan came to believe that Darwinism laid the foundation for, as he put it, the bloodiest war in history, and provided the rationale for all the cruelties and atrocities committed by the German military. He felt that it was also responsible for the struggle between capital and labor. "Survival of the fittest," he said, "was driving both capitalist and laborer into a life and death struggle from which sympathy and the spirit of brotherhood are eliminated. It is transforming the industrial world into a slaughter-house" (Cherny, 1985, pp. 172–173). And of course, he blamed evolution for the conflict between church and school, the two institutions that he believed formed the foundation of rural life.

Thus Bryan's campaign against the teaching of evolution was largely an effort to save religious faith, which, for him, was necessary for solving social problems and addressing human flaws. He had other objections, which we will discuss in the following section, but his final campaign was very much an extension of his political philosophy.

The Scopes Trial: The Setting, the Issues, and the People

The trial of John T. Scopes began on July 10, 1925. The defense tried to get the charges dismissed on the grounds that the Tennessee law violated both the Tennessee and U.S. Constitution; defense attorney Arthur Garfield Hays argued that the state did have the right to determine what is taught, but it can't require that it be taught falsely (Larson, 1997, pp. 159–160). The judge rejected that argument. The prosecution argued that the state had the right to control expenditures, including the right to determine what is taught in its schools.

Bryan gave the first major speech of the trial, in which, with occasional humor, he defended the rights of parents to decide what their children learned in school, claimed that the theory of evolution lacked scientific proof because "never have [scientists] traced one single species to any other" (Kazin, 2006, p. 289) and that the teaching of evolution undermined religious faith, accusing Darrow's team of attempting to take from the people of Tennessee "every moral standard that the Bible gives us" (Larson, 1997, pp. 98–99).

Darrow then spoke; his main argument was that the antievolution statute was illegal because it established a particular religious viewpoint in the public schools. He then read from the Tennessee Constitution:

> "'All men have a natural and indefeasible right to worship Almighty God according to the dictates of their own conscience.' That takes care of the despised modernist who dares to be intelligent." He continued reading: "and that 'no preference shall be given by law to any religious establishment or mode of worship.' Does it? Could you get any more preference, your honor, by law?" Darrow explained, "Here is the state of Tennessee going along its own business, teaching evolution for years." And, turning toward Bryan, "And along comes somebody who says we have to believe it as I believe it. It is a crime to know more than I know. And they publish a law inhibiting

learning. . . . It makes the Bible the yard stick to measure every man's intellect, to measure every man's intelligence and to measure every man's learning." "Bryan is responsible for this foolish, mischievous and wicked act," Darrow said. "Nothing was heard of all that until the Fundamentalists got into Tennessee." (Larson, 1997, p. 163)

Darrow continued by saying the state of Tennessee has no more right to dictate the Bible as the major source of knowledge than it has the right to say that the Koran, the Book of Mormon, the book of Confucius, or the essays of Emerson are the major source of knowledge. "There is nothing else your Honor," he said, "that has caused the difference of opinion, of bitterness, or hatred, of war, of cruelty, that religion has caused." "To strangle puppies is good," he said following an old maxim, "when they grow up into mad dogs," applying the maxim to fundamentalism, which, he said, threatened "to kindle bigotry and hate" (Larson, 1997, pp. 163–164).

It was a triumphant presentation that went on for over two hours. Newspapers printed the entire speech and Darrow's hometown paper called it the greatest speech he ever made. What Darrow had done, of course, was turn the case into an attack on religious bigotry and intolerance and an attempt by the state to impose a religious doctrine.

But perhaps the most stirring speech of the trial was given by another of the defense attorneys, Dudley Field Malone. Malone began by scolding Bryan for attacking teachers and went on to praise the Bible as a wonderful book, but not a work of science. "Keep it as your consolation, keep it as your guide," he said, "but keep it where it belongs in the world of your own conscience, in the world of individual judgment, in the world of the Protestant conscience that I heard so much

Bryan consented to being a witness in the trial, but only if he could also question Darrow. However, because Darrow requested that the judge direct the jury to return a guilty verdict, he avoided being questioned and also prevented Bryan from giving his closing speech.

about when I was a boy." He then attacked the idea that the young needed to be protected; shouldn't they have the opportunity to decide for themselves, he asked? He concluded that we should not be afraid of new ideas; "The truth is no coward," he said. At the conclusion of his speech, the anti-Darwinist audience exploded with applause; even Bryan congratulated him and said, "Although we differ, I have never heard a better speech," to which Malone replied, "I am terribly sorry I had to do it." (Kazin, 2006, p. 290).

Then the defense team called Bryan to testify as an expert on the Bible, which he agreed to do against the advice of the rest of the prosecution team. Bryan had stipulated that he would testify, but only if he could put members of the defense team of Darrow, Malone, and Hays on the stand also, to which the judge replied that he could call whomever he wished. Bryan then took the stand.

DARROW	You claim that everything in the Bible should be literally interpreted?
BRYAN	I believe everything in the Bible should be accepted as it is given there: some of the Bible is given illustratively. For instance: "Ye are the salt of the earth." I would not insist that man was actually salt, or that he had flesh of salt, but it is used in the sense of salt as saving God's people.
DARROW	But when you read that Jonah swallowed the whale—or that the whale swallowed Jonah—excuse me please—how do you literally interpret that?
BRYAN	When I read that a big fish swallowed Jonah—it does not say whale. . . . That is my recollection of it. A big fish, and I believe it, and I believe in a God who can make a whale and can make a man and make both do what He pleases.
DARROW	Now, you say, the big fish swallowed Jonah, and he there remained how long—three days—and then he spewed him upon the land. You believe that the big fish was made to swallow Jonah?
BRYAN	I am not prepared to say that; the Bible merely says it was done.
DARROW	You don't know whether it was the ordinary run of fish, or made for that purpose?
BRYAN	You may guess; you evolutionists guess. . . .
DARROW	You are not prepared to say whether that fish was made especially to swallow a man or not?
BRYAN	The Bible doesn't say, so I am not prepared to say.
DARROW	But do you believe He made them—that He made such a fish and that it was big enough to swallow Jonah?
BRYAN	Yes, sir. Let me add: One miracle is just as easy to believe as another.
DARROW	Just as hard?
BRYAN	It is hard to believe for you, but easy for me. A miracle is a thing performed beyond what man can perform. When you get within

the realm of miracles; and it is just as easy to believe the miracle of Jonah as any other miracle in the Bible.

DARROW   Perfectly easy to believe that Jonah swallowed the whale?

BRYAN   If the Bible said so; the Bible doesn't make as extreme statements as evolutionists do. . . .

At various points the prosecutors attempted to stop the testimony, but Bryan insisted on continuing. Darrow began again:

DARROW   Have you any idea how old the earth is?

BRYAN   No.

DARROW   The Book you have introduced in evidence tells you, doesn't it?

BRYAN   I don't think it does, Mr. Darrow.

DARROW   Let's see whether it does; is this the one?

BRYAN   That is the one, I think.

DARROW   It says B.C. 4004?

BRYAN   That is Bishop Usher's calculation.

DARROW   That is printed in the Bible you introduced?

BRYAN   Yes, sir. . . .

DARROW   Would you say that the earth was only 4,000 years old?

BRYAN   Oh, no; I think it is much older than that.

DARROW   How much?

BRYAN   I couldn't say.

DARROW   Do you say whether the Bible itself says it is older than that?

BRYAN   I don't think it is older or not.

DARROW   Do you think the earth was made in six days?

BRYAN   Not six days of twenty-four hours.

DARROW   Doesn't it say so?

BRYAN   No, sir. . . .

As the judge intervened, Bryan said:

Your honor, they have not asked a question legally and the only reason they have asked any question is for the purpose, as the question about Jonah was asked, for a chance to give this agnostic an opportunity to criticize a believer in the word of God; and I answered the question in order to shut his mouth so that he cannot go out and tell his atheistic friends that I would not answer his questions. That is the only reason, no more reason in the world.

Darrow continued his questioning until the judge once again intervened:

BRYAN   Your Honor, I think I can shorten this testimony. The only purpose Mr. Darrow has is to slur at the Bible, but I will answer his question.

	I will answer it all at once, and I have no objection in the world, I want the world to know that this man, who does not believe in a God, is trying to use a court in Tennessee—
DARROW	I object to that.
BRYAN	(Continuing) to slur at it, and while it will require time, I am willing to take it.
DARROW	I object to your statement. I am exempting you on your fool ideas that no intelligent Christian on earth believes.
THE COURT	Court is adjourned until 9 o'clock tomorrow morning.[1]

Most of the newspapers of the day concluded that the cross-examination of Bryan was a huge victory for Darrow: Darrow himself wrote to H. L. Mencken, who had left Dayton before Bryan's testimony, that "I made up my mind to show the country what an ignoramus he was and I succeeded" (Larson, 1997, p. 190). The next day the judge ordered Bryan's testimony expunged from the court record, ruling that the only question to be decided was whether or not John T. Scopes taught that humans descended from a lower form of animal. At that point Darrow requested that the judge direct the jury to return a guilty verdict, thus laying the groundwork for an appeal, and also preventing Bryan from giving his closing speech. In yet another irony of the case, an appeals judge overthrew the guilty verdict because the fine Scopes was ordered to pay was improperly imposed by the judge instead of the jury, thus preventing the ACLU and Darrow from appealing the guilty verdict and testing the Tennessee law.[2]

The Depiction of the Trial

The Scopes trial occupies a special place in U.S. history. It is often portrayed as a victory for science over religious bigotry while Bryan is depicted as a once-influential politician trapped in an outmoded viewpoint. Certainly the bulk of the newspapers saw the trial as a victory for science and a defeat of fundamentalism. "Bryan was broken," said one reporter. "Darrow never spared him. It was masterful, but it was pitiful" (Cherny, 1985, p. 181).

The contemporary assessment of the Scopes trial is dominated by three things: the newspaper reports, particularly those of H. L. Mencken; a book written in 1931 by journalist Frederick Lewis Allen, *Only Yesterday: An Informal History of the Nineteen-Twenties*; and the play and movie *Inherit the Wind*.

Mencken's role is curious. He clearly hated Bryan, largely because of Mencken's disregard for politicians who, as Michael Kazin puts it, "allied themselves with the 'common folk.'" His experience in Dayton, says Kazin (2006),

hardened his conviction that democracy was simply a way to free the hatred of the lower orders against their mental superiors. And Bryan was the leader of the mob.

---

[1] *www.law.umkc.edu/faculty/projects/ftrials/scopes/day7.htm.*
[2] The antievolution law (the Butler Act) stood until 1967.

H. L. Mencken's accounts of the trial and his attacks on Bryan dominated the news and helped forge the popular opinion of the event.

"He seemed only a poor clod like those around him," wrote Mencken, "deluded by a childish theology, full of an almost pathological hatred of all learning, all human dignity, all beauty, all fine and noble things. He was a peasant come home to the barnyard." (p. 298)

Mencken's loathing was, says Kazin (2006), driven by a fear of the establishment of "a theocratic state run by idiots" (p. 299). But few noted the irony of the fact that Mencken was a lifelong anti-Semite who admired German culture to such an extent that he was blinded to the menace of Nazism. He was also a blistering critic of Franklin D. Roosevelt during the 1930s. Thus, as Kazin (2006, p. 299) put it, the writer who was most responsible for molding Bryan's image for liberals and Progressives, admired the Nazis and hated their most admired politician. Even in 2000 historian Ronald Steele (2006) marveled that Bryan, "who today would be considered a windbag fit only for a career as a TV evangelist, mesmerized crowds for hours with his mellifluous prose."

The second thing that most contributed to the general account of the Scopes trial was Frederick Lewis Allen's book *Only Yesterday: An Informal History of the Nineteen-Twenties*. Allen based his account largely on newspaper reports of the trial, and it became the leading source used by historians to describe the trial and its aftermath as a defeat for fundamentalism and the major event that drove it "underground," until its reemergence in the 1970s as the "moral majority" (Numbers, 1998, p. 85).

Finally, there was the play and movie *Inherit the Wind*. First produced on Broadway in 1955, it was made into a movie in 1960, and is still widely shown in schools as an accurate historical account of the Scopes trial. The story turns Darrow (Henry Drummond played by Spencer Tracy) into a hero and Bryan (Matthew Harrison Brady played by Fredric March) into a dolt. The stage instructions, as

Numbers points out, specify that the turning point in the film is when Drummond questions Brady about the age of the earth: "Drummond's got him. And he knows it! *This is the turning point.* From here on, the tempo mounts, Drummond is now fully in the driver's seat" (see Numbers, 1998, pp. 86–87). *Inherit the Wind* was intended as a critique of the McCarthy era and the communist "witch hunt" of the 1940s and 1950s. As such it takes considerable liberties with the actual trial, including showing Scopes in jail, altering the testimony, and depicting a crestfallen Brady dying immediately after the trial. Numbers (1998, p. 87) recognizes that the play must invent dialog and even characters to heighten the dramatic effect of the trial and to make its points about McCarthy and the fear tactics of politicians of that era. But he does

> question the judgment of the historians who drafted the National Standards for United States History, which recommended the movie as an aid to understanding Bryan's mind and "Fundamentalist thinking" in general. This strikes me as being a little like recommending Gone with the Wind as a historically reliable account of the Civil War. (Numbers, 1998, p. 87).

In actuality, fundamentalists thought that they had won; Scopes was convicted and Bryan used the publicity to give his planned trial summation at a local church. In his speech he summarized his main objections against evolution and said of science that it "is a magnificent material force, but it is not a teacher of morals. It can perfect machinery, but it adds no moral restraints to protect society from the misuse of the machine." Then toward the end he said that science "not only fails to supply the spiritual element needed but some of its unproved hypotheses rob [society of its moral] compass" and this "endangers humanity" (Larson, 1997, p. 198).

Even Mencken concluded that Genesis emerged "completely triumphant," and *The Nation* concluded that the fundamentalists' "success at Dayton" was so complete that, in 1926, we would witness "a flood of bills introduced into the legislature of every state in the Union" (Numbers, 1998, p. 87). In fact, from 1921 to 1929, of all the thirty-seven antievolution measures that had been introduced into state legislatures, twenty-three (62 percent) occurred after 1925, the year of the Scopes trial.

A Reexamination of the Case against Evolution

It is probably fair to say that, by forcing Bryan to defend a literal interpretation of the Bible (which Bryan never actually advocated), Darrow accomplished his goal of debunking religion, but also precluded any discussion of the other grounds for the attack on evolution. The question is, is it possible to make a good case against the teaching of evolution, at least as the situation stood in 1925? There are four areas in which Darwinism and the teaching of evolution were being criticized that might resonate today: (1) the democratic argument that parents should be able to determine what is taught in schools and have a say in what is accepted as valid science; (2) the scientific standing of Darwin as it existed in the 1920s; (3) Darwinism's association with eugenics; and (4) the moral implications of evolution. Let's briefly examine each one.

Democracy, Education, and Science

We tend to take U.S. democracy for granted, but the elite in the United States have always been suspicious and fearful of a takeover of the government by the "mob." For example, Gustave Le Bon, in his influential book *The Crowd* (1895), warned of the power of the masses, which had been set loose and was overtaking the historical stage. The crowd, he said, is little adapted to reasoning and is only capable of reacting, and the question was how to control it (Ewen, 1996). This theme dominated the Progressive era as citizens began to demand changes: women's rights, regulation of corporations, democratic election of senators, protection of unions. All issues central to Bryan's politics were seen by some as signs of mob control. And Bryan, "The Great Commoner," was their spokesperson.

In demanding that parents had a right to determine the content of their child's education, Bryan was simply following Thomas Jefferson's dictate contained in the Virginia Statute for Religious Freedom,[3] which says, "to compel a man to furnish contributions of money for the propagation of opinions which he disbelieves, is sinful and tyrannical." "The real issue," said Bryan, "is not *what* can be taught in public schools, but *who* shall control the education system" (Larson, 1997, p. 104).

Other than parents, he said, there were only two possibilities: individual teachers, which he rejected as impractical, and scientists, which he rejected as undemocratic (Larson, 1997, p. 104). Bryan, in fact, viewed science as undemocratic and feared that a "scientific soviet" would "establish an oligarchy over forty million American Christians" (Numbers, 1982, p. 538).

In an exchange with Bryan in the *New York Times* and then in a small book *The Earth Speaks to Bryan*, Henry Fairfield Osborn, president of the American Museum of Natural History, had denounced Bryan's antievolutionism, claiming that science was the province of professionals, not commoners with Bibles. Bryan, however, did not want to give up science as a democratic endeavor; in fact, Bryan was a great admirer of science and in 1924 he paid his five dollars to join the American Association for the Advancement of Science (Witham, 2002, p. 26).

The Scientific Standing of Darwinism in the 1920s

Bryan often called evolution a guess that was unsubstantiated by any evidence. In fact, at the time of the Scopes trial, Darwin's theory of natural selection had gone into eclipse. Some historians of science argued that "Darwin's theory of natural selection was later shown to be of little value and mainly disproved" (Lack, 1957, p. 15). One book on the history of biology written in 1920–1924 concluded, "To raise the theory of selection as has often been done, to the rank of a 'natural law' comparable in value with the law of gravity established by Newton is, of course, quite irrational, as time has already shown; Darwin's theory on the origin of species was long ago abandoned" (quoted in Young, 1971, p. 197).

Among the reasons why the idea of natural selection was in eclipse in the 1920s was the lack of direct evidence for the formation of new species by natural selection and absurd speculations such as explaining that flamingos were pink to conceal them against the sunset, and that the eye began as a pigment on the skin.

---

[3] http://worldpolicy.org/globalrights/religion/va-religiousfreedom.html.

Bryan collected these kinds of speculations and included a number of them in a 1922 *New York Times* article. It did not help that some fossil evidence for human evolution was in dispute: There were serious doubts about the so-called Piltdown discovery (later discovered to be a fraud), and a tooth found in Nebraska and claimed in 1922 by Osborn to be from a million-year-old human (in an exchange with Bryan he jokingly offered to name it *Bryopithecus* "after the most distinguished Primate the State of Nebraska has thus far produced"), but later acknowledged by Osborn to be a pig's tooth (Numbers, 1998, p. 90).

It was not until a more general understanding of genetics began to take hold in 1930 that scientists almost unanimously accepted Darwin's ideas on natural selection.

Eugenics and Race

Perhaps the most telling critique of Darwinism was its association with eugenics. Bryan's objection to evolution, as Kazin (2006) puts it, was "mitigated somewhat by his revulsion at the prospect of sterilizing the slow-witted and the disadvantaged" (p. 263).

The antievolution crusade corresponded with the development of such groups as the National Eugenics Education Society in Great Britain headed by Darwin's son, Leonard, and the growth in the United States of sexual segregation and sterilization laws in thirty-five states to discourage or prevent people deemed "inferior" (those who were mentally ill, retarded, criminals, and epileptics) from having children. Eugenicists actually criticized Bryan for not supporting eugenics and its "profound ethical and religious significance." In another irony of the Scopes trial, Scope's defense had trouble getting scientists to testify because, as eugenicists, they were fearful of Darrow who had denounced eugenic measures as incompatible with human rights (Larson, 1997, p. 135).

But perhaps the most telling document in the debate, which was never mentioned in the trial, was the text that was being used in Tennessee and around the country for teaching high school biology—George William Hunter's *A Civic Biology Presented in Problems*. The book was published in 1914 and presented the standard materials on cells, muscles, respiration, and so on. But it also included lots of material on eugenics. In fact, the book's title, *Civic Biology*, was another term for *eugenics*.

In Chapter 17 (pp. 261–265) of *Civic Biology* Hunter says:

If the stock of domesticated animals can be improved upon, it is not unfair to ask if the health and vigor of the future generations of men and women on the earth might not be improved by applying to them the laws of selection.[4]

In a description of eugenics, Hunter continues,

When people marry there are certain things that the individual as well as the race should demand. The most important of these is freedom from germ diseases which might be handed down to the offspring. Tuberculosis, syphilis, that dread disease which cripples and kills hundreds of thousands of innocent children, epilepsy, and

---

[4] *www.eugenics-watch.com/roots/chap08.html.*

feeble-mindedness are handicaps which it is not only unfair but criminal to hand down to posterity. The science of being well born is called eugenics.

He cites the now discredited study of the Jukes and the Kallikaks to confirm the inheritance of "undesirable" characteristics; the former, he said, produced over a hundred feeble-minded, alcoholic, immoral, or criminal persons. Of 480 descendants, the latter produced 33 sexually immoral individuals, 24 confirmed drunkards, 3 epileptics, and 143 who were feeble-minded.

The cost to society of these families, says Hunter, is severe:

They not only do harm to others by corrupting, stealing, or spreading disease, but they are actually protected and cared for by the state out of public money. Largely for them the poorhouse and the asylum exist. They take from society, but they give nothing in return. They are true parasites.

The remedy, says Hunter, is separating the sexes in asylums or preventing the marriage of "defectives."

The Moral Implications of Evolution

Finally there were the ethical and moral implications of Darwinism. We have already addressed some of these in the introduction to this volume, but it is useful to explore Bryan's reasoning. He believed, as mentioned, that any solution to human and social problems required religious faith. Consequently, he was alarmed at studies showing that education undermined such faith.

In his 1922 article solicited by the *New York Times*, "God and Evolution," in which Bryan sets out his main objections to Darwin, he cites the fact that Darwin's research drove him to agnosticism and that research concluded that religious disbelief increases for each year a student spends in college. He mentions that parents are concerned about their children losing interest in religion and says, "This begins when they come under the influence of a teacher who accepts Darwin's guess, ridicules the Bible story of creation and instructs the child upon the basis of the brute theory" (Bryan, 1922, p. 84).

He was also alarmed at the writings of such people as Alexander Tille who advocated "evolutionary ethics" that justified eugenics and militarism. Tille rejected love and compassion because they led to the survival of the weak and unhealthy (Weikart, 2004, pp. 45–46). Other writers argued that Christian ideas about morality, such as love, sympathy, humility, loving one's enemy, and so on, hindered evolutionary progress, which they saw as the ultimate good. Christian love, they argued, needs to be balanced with self-preservation and a concern for biological improvement (Weikart, 2004, p. 52).

Bryan could also cite two influential disciples of Darwin to buttress his argument concerning evolution and morality. Vernon Kellogg, a Stanford professor who wrote widely about evolution, wrote a book in 1917 after spending several weeks with officers on the Kaiser's general staff. He reported that

to these men, natural selection meant "a violent and competitive struggle" that could end only with "the most advanced" nation dominating or destroying the others. (Quoted in Kazin, 2006, pp. 273–274)

British author Benjamin Kidd wrote in 1918 a repudiation of his earlier defense of Darwin:

Theorists of evolution, Kidd now maintained, sought to replace Christian ethics with a philosophy "resting on inequality. . . . If in the struggle for existence A was able to kill B before B killed A, then the [human] race became a race of A's inheriting A's qualities." (p. 273)

Thus, as Kazin points out (2006),

In the writings of Kellogg and Kidd, Bryan found an explanation for these evils that might convince Christians to trust in the gospel of brotherhood against a science that made brutality seem inevitable and thus legitimate. (pp. 273–274)

The Relevance of William Jennings Bryan Today

After the Scopes trial, journalists, historians, and others dismissed Bryan as a political anachronism who had squandered his legacy in his ill-thought crusade against evolution. But recent biographies and accounts of the Scopes trial (see, for example, Cherny, 1985; Gould, 1991c; Kazin, 2006; Larson, 1997; Numbers, 1993, 1998) have prompted a reappraisal and raised the question of Bryan's relevance today.

Clearly his progressive political agenda is very much alive within segments of his Democratic Party. Civil rights, regulation of corporate power, the progressive income tax, federal regulation of food and drugs, and government support for disadvantaged people are only some of the issues that still resonate among members of the political left and promote struggle in the political arena.

Ironically, many of these issues had their origin for Bryan in his religious faith, which the largely secular left has rejected. One of the issues worthy of discussion is when and why did the Progressive movement jettison the religious impetus from which it arose? One clue in Bryan's biography is in his meeting with the journalist John Reed. Just after his reporting on the Mexican Revolution (and prior to his first-hand account of the Russian Revolution popularized in Warren Beatty's movie *Reds*), *Collier's Weekly* sent Reed to Florida to interview Bryan. Reed, the romantic leftist and urban bohemian who praised Bryan for his policies and who shared Bryan's condemnation of the war in Europe, portrayed him as "little more than a sideshow for yokels and Bible-thumpers, a man whose time had decisively passed" (Kazin, 2006, p. 143). Reed, the Harvard-educated son of a wealthy Oregon merchant, represented a secular political left that drew its inspiration from European, largely Marxist, sources. Bryan's progressivism, on the other hand, was largely home-grown, rural, and Protestant. It was typified by the Social Gospel movement that believed that social justice and improvement could be attained by following Christ's teaching.

Thus the Democratic left, which still struggles to fulfill the social and political agenda that Bryan played a major role in creating, rejected him for his religiosity. In the meantime, in just one more of the many ironies of the Bryan saga, when large numbers of white evangelical Protestants, who had been and largely remain admirers of Bryan, again threw themselves into electoral politics, they allied themselves with largely procorporate Republicans whose economic and social policies Bryan would have loathed (Kazin, 2006, p. 302).

Bryan's message of civic participation is also one that remains relevant today. Study after study (see, e.g., Putnam, 2000; Skocpol, 2003) shows that civic participation has dramatically declined in the United States. In fact, the present level is often compared to the high rate of participation during the Progressive era; voter turnout in Bryan's presidential campaign against William McKinley was 80 percent and has never again reached that level (Cherny, 1985, p. 70).

Each citizen, Bryan said, had a clear duty to help others. "Each individual," he said, "finds his greatest security in the intelligence and happiness of his fellows," and that "the welfare of each [is] the concern of all." Each citizen, he concluded, "should therefore exert himself to the utmost to improve conditions for all and to raise the level upon which all stand.... He renders the largest service to others when he brings himself into harmony with the law of God, who has made service the measure of greatness" (Cherny, 1985, p. 96).

Finally, Bryan raises the issue of whether or not people can or will devote themselves to helping others without some religious faith to inspire them. This dilemma was aptly posed by the former governor of New York, Mario Cuomo (2004). Speaking about the importance of religion for reform, Cuomo said: "I do desperately want to believe in something better than I am. If all there is is me in this society, then I have wasted an awful lot of time, because I am not worth it" (pp. 17–18).

CHAPTER 8

Postmodern Developments in the Debate

by Edward J. Larson

In his book on the history of the theory of evolution, Edward J. Larson explores also, at least implicitly, the history of the debate with creationists, but, more important, the debates among scientists as well. In the following excerpted chapter, Larson explores the role of what is termed the new synthesis in the debate over evolution. This refers to the pioneering work of Ronald Fisher in the 1920s and 1930s, and the union of natural selection with the then emerging field of genetics. Simply put, the new synthesis shifted the emphasis in the study of evolution from individual organisms and species to genes and the process of genetic transmission. The question now was not only how organisms and species survived, but how genes replicated themselves. It also boosted the role of molecular biology into the forefront in the study of evolution and led, as we'll see, to new theories and explanations of human characteristics central to the debate over evolution. Most important, it offered biologists an opportunity to propose a response to one of the primary arguments against natural selection. If nature selects, creationists asked, only for traits leading to an individual's survival or reproductive success, as classical Darwinism suggested, then mustn't self-sacrifice (except to aid one's own descendents) have a supernatural source? Yet the new theories proposed to address that question did little, as we shall see, to mute the argument over Darwin and the Bible. In fact, among other things, it inspired spirited debate among scientists regarding just how far science could go in tying a person's behavior and beliefs to his or her DNA. Much of this chapter addresses the arguments among scientists themselves regarding the role of genes in human evolution and behavior. But these arguments gave creationists and proponents of intelligent design much to argue over and attack.

Reprinted with permission from Evolution: The Remarkable History of a Scientific Theory (pp. 267–286), by Edward J. Larson, 2004, New York: Modern Library. Editors' note: All citations have been formatted to APA style.

Francis Crick winged into the Eagle, a pub popular with researchers at Cambridge University's nearby Cavendish Laboratory, boasting to one and all, "We have found the secret of life." It was early in 1953, and the "we" referred to thirty-six-year-old British biophysicist Crick and twenty-four-year-old American biochemist James D. Watson, then working at the Cavendish on a postdoctoral fellowship. Watson reported feeling "slightly queasy" at Crick's boast, but over the next few decades, many biologists came to see it as fully justified. In one of the great "eureka" experiences of modern science, Watson and Crick had discovered the gene's double-helical structure by brilliantly and rapidly combining the findings of others with insights of their own. This surprisingly simple, highly elegant structure shed new light on the mechanics of evolution by suggesting how genetic reproduction, inheritance, and variation operated at the molecular level (Watson, 1980).

Although the gene stood at the heart of the modern synthesis, it was a black box prior to 1950. Until then, many scientists envisioned the gene as a complex assemblage of proteins that would take decades to decipher. Yet a growing body of evidence suggested that a much simpler macromolecule, deoxyribonucleic acid (or DNA), carries hereditary information. Watson and Crick followed the latter trail, and it led them to glory. They found that DNA is structured somewhat like a twisted railroad track with sturdy rails along its outer edges and a sequence of connecting ties, each composed of one of two different pairings of four base molecules, commonly identified by their initials: A, T, G, and C. If DNA splits lengthwise, then each half replicates the whole by attracting new pairs for its remaining bases from the cell's organic soup, A to T and G to C. The macromolecule carries genetic information in

Francis Crick (left) and James Watson and their model of DNA.

the sequence of its base molecules, which serve as a template for forming ribonucleic acid (or RNA) and, in turn, proteins. Information flows only one way in this mechanism—from the DNA to the proteins that construct the organism; never from the organism back to the DNA. The result nicely matches the neo-Darwinian principle that inborn hereditary information guides individual development without any gene-altering feedback from the environment. In these and other respects, DNA structure provides a serviceable molecular foundation for evolution to proceed in a manner fitting the modern synthesis. Both concepts are starkly materialistic and functionally reductionist. Still, tensions developed between molecular biologists and neo-Darwinian evolutionists.

Watson and Crick did not work out all the implication of DNA structure themselves. In their initial 1953 papers, they simply noted that it "immediately suggests a possible copying mechanism for the genetic material," which they spelled out in some detail, and that "spontaneous mutations may be due to a base occasionally occurring in one of its less likely tautomeric forms" (Watson, 1980) These and other implications inspired a generation of scientists to pursue molecular biology. Traditional ways of studying evolution suddenly seemed terribly old-fashioned. "For those not studying biology at the time in the early 1950s it is hard to imagine the impact the discovery of the structure of DNA had on our perception of how the world works," zoologist Edward O. Wilson later recalled. "If heredity can be reduced to a chain of four molecular letters—granted, billions of such letters to prescribe a whole organism—would it not also be possible to reduce and accelerate the analysis of ecosystems and complex animal behavior?" (Wilson, 1994, pp. 223–224).

Watson and Wilson, who became two of the most influential scientists of the late twentieth century, both joined Harvard's biology department as assistant professors in 1956. Watson led the shock troops for the newer forms of molecular biology. Wilson, who studied ants, upheld the older naturalist tradition associated with Ernst Mayr and the modern synthesis. The two young biologists rarely spoke to each other during their years together at Harvard. Their department, in a microcosm of larger developments within the profession, eventually split into separate ones for molecular and evolutionary biology. Wilson later described Watson as "the most unpleasant human being that I had ever met" (Wilson, 1994, p. 219). Their relations worsened after Wilson (whom Watson regarded as a mere bug collector) received tenure before Watson. Mayr, Wilson, and others in their camp viewed molecular biology as too narrow and limited to comprehend all aspects of the evolutionary process. To them, organisms and ecosystems still mattered. For his part, in the best-selling book *The Double Helix*, Watson dismissed most zoologists and botanists of the 1950s as "a muddled lot [who] wasted their efforts in useless polemics about the origin of life." Geneticists of the era fared little better in Watson's account. "You would have thought that with all their talk about genes they should worry about what they were," he wrote. "All that most of them wanted out of life was to set their students onto uninterpretable details of chromosome behavior or to give elegantly phrased, fuzzy-minded speculations over the wireless on topics like the role of the geneticist in this transitional age of changing values" (Watson, 1980, p. 46). Yet over time, and from their separate departmental homes, evolutionary and molecular biology grew to complement and reinforce each other.

At the elemental level, the discovery that all species (even the most primitive unicellular ones) shared a common genetic code suggested that they have a common ancestry. In turn, the comparative study of DNA from various organisms elucidated their evolutionary relationships. In one spectacular example of this from the 1960s, Dobzhansky's protégé Richard C. Lewontin used a technique called "gel electrophoresis" to measure genetic variation among individuals of the same species. This analysis tested his mentor's hypothesis that enough latent variability exists in recessive alleles to feed the evolutionary process in response to changed environmental conditions without added mutations. Lewontin found what he was looking for—indeed, he found so much genetic variability within species that much of it must have little or no effect on individuals (Lewontin, 1974). Taking the position that all the variation may be meaningless, diehard opponents of Dobzhansky's hypothesis clung to the classical view (historically associated with Thomas Hunt Morgan and Hermann Muller) that mutations feed evolution.

Further, Watson's success in reducing much of biology to molecules inspired even his adversaries. "He and other molecular biologists conveyed to his generation a new faith in the reductionist method of the natural sciences," Wilson later noted. "A triumph of naturalism, it was part of the motivation for my own attempt in the 1970s to bring biology into the social sciences through a systematization of the new discipline of sociobiology" (Wilson, 1994, p. 225). Watson came to appreciate Wilson's work in sociobiology—and it helped mend their relationship in the years after Watson left Harvard to run the Cold Spring Harbor genetics laboratory, a traditional center for research in applied human genetics, dating from the heyday of eugenics.

Yet Wilson never took a molecular approach to sociobiology. Indeed, his initial foray into the field grew out of his interest in how insect colonies function, which he pursued in opposition to the molecular focus of biologists who followed in Watson's wake. Early on, for example, Wilson explored the impact of population size and density on the caste system of ant colonies and on aggressive behavior by various types

William Hamilton saw evolution "from a gene's point of view," and inspired Wilson and other sociobiologists to do the same.

of "social animals" (or animals that live in groups). Molecules alone could not explain these developments, he argued.

Instead, the fundamental breakthrough to sociobiology came in a brilliant two-part 1964 article by William D. Hamilton (1996), a British graduate student who also rejected the molecular approach to biology. As a self-proclaimed disciple of Ronald Fisher, Hamilton focused his powerful intellect on interactions among genes rather than on the gene's molecular composition. Here, he believed, lay the true secret of life. While still a college student at Cambridge during the 1950s, Hamilton later wrote, "I was convinced that none of the DNA stuff was going to help me understand the puzzles raised by my reading of Fisher and Haldane or to fill the gaps they had left. Their Mendelian approach had certainly not been outdated by any new findings. But ultimately, Hamilton exceeded even Fisher in seeing evolution (as he put it in his 1964 article) "from a gene's point of view," and he inspired Wilson and other sociobiologists to do so, as well.

The origins of altruism stood out as the most prominent evolutionary puzzle unsolved by the synthetic theorists. They had melded Darwinism and Mendalism without accounting for self-sacrifice. This left a glaring gap. Critics of selection theory had long pointed to altruistic behavior (particularly by humans) as evidence that a Darwinian struggle for existence could not explain all aspects of life. If nature selects solely for traits leading to an individual's survival or reproductive success, as classical Darwinism suggested, then self-sacrifice and (except to aid one's own descendents) must have a supernatural source. Such thinking led Darwinists from Alfred Russel Wallace through David Lack to reserve space for the spiritual within their science. Darwin held out for a naturalistic explanation for altruism, but never devised a wholly satisfactory one. Although he otherwise thought that selection acted among individuals, here Darwin bowed to group selection.

Altruism aids the group at the expense of the individual, he reasoned, such as when a bird warns the flock of approaching predators by a self-endangering cry or when childless soldiers die for their country. Castes of sterile worker ants, wasps, and bees present even more dramatic examples of self-sacrificing social behavior. Inasmuch as such traits promote the group's survival, Darwin noted, perhaps nature selects groups that possess them. Unless members of the group jointly learn and pass along such traits in a Lamarckian manner, however, those traits should fail because single individuals displaying them would tend to die earlier than others. In short, as a randomly generated inborn trait, altruism should not persist. Such thinking led Darwin to admit an element of Lamarckism into his system—but the modern synthesis rejected this solution.

Hamilton proposed a purely Darwinist account for altruism by shifting the level of selection to the gene. Take social insects, he proposed. Because of the peculiar way they reproduce, female ants, wasps and bees share more genes in common with their sisters (75 percent) than with their own children (50 percent) or brothers (25 percent). Thus, from the gene's point of view, female ants achieve greater reproductive success by aiding their sisters than their offspring. Fitting the model, all sterile worker ants are female and, as Hamilton noted, "working by males seems to be unknown in the group." Similarly, but less spectacularly, any animal (including a human) that shares genes with its collateral kin (as well as with its lineage) can maximize the survival of those genes held in common by those relatives provided the number of genes held in common by those relatives exceed those lost by its sacrifice.

In his 1964 article, Hamilton worked out the algebra of such so-called "kin selection" to show that, at least in theory, it could account for apparently altruistic behavior in terms of selfish genes. "In the world of our model organisms," he concluded, "we expect to find that no one is prepared to sacrifice his life for a single person but that everyone will sacrifice it when he can thereby save more than two bothers, or four half brothers, or eight first cousins" (Hamilton, 1964, p. 31). Genetic tendencies in this direction should survive and spread. In this manner, a starkly naturalistic struggle for existence should lie at the heart of seemingly selfless acts of individual love. With this conceptual breakthrough, the way seemed open to find biologic bases for all manners of human and other-animal behavior.

Wilson first read Hamilton's paper in 1965, on a train trip from Boston to Miami. By his own account, Wilson left New England with a casual interest in Hamilton's ideas, became increasingly "frustrated and angry" about them during the journey, but arrived in Florida fully convinced. "Because I modestly thought of myself as the world authority on social insects," Wilson related, "I also thought it unlikely that anyone else could explain their origin, certainly not in one clean stroke," but Hamilton had (Wilson, 1994, p. 319). Like Hamilton, Wilson believed that whatever explained the behavior of social insects also shed light on the behavior of other social animals, including humans. A core group of evolutionary biologists agreed. An outburst of research ensued, testing and extending Hamilton's insight and other sociobiologic theories (collectively called "evolutionary psychology" when applied to humans).

These efforts sought to explain behavior in terms of its impact on the survival and reproductive success of genes and individuals. Models, metaphors, and concepts proliferated, such as reciprocal altruism (where organisms evolve to help one another survive), and an arms race (where predator and prey evolve in response to one another's developments). By factoring in circumstances impacting populations, sociobiologists used such theories to predict and explain all manners of animal behavior.

Wilson pulled many of these threads together in his 1975 survey, *Sociobiology: The New Synthesis*. Because of its emphasis on adaptations aiding reproduction, the book featured biologic accounts of gender-based behaviors. Males naturally tend to spread their ample sperm (including through multiple mates), Wilson suggested, while females tend to conserve their scarce eggs (such as investing heavily in mate-selection and child-rearing). Indeed, some sociobiologists accounted for aggressive behavior by

Edward O. Wilson believed that whatever explained the behavior of social insects also shed light on the behavior of other social animals, including humans.

young males as a genetic holdover from a time when it carried reproductive benefit. To some readers, such explanations sounded like justifications for traditional gender roles and sociobiology seemed to endorse the social status quo (or worse)—especially given Wilson's insistence that humans disregard nature at their peril.

Characteristically, the chapter of *Sociobiology* dealing with human behavior opened with a deliberately provocative challenge. "Let us now consider man in the free spirit of natural history," Wilson wrote. "In this macroscopic view the humanities and social sciences shrink to specialized branches of biology; history, biography, and fiction are the research protocols of human ethology; and anthropology and sociology together constitute the sociobiology of a single primate species." Ethics, he suggested, should "be removed temporarily from the hands of the philosophers and biologicized" (Wilson, 2000, pp. 547, 562). These were bold claims for a discipline supposedly chastened by the excesses of Social Darwinism, eugenics, and Nazi race theory. Wilson (1978) did not assert that nature alone shaped human behavior, but he clearly wanted to push the pendulum back from the extreme nurture position taken by most mid-twentieth-century social scientists. They envisioned human culture as infinitely malleable for good or ill while he declared that "the gene holds Culture on a leash" (p. 167).

The reaction came swiftly. Steeped in environmentalism, many social scientists and humanists hotly contested Wilson's claims, with protesters once going so far as to pour ice water on him during an academic address. Following the lead of T. H. Huxley, who in 1893 called it a "fallacy" to base ethics on evolution, many biologists had conceded the study of human behavior to the social scientists (Huxley, 1997, p. 327). "Culture is acquired, not transmitted through genes," Dobzhansky (1963, p. 146) assured anthropologists in 1963. Beginning in 1975, Dobzhansky's former student and Wilson's colleague, Richard Lewontin, led the scientific assault on sociobiology. Another distinguished Harvard evolutionist with a popular following, paleontologist Stephen Jay Gould, joined the attack. Both acknowledged that genetic determinism offended their Marxist ideology, just as it had offended Dobzhansky's Christian beliefs, but they focused their criticisms on Wilson's science. Likening sociobiologic explanations of human behavior to Rudyard Kipling's "just so" fables of how primitive peoples account for animal origins, Lewontin and Gould damned sociobiology as scientifically flawed and socially dangerous. "Wilson joins the long parade of biological determinists whose work has served to buttress the institutions of their society by exonerating them from responsibility for social problems," they wrote in a 1975 critique of *Sociobiology*, cosigned by a dozen other Boston-area academics (Allen et al., 1975, p. 43).

Wilson replied with an expanded defense of human sociobiology in his award-winning 1978 book, *On Human Nature*. The sparring continued into the twenty-first century, with Wilson gradually gaining allies among evolutionary biologists and a new generation of social scientists. "Overall," he boasted in the foreword to a commemorative twenty-fifth anniversary edition of *Sociobiology*, "there is a tendency at the century's close to accept that *Homo sapiens* is an ascendent primate, and that biology matters" (Wilson, 2000, p. vii). Indeed, by offering edgy, materialistic explanations for human interactions, sociobiology and gene-centered evolutionism attracted a popular (as well as an academic) following. It fit the secular, consumer-oriented culture commonly associated with America in the 1980s. Although books by Wilson on the topic sold well, they were eclipsed on both sides of the Atlantic by those of a younger British evolutionist, Richard Dawkins, who as an Oxford student in the late 1960s had taken Hamilton as his "intellectual hero" (Dawkins, 2001, p. xv).

In his intoxicating prose, Dawkins popularized Hamilton's vision of organisms (including humans) as elaborate apparatuses evolved to propagate their genes. We are survival machines—robot vehicles blindly programmed to preserve the selfish molecules known as genes," he explained. "This is a truth which still fills me with astonishment" (Dawkins, 1976, p. v). The genes themselves cannot plan ahead or respond to their environment, Dawkins stressed. They simply reproduce themselves with occasional random mutations that may or may not assist their survival, and we ("climbing Mount Improbable" of Sewall Wright's adaptive landscape over some four billion years of trial-and-error organic evolution) are the result (Dawkins, 1996). Dawkins found this view of life exhilarating. For him, it freed humans from the burden of purposeful design in nature, which he identified as "the most influential of the arguments for the existence of God." Unlike the controlling purposes of a Designing God, Dawkins noted, "Natural selection, the blind, unconscious, automatic process which Darwin described, and which we now know is the explanation for the existence and apparently purposeful form of all life, has no purpose in mind." By banishing the argument for God from design, he proclaimed, "Darwin made it possible to be an intellectually fulfilled atheist" (Dawkins, 1986, pp. 4–5).

Agreeing with Dawkins's naturalistic gospel insofar as it went, Wilson nevertheless hoped for something more from scientific materialism. "It presents the human mind with an alternative mythology that until now has always, point for point in zones of conflict, defeated traditional religion," he stated. "Its narrative form is epic: the evolution of the universe from the big bang . . . [to] life on earth" (Wilson, 1978, p. 192). Reared in the Bible Belt of Alabama by fundamentalist parents, Wilson maintained that people need to believe in something larger than themselves to justify the individual sacrifices that propagate genes through kin selection. Indeed, in an article coauthored by Darwinian philosopher Michael Ruse, Wilson described religion (or at least ethics based on religion) as "an illusion fobbed off on us by our genes to get us to cooperate" (Ruse & Wilson, 1985, p. 52). As people shed spiritual belief in the light of scientific understanding, he believed that some other source of larger meaning must takes its place.

In his 1998 book *Consilience* and elsewhere, Wilson offered evolutionism as a new "sacred narrative" capable of enshrining essential ethical principles calculated to advance human development and preserve genetic diversity (Wilson, 1998, pp. 264–265). Although Wilson's vision of a naturalistic religion based on modern evolutionary thought stirred widespread comment, most scientists kept their professional distance. "He is a good and gentile man, generous to a fault, with a real concern for . . . biodiversity and ecological preservation," Ruse noted. "But I do not see that his fellow evolutionists have to follow him in making a religion out of their shared science" (Ruse & Wilson, 2001, p. 284). Of course, scientists can see their science as important without making it their religion. Certainly most evolutionary biologists view the theory of evolution as extremely important: That is why they study it. Hamilton, for example, like Fisher before him, entered the field in pursuit of the eugenicist's dream of enhancing the human stock. "I had come to Galton's ideas by my own parallel reasoning spurred by the common youthful wish to improve the world, and by reading Fisher," Hamilton wrote shortly before his death in 2000. "I much liked the notion that human-directed selection, whether to maintain standards or to speed the intellectual and physical progress of humanity, could be made more effective and more merciful than the obviously inefficient and cruel natural process" (Hamilton, 1996, p. 15). Although the dream sustained his early studies of altruistic behavior, Hamilton's later work on another major evolutionary puzzle—left unsolved by Fisher—the so-called "problem of sex"—dampened his enthusiasm for state-controlled eugenics and deepened his appreciation for the efficiency of natural selection.

Sexual (as opposed to asexual) reproduction comes at a huge biologic cost to the individual. The birthing female transmits only half of her individual genetic identity to her offspring.

The payoff comes in variation as the genetic material from two parents passes on in new combinations. Under evolutionary models that rely exclusively on individual or gene-level selection (rather than group selection or intelligent design), synthetic theorists began questioning whether the payoff justified the cost. Among biologists taking up this puzzle, which included such leading neo-Darwinists as George C. Williams and John Maynard Smith, Hamilton offered perhaps the most convincing (though far from universally accepted) reason why sexual reproduction predominates among species that produce few offspring. He called it the "*parasite Red Queen hypothesis*," in reference to the character in *Through the Looking-Glass* who had to run as fast as she could just to stay in place—a name borrowed from biologist Leigh Van Valen's more-general "Red Queen" hypothesis of an evolutionary arms race. It relied on the premise that sexual reproduction produces more genetic variation than asexual reproduction. Hamilton proposed that slow-reproducing organisms need the added variation coming from sexual reproduction to stay ahead of the rapidly reproducing asexual parasites. "The host's best defense may be based on genotypic diversity, which, if recombined each generation can present to the parasites what amounts to a continually moving target," he explained in a coauthored 1988 article (Seger & Hamilton, 1988, p. 176).

The parasitic Red Queen hypothesis, with its emphasis on random genotypic diversity, convinced Hamilton that any controlled scheme of eugenic breeding would fail through a lack of genetic variation. Better let natural selection take its course, he concluded, whatever the pain (Hamilton, 1996, p. 17). Yet his youthful enthusiasm for planned reproduction merely gave way to later-life concerns about the dysgenic effects of advances in health care that allow people (such as diabetics, he noted) to survive and reproduce their deleterious genes. "I predict that in two generations the danger being done to the human genome by the anti- and postnatal life-saving efforts of modern medicine will be obvious to all," he warned in a posthumously published autobiographical account (Hamilton, 1998, p. 456). Hamilton simply could not stop worrying about humanity's future: Perhaps it was in his genes.

Just as Gould joined in leading the scientific opposition to sociobiology, he loudly protested any return to eugenic thinking. Gould saw the two as inexorably linked in a damnable hereditarian view of humanity. During the 1980s, he wrote popular books and articles exposing "the mismeasure of man" that bedeviled earlier efforts to devise eugenic standards for human reproduction. (See Gould 1981.) Hamilton attributed Gould's position to a Marxist's misguided commitment to human equality, while Ruse viewed it as at least partially rooted in a Jew's memory of the Holocaust (Hamilton, 1996, pp. 490–491; Ruse & Wilson, 2001). Indeed, Gould did not limit his assault to sociobiology and eugenics, but took on fundamental tenets of the modern synthesis that supported them. In doing so, he offered an alternative scientific view of how evolution operates that challenged genetic reductionism.

Gould complained that exclusive reliance on the natural selection of genes to account for evolution ignored factors that shape organisms. With Richard Lewontin in 1979, Gould argued that developmental constraints limit and channel adaptations. Certain features (such as the *Tyrannosaurus*'s reduced front legs) may serve no adaptive purpose, they suggested, but instead arise as a by-product of other adaptations (such as larger hind legs) (Gould & Lewontin, 1979, p. 587). Over the years, Gould expounded the view that form does not inexorably follow function, and that much is left to chance in the lottery of life. "If a large extraterrestrial object—the ultimate random bolt from the blue—had not triggered the extinction of dinosaurs 65 million years ago, mammals would still be small creatures, confined to nooks and crannies of a dinosaur's world, and incapable of evolving the larger size that brains big enough for self-consciousness require," he commented in 1996 (Gould, 1996, p. 216). Gould's view flew in the face of the progressivism implicit in much neo-Darwinian thinking. Given the enormous adaptive advantage of intelligence and cooperation, for example, both Hamilton and Wilson believed that the evolution of self-conscious, altruistic beings was far from accidental. Their depictions of kin-based and reciprocal altruism in various types of social animals supported their faith in evolutionary progress. "Since natural selection has invented both kinds of altruism numerous times," the like-minded science writer Robert Wright explained, "it is not too wild to suggest that this expansive sentiment was probable all along" (Wright, 1999, p. 64).

Beginning in the 1970s, Gould worked with American Museum of Natural History paleontologist Niles Eldredge in formulating the theory of punctuated equilibria to account for the pattern of organic life preserved in sedimentary rock. "The oldest truth of paleontology proclaimed that the vast majority of species appear fully formed in the fossil record and do not change substantially during the long period of their later existence," Gould noted in an obvious reference to Cuvier's findings. "In other words, geologically abrupt appearance followed by subsequent stability" (Gould, 1991, p. 14). The modern synthesis, in contrast, presented evolution proceeding gradually, by minute adaptations, without sharp divisions of individuals into enduring species. For generations, Darwinists confidently predicted that further research would smooth out the fossil record into the predicted pattern of gradual change, but it never happened. Increasingly, synthetic theorists extrapolated from their mathematical models and population studies to chart the course of evolution, while relegating fossils to museum exhibits calculated to impress the public that evolution happens. Gould and Eldredge resisted this role for their field. Instead they took its findings seriously and tried to explain them in evolutionary terms. To do so, they drew on Sewall Wright's classic (but unfashionable) notion of non-adaptive genetic drift as developed in Ernst Mayr's so-called "founder principle" of allopatric speciation.

Mayr had proposed that new species form when a small population becomes geographically isolated from the main group—such as a few mainland finches blown to the Galapagos Islands. The new or particularized environment, coupled with a greatly restricted gene pool, accelerates the evolutionary process and facilitates the formation of new species, Mayr suggested. Once established, though, the new species should become as stable as the old one. This process, Eldredge and Gould observed, should generate the pattern they found in the fossil record: long periods of equilibria or stasis in species, punctuated with the abrupt appearance of new ones. "If new species arise very rapidly in small, peripherally isolated populations, then the great expectation of insensibly graded fossil sequences is a chimera," they wrote in 1972. "A new species does not arise from the slow transformation of all its forebears. Many breaks in the fossil record are real" (Eldredge & Gould, 1972, p. 84).

By the time Eldredge and Gould proposed their theory, however, Mayr's founder principle played little part in mainstream evolutionary thought, which Eldredge characterized as having become "ultra-Darwinian." "Ultra-Darwinians are really followers of Ronald Fisher," he asserted, "seeking to explain all evolutionary phenomena strictly in terms of natural selection acting on heritable variations within populations" (Eldredge, 1995, p. 86). Like Wright's concept of genetic drift, synthetic theorists came to view the founder principle as insignificant in evolutionary effect as compared with gene-based adaptations in large populations—such as the selection of black peppered moths in a darkened environment. Now Eldredge and Gould sought to revive it as a primary explanation for the patterns preserved in the fossil record and, in doing so, to give special significance to speciation within the overall evolutionary process. "Species represent a level of performance that acts to conserve adaptive change far beyond the ephemeral capabilities of local populations," Eldredge asserted (Eldredge, 1995, p. 87). Drifting further from the neo-Darwinian mainstream, Gould later proposed that nonadaptive developmental constraints and macromutations might also impact evolution, at least at higher levels of the process. There is something real about species, he stressed, that resists change without a jolt beyond that required for lower-level variation among individuals within populations. Using language certain to inflame synthetic theorists who believed that evolution operated the same way at all levels, Gould differentiated between "microevolution" within species and "macroevolution" of higher level taxa. (See, e.g., Gould, 2002, pp. 774–784.)

Gould's ability to communicate his heresies to an educated audience through best-selling books and popular articles fed the public perception of a revolution within evolutionary thought, when in reality the rebellion was limited largely to one wing of paleontology. For his part, Eldredge maintained that the "abrupt appearance" of any new species under the punctuated-equilibrium model would still take generations of gradual change—he estimated it as ranging "from five to fifty thousand years"—and did not involve macromutations. (Gould, 2002, p. 99). Any plausible version of punctuated equilibria, Mayr insisted, is compatible with the modern synthesis. Nevertheless, purporting to speak for mainline neo-Darwinists generally, John Maynard Smith dismissed Gould's view of evolution as "so confused as to be hardly worth bothering with" (Smith, 1995, p. 46). Robert Wright added, "He stresses its flukier aspects—freak environmental catastrophes and the like—and downplays natural selection's power to design complex life forms. In fact, if you really pay attention to what he is saying, and accept it, you might start to wonder how evolution could have created anything as intricate as a human being." Gould's view thus contrasted sharply with that of Hamilton, and other ultra-Darwinists who saw the creation of humans as all but inevitable in the naturalistic processes envisioned by the modern synthesis. Wright dlsmissively dubbed Gould as "the accidental creationist," even though Gould steadfastly proclaimed his commitment to evolutionary materialism (Wright, 1999, p. 56).

Of course, many evolutionists still dissent on the critical issue of materialism, particularly when it comes to the ascent of humans. Calling himself a "theistic evolutionist," for example, noted American geneticist Francis Collins, who directed the human genome project during the 1990s and beyond, followed the path trod by God-fearing Darwinists from Wallace to Lack in rejecting naturalistic explanations for altruism and other distinctly human traits. "Science," Collins wrote in 2002, "will certainly not shed any light on what it means to love someone, what it means to have a spiritual dimension to our existence, nor will it tell us much about the character of God" (Collins, 2002, p. 16). Surveys from the 1990s suggested that Collins speaks for about 40 percent of the American people—and almost a like percentage of American scientists—when he posits God as somehow involved in the evolutionary process, at least to the extent of breathing a supernaturally created soul into a naturally evolved body (see, e.g., Giberson & Yerxa, 2002, pp. 53–57; Larson & Witham, 1997, p. 435). For the record, the Roman Catholic Church approves the latter position. "Rather than the theory of evolution, we should speak of several theories of evolution . . . materialistic, reductionist and spiritualist," Pope John Paul II declared in a 1996 message to the Pontifical Academy of Sciences. "Theories of evolution which, in accordance with the philosophies inspiring them, consider the mind as emerging from the forces of living matter, or as a mere epiphenomenon of this matter, are incompatible with the truth about man" (John Paul II, 1997, pp. 382–383).

Despite challenges, the naturalistic modern synthesis stands at the heart of current evolutionary science. Genetic mutations and recombinations, this view maintains, cause organisms to vary. The fittest of these various individuals survive to pass along their genes. Change builds incrementally, without discrete breaks. As synthetic biologists have asserted all along, hybrid crosses between nearly related species add to the gene flows that cause individuals to vary (Arnold, 1977, pp. 182–185). Recent research suggests that (much as happens in genetic engineering) viruses and bacteria can invade the cells of other organisms and implant their own genes or genes from other organisms into the host's DNA (Margulis & Sagan, 2002, pp. 71–77). Again, variation can result. Natural hybridization and gene acquisition join mutation and recombination as the genetic fodder for natural selection to sift and winnow in evolving the diversity of life. Two centuries of research in biology since Lamarck's day have enriched the scientific account of origins that Wilson now calls "epic." "It is indeed remarkable that this theory has been progressively accepted by researchers, following a series of discoveries in various fields of knowledge," John Paul II noted in his 1996 message. "The convergence, neither sought nor fabricated, of results of work that was conducted independently is in itself a significant argument in favor of this theory" (John Paul II, 1997, p. 382). Indeed, its proponents describe it as a "fact," not a theory (see, e.g., Mayr, 1997, p. 178). The evolutionary epic began with the appearance of self-replicating cells on earth some four billion years ago, scientists estimate. Multicellular life came more than three billion years later; hominids stood erect on the plains of Africa beginning about five million years ago and the first of our species walked into history within the past hundred thousand years. "There is a grandeur in this view of life," Darwin wrote in the last sentence of

Origin of Species, "that, whilst this planet has gone cycling on according to the fixed law of gravity, from so simple a beginning endless forms most beautiful and most wonderful have been, and are being, evolved" (Darwin, 1964, p. 490). With this, all manner of modern evolutionists would agree. Even if they cannot wholly accept Wilson's depiction of "a cause-and effect continuum from physics to the social sciences, from this world to all other worlds in the visible universe, and backward through time to the beginning of the universe," they share the awe implicit in a well-known movie's title that Gould adapted in naming his most popular book, *Accident or Not, It's a Wonderful Life* (Gould, 1989, p. 14).

Darwin's Influence on Modern Thought

by Ernst Mayr

Ernst Mayr describes the changes that the Origin of Species made not only in our sense of evolution per se, but in much of our more general sense of the world (Zeitgeist in his terms) by challenging the idea that world was controlled directly by the supernatural; and the idea of a stable unvarying world divisible into strict classes of things or types substituting the concept of a natural range of variability. He challenged the idea that history was defined by teleology (the sense of an ultimate, predefined goal) substituting a sense of the randomness of nature. And he suggested that human beings were part of the general pattern of nature, not uniquely above it. Great minds shape the thinking of successive historical periods. Luther and Calvin inspired the Reformation; Locke, Leibniz, Voltaire, and Rousseau, the Enlightenment. Modern thought is most dependent on the influence of Charles Darwin.

Clearly, our conception of the world and our place in it is, at the beginning of the twenty-first century, drastically different from the Zeitgeist at the beginning of the nineteenth century. But no consensus exists as to the source of this revolutionary change. Karl Marx is often mentioned; Sigmund Freud has been in and out of favor; Albert Einstein's biographer Abraham Pais made the exuberant claim that Einstein's theories "have profoundly changed the way modern men and women think about the phenomena of inanimate nature." No sooner had Pais said this, though, than he recognized the exaggeration. "It would actually be better to say 'modern scientists' than 'modern men and women,'" he wrote, because one needs schooling in the physicist's style of thought and mathematical techniques to appreciate Einstein's

---

This article is based on the September 23, 1999, lecture that Mayr delivered in Stockholm on receiving the Crafoord Prize from the Royal Swedish Academy of Science. Adapted with permission.

Ernst Mayr challenged the idea that history was defined by teleology substituting a sense of randomness of nature.

contributions in their fullness. Indeed, this limitation is true for all the extraordinary theories of modern physics, which have had little impact on the way the average person apprehends the world.

The situation differs dramatically with regard to concepts in biology. Many biological ideas proposed during the past 150 years stood in stark conflict with what everybody assumed to be true. The acceptance of these ideas required an ideological revolution. And no biologist has been responsible for more—and for more drastic—modifications of the average person's worldview than Charles Darwin.

Darwin's accomplishments were so many and so diverse that it is useful to distinguish three fields to which he made major contributions: evolutionary biology, the philosophy of science, and the modern Zeitgeist. Although I will be focusing on the last domain, for the sake of completeness I will put forth a short overview of his contributions—particularly as they inform his later ideas—to the first two areas.

A Secular View of Life

Darwin founded a new branch of life science, evolutionary biology. Four of his contributions to evolutionary biology are especially important, as they held considerable sway beyond that discipline. The first is the nonconstancy of species, or the modern conception of evolution itself. The second is the notion of branching evolution, implying the common descent of all species of living things on earth from a single unique origin. Up until 1859, all evolutionary proposals, such as that of naturalist Jean-Baptiste Lamarck, instead endorsed linear evolution, a teleological march toward greater perfection that had been in vogue since Aristotle's concept of *Scala Naturae*, the chain of being. Darwin further noted that evolution must be gradual, with no major breaks or discontinuities. Finally, he reasoned that the mechanism of evolution was natural selection.

These four insights served as the foundation for Darwin's founding of a new branch of the philosophy of science, a philosophy of biology. Despite the passing of a century before this new branch of philosophy fully developed, its eventual form is based on Darwinian concepts. For example, Darwin introduced historicity into science. Evolutionary biology, in contrast with physics and chemistry, is an historical science—the evolutionist attempts to explain events and processes that have already taken place. Laws and experiments are inappropriate techniques for the explication of such events and processes. Instead, one constructs an historical narrative, consisting of a tentative reconstruction of the particular scenario that led to the events one is trying to explain.

For example, three different scenarios have been proposed for the sudden extinction of the dinosaurs at the end of the Cretaceous: a devastating epidemic; a catastrophic change of climate; and the impact of an asteroid, known as the Alvarez theory. The first two narratives were ultimately refuted by evidence incompatible with them. All the known facts, however, fit the Alvarez theory, which is now widely accepted. The testing of historical narratives implies that the wide gap between science and the humanities that so troubled physicist C. P. Snow is actually nonexistent—by virtue of its methodology and its acceptance of the time factor that makes change possible, evolutionary biology serves as a bridge.

The discovery of natural selection, by Darwin and Alfred Russel Wallace, must itself be counted as an extraordinary philosophical advance. The principle remained unknown throughout the more than two-thousand-year history of philosophy ranging from the Greeks to Hume, Kant, and the Victorian era. The concept of natural selection had remarkable power for explaining directional and adaptive changes. Its nature is simplicity itself. It is not a force like the forces described in the laws of physics; its mechanism is simply the elimination of inferior individuals. This process of nonrandom elimination impelled Darwin's contemporary, philosopher Herbert Spencer, to describe evolution with the now familiar term "survival of the fittest." (This description was long ridiculed as circular reasoning: "Who are the fittest? Those who survive." In reality, a careful analysis can usually determine why certain individuals fail to thrive in a given set of conditions.)

The truly outstanding achievement of the principle of natural selection is that it makes unnecessary the invocation of "final causes"—that is, any teleological forces leading to a particular end. In fact, nothing is predetermined. Furthermore, the objective of selection even may change from one generation to the next, as environmental circumstances vary.

A diverse population is a necessity for the proper working of natural selection. (Darwin's success meant that typologists, for whom all members of a class are essentially identical, were left with an untenable viewpoint.) Because of the importance of variation, natural selection should be considered a two-step process: The production of abundant variation is followed by the elimination of inferior individuals. This latter step is directional. By adopting natural selection, Darwin settled the several-thousand-year-old argument among philosophers over chance or necessity. Change on the earth is the result of both, the first step being dominated by randomness, the second by necessity.

Darwin was a holist: For him the object, or target, of selection was primarily the individual as a whole. The geneticists, almost from 1900 on, in a rather reductionist spirit preferred to consider the gene the target of evolution. In the past twenty-five years, however, they have largely returned to the Darwinian view that the individual is the principal target.

For eighty years after 1859, bitter controversy raged as to which of four competing evolutionary theories was valid. "Transmutation" was the establishment of a new species or new type through a single mutation, or saltation. "Orthogenesis" held that intrinsic teleological tendencies led to transformation. Lamarckian evolution relied on the inheritance of acquired characteristics. And now there was Darwin's variational evolution, through natural selection. Darwin's theory clearly emerged as the victor during the evolutionary synthesis of the 1940s, when the new discoveries in genetics were married with taxonomic observations concerning systematics, the classification of organisms by their relationships. Darwinism is now almost unanimously accepted by knowledgeable evolutionists. In addition, it has become the basic component of the new philosophy of biology.

A most important principle of the new biological philosophy, undiscovered for almost a century after the publication of *On the Origin of Species*, is the dual nature of biological processes. These activities are governed both by the universal laws of physics and chemistry and by a genetic program, itself the result of natural selection, which has molded the genotype for millions of generations. The causal factor of the possession of a genetic program is unique to living organisms, and it is totally absent in the inanimate world. Because of the backward state of molecular and genetic knowledge in his time, Darwin was unaware of this vital factor.

Another aspect of the new philosophy of biology concerns the role of laws. Laws give way to concepts in Darwinism. In the physical sciences, as a rule, theories are based on laws; for example, the laws of motion led to the theory of gravitation. In evolutionary biology, however, theories are largely based on concepts such as competition, female choice, selection, succession, and dominance. These biological concepts, and the theories based on them, cannot be reduced to the laws and theories of the physical sciences. Darwin himself never stated this idea plainly. My assertion of Darwin's importance to modern thought is the result of an analysis of Darwinian theory over the past century. During this period, a pronounced change in the methodology of biology took place. This transformation was not caused exclusively by Darwin, but it was greatly strengthened by developments in evolutionary biology. Observation, comparison, and classification as well as the testing of competing became the methods of evolutionary biology, outweighing experimentation.

I do not claim that Darwin was single-handedly responsible for all the intellectual developments in this period. Much of it, like the refutation of French mathematician and physicist Pierre-Simon Laplace's determinism, was "in the air." But Darwin in most cases either had priority or promoted the new views most vigorously.

The Darwinian Zeitgeist

A twenty-first-century person looks at the world quite differently than a citizen of the Victorian era did. This shift had multiple sources, particularly the incredible advances in technology. But what is not at all appreciated is the great extent to which this shift in thinking indeed resulted from Darwin's ideas.

Remember that in 1850 virtually all leading scientists and philosophers were Christian men. The world they inhabited had been created by God, and as the natural theologians claimed, He had instituted wise laws that brought about the perfect adaptation of all organisms to one another and to their environment. At the same time, the architects of the scientific revolution had constructed a worldview based on physicalism (a reduction to spatiotemporal things or events or their properties), teleology, determinism, and other basic principles. Such was the thinking of Western humans prior to the 1859 publication of *On the Origin of Species*. The basic principles proposed by Darwin would stand in total conflict with these prevailing ideas.

First, Darwinism rejects all supernatural phenomena and causations. The theory of evolution by natural selection explains the adaptedness and diversity of the world solely materialistically. It no longer requires God as creator or designer (although one is certainly still free to believe in God even if one accepts evolution). Darwin pointed out that creation, as described in the Bible, and the origin accounts of other cultures, was contradicted by almost any aspect of natural world. Every aspect of the "wonderful design" so admired by the natural theologians could be explained by natural selection. (A closer look also reveals that design is often not so wonderful; see Nesse & Williams, 1998.) Eliminating God from science made room for strictly scientific explanations of all natural phenomena; it gave rise to positivism, and it produced a powerful intellectual and spiritual revolution, the effects of which have lasted to this day.

Second, Darwinism refutes typology. From the time of the Pythagoreans and Plato, the general concept of the diversity of the world emphasized its invariance and stability. This viewpoint is called typology, or essentialism. The seeming variety was seen as a limited number of natural kinds each one forming a class. The members of each class were thought to be identical, constant, and sharply separated from the members of other essences.

Variation, in contrast, is nonessential and accidental. A triangle illustrates essentialism: All triangles have the same fundamental characteristics and are sharply delimited against quadrangles or any other geometric figures. An intermediate between a triangle and a quadrangle is inconceivable. Typological thinking, therefore, is unable to accommodate variation and gives rise to a misleading conception of human races. For the typologist, Caucasians, Africans, Asians, or Inuits are types that conspicuously differ from other human ethnic groups. This mode of thinking leads to racism. (Although the ignorant misapplication "social Darwinism" often gets blamed for justifications of racism, adherence to the disproved essentialism preceding Darwin in fact can lead to a racist viewpoint.)

Darwin completely rejected typological thinking and introduced instead the entirely different concept now called population thinking. All groupings of living organisms, including humanity, are populations that consist of uniquely different individuals. No two of the six billion humans are the same. Populations vary not by their essences but only by mean statistical differences. By rejecting the constancy of populations, Darwin helped introduce history into scientific thinking and promote a distinctly new approach to explanatory interpretation in science.

Third, Darwin's theory of natural selection made any invocation of teleology unnecessary. From the Greeks onward, there existed a universal belief in the existence of a teleological force in the world that led to ever greater perfection. This "final cause" was one of the causes specified by Aristotle. After Kant, in *Critique of Judgment*, had unsuccessfully attempted to describe biological phenomena with the help of a physicalist Newtonian explanation, he then invoked teleological forces. Even after 1859, teleological explanations (orthogenesis) continued to be quite popular in evolutionary biology. The acceptance of the *Scala Naturae* and the explanations of natural theology were other manifestations of the popularity of teleology. Darwinism swept away such considerations.

(The designation "teleological" actually applied to various different phenomena. Many seemingly end-directed processes in inorganic nature are the simple consequence of natural laws—as one falls or a heated piece of metal cools because of laws of physics, not some end-directed process. Processes in living organisms owe their apparent goal-directedness to the operation of an inborn genetic or acquired program. Adapted systems, such as the heart or kidneys, may engage in activities that can be considered goal seeking, but the systems themselves were acquired during evolution and are continuously fine-tuned by natural selection. Finally, there was a belief in cosmic teleology, with a purpose and predetermined goal ascribed to everything in nature. Modern science, however, is unable to substantiate the existence of any such cosmic teleology.)

Fourth, Darwin does away with determinism. Laplace notoriously boasted that a complete knowledge of the current world and all its processes would enable him to predict the future to infinity. Darwin, by comparison, accepted the universality of randomness and chance throughout the process of natural selection. (Astronomer and philosopher John Herschel referred to natural selection contemptuously as "the law of the higgledy-piggledy.") That chance should play an important role in natural processes has been an unpalatable thought for many physicists. Einstein expressed this distaste in his statement, "God does not play dice." Of course, as previously mentioned, only the first step in natural selection, the production of variation, is a matter of chance. The character of the second step, the actual selection, is to be directional.

Despite the initial resistance by physicists and philosophers, the role of contingency and chance in natural processes is now almost universally acknowledged. Many biologists and philosophers deny the existence of universal laws in biology and suggest that all regularities be stated in probabilistic terms, as nearly all so-called biological laws have exceptions. Philosopher of science Karl Popper's famous test of falsification therefore cannot be applied in these cases.

Fifth, Darwin developed a new view of humanity and, in turn, a new anthropocentrism. Of all of Darwin's proposals, the one his contemporaries found most difficult to accept was that the theory of common descent applied to Man. For theologians and philosophers alike, Man was a creature above and apart from other living beings. Aristotle, Descartes, and Kant agreed on this sentiment, no matter how else their thinking diverged. But biologists Thomas Huxley and Ernst Haeckel revealed through rigorous comparative anatomical study that humans and living apes clearly had common ancestry, an assessment that has never again been seriously questioned in science. The application of the theory of common descent to Man deprived man of his former unique position.

Ironically, though, these events did not lead to an end to anthropocentrism. The study of man showed that, in spite of his descent, he is indeed unique among all organisms. Human intelligence is unmatched by that of any other creature. Humans are the only animals with true language, including grammar and syntax. Only humanity, as Darwin emphasized, has developed genuine ethical systems. In addition, through high intelligence, language, and long parental care, humans are the only creatures to have created a rich culture. And by these means, humanity has attained, for better or worse, an unprecedented dominance over the entire globe.

Sixth, Darwin provided a scientific foundation for ethics. The question is frequently raised—and usually rebuffed—as to whether evolution adequately explains healthy human ethics. Many wonder how, if selection rewards the individual only for behavior that enhances his own survival and reproductive success, such pure selfishness can lead to any sound ethics. The widespread thesis of social Darwinism, promoted at the end of the nineteenth century by Spencer, was that evolutionary explanations were at odds with the development of ethics.

We now know, however, that in a social species not only the individual must be considered—an entire social group can be the target of selection. Darwin applied this reasoning to the human species in 1871 in *The Descent of Man*. The survival and prosperity of a social group depends to a large extent on the harmonious cooperation of the members of the group, and this behavior must be based on altruism. Such altruism, by furthering the survival and prosperity of the group, also indirectly benefits the fitness of the group's individuals. The result amounts to selection favoring altruistic behavior.

Kin selection and reciprocal helpfulness in particular will be greatly favored in a social group. Such selection for altruism has been demonstrated in recent years to be widespread among many other social animals. One can then perhaps encapsulate the relation between ethics and evolution by saying that a propensity for altruism and harmonious cooperation in social groups *is* favored by natural selection. The old thesis of social Darwinism—strict selfishness—was based on an incomplete understanding of animals, particularly social species.

The Influence of New Concepts

Let me now try to summarize my major findings. No educated person any longer questions the validity of the so-called theory of evolution, which we now know to be a simple fact. Likewise, most of Darwin's particular theses have been fully confirmed, such as that of common descent, the gradualism of evolution, and his explanatory theory of natural selection.

I hope I have successfully illustrated the wide reach of Darwin's ideas. Yes, he established a philosophy of biology by introducing the time factor, by demonstrating the importance of chance and contingency, and by showing that theories in evolutionary biology are based on concepts rather than laws. But furthermore—and this is perhaps Darwin's greatest contribution—he developed a set of new principles that influence the thinking of every person: The living world, through evolution, can be explained without recourse to supernaturalism; essentialism or typology is invalid, and we must adopt population thinking, in which all individuals are unique (vital for education and the refutation of racism); natural selection, applied to social groups, is indeed sufficient to account for the origin and maintenance of altruistic ethical systems; cosmic teleology, an intrinsic process leading life automatically to ever greater perfection, is fallacious, with all seemingly teleological phenomena explicable by purely material processes; and determinism is thus repudiated, which places our fate squarely in our own evolved hands.

To borrow Darwin's phase, there is grandeur in this view of life. New modes of thinking have been, and are being, evolved. Almost every component in modern man's belief system is somehow affected by Darwinian principles.

CHAPTER 10

Creationism as a Global Phenomenon

by Glenn Branch

The debate over Darwin and the Bible is no longer solely a phenomenon of the United States. It is clearly global, as Ronald Numbers demonstrated in his classic history of creationism and as Glenn Branch documents in this article. The global spread of the debate promises to keep it alive and thriving, aided by the global spread of a conservative brand of Christianity and, in some parts of the world, hostility toward the West, particularly the United States.

Discussing creationism, Stephen Jay Gould once contended, "This controversy is as locally and distinctively American as apple pie and Uncle Sam" (Gould, 1999, p. 129). Coming from a leading paleontologist and the de facto public voice for evolution, thanks to his voluminous writing for the public, his opinion was doubtless respected. But was it right? Seven years before Gould offered his view, the historian Ronald L. Numbers had already devoted a section of his monumental history of creation science, *The Creationists*, to the global spread of creationism, observing, "By the 1990s scientific creationism, though made in America, had become a small-scale international phenomenon" (Numbers, 1992, p. 323). Through the 1990s and the first years of the twenty-first century, creationism continued to thrive outside its American milieu; indeed, when Numbers updated his book, he added a new chapter on the global spread of creationism, remarking, "Although Gould remained oblivious to it, the worldwide growth of creationism by 2000 had already proven him utterly wrong. Antievolutionism had become a global phenomenon, as readily exportable as hip-hop and blue jeans" (Numbers, 2006, p. 399). But Gould was not utterly wrong, after all, for his "apple pie and Uncle Sam" comment was immediately followed by his clarifying assertion that "no other Western nation faces such an incubus as a serious political movement" (Gould, 1999, p. 129)—a judgment that, despite the worldwide panoply of creationist sentiment, organizations, and activities documented by Numbers, continues to be plausible.

Especially in a global context, it is important not to define creationism too narrowly. Even in the United States, it exists in a variety of forms (Scott, 2005, pp. 57–64). The main distinction is between young-earth creationism (YEC; e.g., Morris & Parker, 1987)—which, as the dominant form, provides the stereotype— and old-earth creationism (OEC; e.g., Ross, 2006). Both positions are typically, if not invariably, motivated by inerrantism, the belief that the Bible, as God's Word, is necessarily accurate and authoritative in matters of science and history as well as in matters of morals and doctrine. They therefore seek to argue that science confirms their differing interpretations of the Bible. As the labels suggest, YEC and OEC differ on the age of the universe and the earth; they usually differ about Noah's flood as well, which YEC typically regards as responsible for the fossil record and for geological features like the Grand Canyon. They agree, however, in rejecting evolution (in the sense of common ancestry, particularly with respect to humans) in favor of creation by a supernatural agent; such a rejection is plausibly identified as the defining principle of creationism (Pennock, 2003). There are people within Islamic, Jewish, Hindu, New Age, and indigenous religious traditions who, adopting a similar attitude toward their scriptures (or whatever religious authority is appropriate), similarly reject evolution in favor of creation by a supernatural agent. It is thus natural to speak of, for example, Islamic or Qur'anic creationism among Muslims and others.

Intelligent design (ID) presents a momentary taxonomic puzzle, for its proponents tend to disavow any commitment to any sacred texts, deny the necessity of any appeal to the supernatural, and shudder at the word *creationism* (Meyer, 2006). Yet according to its critics, intelligent design—or intelligent design creationism (IDC)—is riddled with the same scientific errors endemic to creationism (Pennock, 1999; Young & Edis, 2006) and is entangled historically and conceptually with creationism (Forrest & Gross, 2007; Scott, 2007). IDC, say its critics, is "creationism lite" or "mere creation" (as in the revealing title of Dembski, 1998): creationism divested of its visible religiosity simply to acquire a broad base of support and to circumvent the constitutional strictures on teaching creationism. When the constitutionality of teaching ID was successfully challenged in 2005, the critics were vindicated; the judge observed, "ID cannot uncouple itself from its creationist, and thus religious, antecedents" (*Kitzmiller* v. *Dover*, 400 F.Supp.2d 707 [M.D. Pa. 2005]). Despite the setback of the *Kitzmiller* case, the proponents of IDC are still hopeful of successes not only in the United States but also abroad. The hope is that, as a minimal version of creationism, IDC will be able to flourish in cultural climates to which YEC and OEC, as the products of American fundamentalist Protestantism, are not so easily habituated. Before discussing creationism as it exists beyond the United States, however, it is useful first to consider it at home—with respect to public opinion regarding creationism, the presence of organized support for creationism, and the effect of both on the teaching of evolution in the public schools.

In the United States, the results of Gallup polls on creationism have been basically constant over the years, with responses ranging from 44 to 47 percent for "God created human beings pretty much in their present form at one time within the last 10,000 years or so; 35 to 40 percent for "Human beings have developed over millions of years from less advanced forms of life, but God guided this process"; 9 to 13 percent for "Human beings have developed over millions of years from less advanced forms of life, but God had no part in this process"; and 4 to 9 percent volunteering a different response or declining to answer ("Polling the Creationism/Evolution Controversy," 2004). (In contrast, a 1996 poll asking the same question of scientists sampled from *American Men and Women of Science* reported responses of 5%, 40%, and 55%; see Witham, 1997.) Versions of the Gallup poll questions are widely used in media polling in the United States. A less theologically fraught statement, "Human beings, as we know them, developed from earlier species of animals," is often included as a response in surveys of scientific literacy; in 2005, 40 percent of surveyed Americans agreed, 39 percent disagreed, and 21 percent were unsure (Table 10.1). Longitudinally, "After 20 years of public debate, the percentage of U.S. adults accepting the idea of evolution has declined from 45 percent to 40 percent and the percentage of adults overtly rejecting evolution declined from 48 percent to 39 percent. The percentage of adults who were not sure about evolution increased from 7 percent in 1985 to 21 percent in 2005" (Miller, Scott, & Okamoto, 2006, p. 765).

Creationist organizations in the United States are rife, ranging from individual itinerant evangelists (usually espousing YEC) to operations with budgets in the millions of dollars, such as the Institute for Creation Research (YEC), Answers in Genesis (AiG), and the Discovery Institute's Center for Science and Culture (IDC). A back-of-the-envelope study by Jim Lippard (2007) suggests that the "market" for creationism in the United States was in the neighborhood of $22 million in 2004, and likely to increase in the future, with AiG dominating the market. Creationist efforts are bolstered by the support of institutions with broader religious agendas, including individual churches, entire denominations (including the Assemblies of God, the Jehovah's Witnesses, the Seventh-day Adventist Church, the Southern Baptist Convention, and the Wisconsin Evangelical Lutheran Synod), religious publishers, and Bible colleges where creationism is routinely taught in science classes. Also important is the support of organizations on the religious right such as James Dobson's Focus on the Family, the Alliance Defense Fund, and Pat Robertson's Christian Broadcasting Network. Although the Republican Party itself is not committed to supporting creationism, there are currently nine state Republican Parties that have officially adopted antievolution positions ("updates," 2006). During his candidacy in 1980, Ronald Reagan endorsed teaching creationism along with evolution (Numbers, 2006, p. 330); during his presidency in 2005, in response to a question about IDC, George W. Bush appeared to endorse teaching creationism along with evolution, eliciting a chorus of condemnation from the scientific and education communities (Branch, 2005).

In light of such a level of sentiment and support for creationism, it is no surprise that the teaching of evolution is a recurring controversy in American science education (Scott, 2005, pp. 71–133), facilitated by the radically decentralized nature of education in the United States. With no national curriculum and with only limited (but increasing) state control over curriculum, local school districts—of which there are over 15,000—offer constant opportunities to creationists, even despite the case law establishing the unconstitutionality of teaching creationism in the public schools (Larson, 2003). Teachers may themselves be creationists, or may mistakenly think it fair to present creationism along with evolution, or may decide to omit evolution to avoid controversy (National Science Teachers Association [NSTA], 2005); local school boards may overtly or covertly promote the teaching of creationism or discourage the teaching of evolution (as in the *Kitzmiller* case). At the state level, antievolution legislation is frequently, but usually unsuccessfully, introduced; in states that have a centralized textbook adoption process, such as Texas, creationists often challenge the proposed biology textbooks for their evolutionary content; and with the advent of state standards, which provide guidelines for local school districts to follow in their individual curricula, challenges to the treatment of evolution are now routine whenever state science standards are under revision (Branch, 2006). In 2005, the National Center for Science Education was monitoring over one hundred challenges to evolution education, varying in scope and severity, but almost all in the United States. But how is creationism faring in the rest of the Anglophone world?

In neighboring Canada, a 1993 poll found that 53 percent of Canadians surveyed disagreed with the statement "Human beings as we know them today developed from earlier species of animals" (Sonderstrom, 2000), but a later poll found that only 33 percent regarded it as probably or definitely false. Although a 2000 poll suggested that "Canadians are about evenly divided in their views about the origin of life" (Compas, 2000, p. 1), the methodology of the survey is suspect (Brown & Delodder, 2003). There is reportedly a creationist organization in almost every province (Wiles, 2006), and fundamentalist organizations often promote creationism. Probably owing to the fact that curriculum is established at the provincial level, however, creationist incursions on public education are rare: A case in Abbotsford, British Columbia, culminating in 1995 was "easily the largest public confrontation over the teaching of origins in Canadian history" (Barker, 2004, p. 91; see also Goodman, 1995). There are sporadic incidents of antievolutionism in the public schools and at the provincial level (Wiles, 2006); it was recently reported that the Quebec government was turning a blind eye to unlicensed private evangelical schools in which creationism is taught (Alphonso & Séguin, 2006). On the national stage, a conservative candidate for prime minister, Stockwell Day, was widely criticized for his acceptance of YEC (Numbers, 2006, pp. 404–405) in 2000, but in 2006, a funding proposal to study the influence of antievolutionism in Canada was rejected in terms that suggested, on the part of the evaluators, skepticism about evolution and sympathy for IDC (Baslaugh, 2006).

According to a report of a national poll in Australia, "45 percent of Australians doubted, or were not sure, if humans evolved from lower species via natural selection, as opposed to about 55 per cent who thought this was definitely or probably true" (Brook, 2000). In neighboring New Zealand, 57 percent of respondents regarded the statement "Human beings developed from earlier species of animals" as definitely or probably true (Table 10.2), and 60 percent of respondents in a later poll preferred "Darwin's theory of evolution" to divine intervention, although 52 percent were open to the teaching of the latter (Barnett, 2006). Creationism flourishes down under, according to Numbers, who writes, "No country outside the United States has given creationism a warmer reception than Australia" (2006, p. 401). In 1980, the Creation Science Foundation was established by YECs in the states of South Australia and Queensland; Numbers notes, "Queensland offered a unique opportunity for Australian creationists, in part because Protestantism in the state had become heavily Americanized since World War II and because 'creation' already appeared in the official science syllabus for public schools" (2006, p. 402). Australian-style creationism as promoted by the CSF was brasher than its counterpart in the United States, and resistance to it was brasher too: The Australian geologist Ian Plimer's spirited if not always accurate

TABLE 10.1

Acceptance of Evolution in Thirty-Four Countries, 2005

Human Beings, as We Know Them Today, Developed from Earlier Species of Animals

Country	Agree	Not Sure	Disagree	N
1 Iceland	85%	8%	7%	500
2 Denmark	83	4	13	1,013
3 Sweden	82	5	13	1,023
4 France	80	8	12	1,021
5 Japan (2001)	78	14	8	2,146
6 United Kingdom	75	8	17	1,308
7 Norway	74	8	18	976
8 Belgium	74	5	21	1,024
9 Spain	73	11	16	1,035
10 Germany	72	7	21	1,507
11 Italy	69	11	20	1,006
12 Netherlands	68	9	23	1,005
13 Hungary	67	12	21	1,000
14 Luxembourg	67	10	23	518
15 Ireland	67	12	21	1,008
16 Slovenia	67	8	25	1,061
17 Finland	66	7	27	1,006
18 Czech Republic	66	7	27	1,037
19 Estonia	64	17	19	1,000
20 Portugal	64	15	21	1,009
21 Malta	62	13	25	500
22 Switzerland	62	10	28	999
23 Slovak Republic	59	12	29	1,241
24 Poland	58	15	27	999
25 Austria	57	15	28	1,034
26 Croatia	57	15	28	1,000
27 Romania	55	20	25	1,005
28 Greece	54	14	32	1,000
29 Bulgaria	50	29	21	1,008
30 Lithuania	49	21	30	1,003
31 Latvia	48	25	27	1,034
32 Cyprus	46	18	36	505
33 United States	40	21	39	1,484
34 Turkey	27	22	51	1,005

Table courtesy of Jon D. Miller, Michigan State University. See Miller et al. (2005) for discussion.

TABLE 10.2

Acceptance of Evolution in Twenty-Seven Countries, 2001

		Human Beings Developed from Earlier Species of Animals					
	Country	Definitely True	Probably True	True	Probably Not True	Definitely Not True	N
1	Germany (East)	60.6%	30.9%		3.4%	5.1%	527
2	Japan	39.7	50.4		6	3.8	1,180
3	Denmark	46.3	42.8		3.7	7.2	1,069
4	Sweden	34.9	51.5		7.2	6.4	1,067
5	Germany (West)	43.6	42.1		6.2	8.1	974
6	Austria	41.7	41.9		8.2	8.3	1,011
7	Portugal	27.4	55.7		13.6	3.3	1,000
8	Switzerland	38.8	43.9		5.5	11.8	1,006
9	Bulgaria	39.6	39.6		7.3	13.4	1,013
10	Great Britain	31.6	46.7		11.7	10.1	972
11	Czech Republic	37.7	39.1		13.7	9.4	1,244
12	Slovenia	31.3	44.6		11.4	12.7	1,077
13	Finland	24.1	51.6		14.6	9.7	1,528
14	Spain	34.7	38.8		8.9	17.7	958
15	Norway	30.4	42.9		9.7	13.4	1,452
16	Ireland	25.1	46.2		13.9	14.8	1,232
17	Chile	8.8	23.6	37.6	14.4	15.7	1,503
18	Netherlands	24.7	44.4		10.8	20.1	1,609
19	New Zealand	25.1	42		11.2	21.7	1,112
20	Canada	26.8	40.3		13.8	19.1	1,115
21	Northern Ireland	15.8	46.2		13.4	24.7	745
22	Russia	17.3	43.8		17	21.9	1,705
23	Mexico	25.6	34.8		9.3	30.3	1,262
24	Israel (Jews and Arabs)	22.9	31		16.3	29.8	1,205
25	Latvia	8.8	41.3		23.3	26.6	1,000
26	Philippines	16.2	32.7		19	32.1	1,200
27	United States	15.7	30.5		17.7	36.1	1,276

The data are from the International Social Survey Programme (2000).
These data were documented and made available by the Zentralarchiv für Empirische Sozialforschung, Köln. They were collected by independent institutions in each country. Neither the original collectors not the Zentralarchiv bear any responsibility for the analyses or interpretation presented here.

Ken Ham is an Australian expatriate who runs the *Answers in Genesis*, perhaps the largest creationist organization in the world.

critique was titled *Telling Lies for God* (1994). A branch of the CSF was opened in New Zealand in 1992 (Riddell, 2002).

CSF's Ken Ham, a former biology teacher with a Lincolnesque beard and a rapid line of creationist patter, emigrated from Australia to the United States, where he worked for seven years as a speaker for the ICR before establishing the YEC ministry Answers in Genesis. AiG, headquartered in northern Kentucky, was remarkably successful at capturing the market for creationism (Lippard, 2007), apparently owing in part to its adopting a style heavier on evangelism and lighter on science and in part to its use of the latest technology, including a well-crafted website. Moreover, AiG is about to open a creation museum in Kentucky—not the first of its kind but certainly, at a reported cost of $27 million, the most elaborate (Redfern, 2007). AiG's success faltered late in 2005, when it underwent a schism; what were the Australian and New Zealand branches of AiG (as well as those in Canada and South Africa) are now part of a new international YEC organization, Creation Ministries International, headquartered in Queensland. Creationism was in the news in Australia when the minister for education, science, and technology, Brendan Nelson, expressed sympathy for teaching IDC along with evolution, eliciting a protest from a coalition of 70,000 scientists and teachers (Lloyd, 2005) as well as a campaign from Campus Crusade for Christ in which the IDC DVD *Unlocking the Mystery of Life* was distributed to schools throughout the country (Numbers, 2006, p. 403). A similar campaign was undertaken in New Zealand by the local branch of Focus on the Family (Barnett, 2006).

In Britain, where Darwin's visage adorns the £10 note, a 2006 poll reported that 48 percent of respondents accepted evolution (defined to include "God had no part in this process") with 22 percent accepting creationism and 17 percent accepting "intelligent design"; 44 percent thought that creationism ought to be taught in the classroom (Ipsos MORI, 2006). The poll is methodologically flawed, however, and

Britain ranks high in the developed world for acceptance of evolution (Tables 10.1 and 10.2). The Creation Science Movement, founded in 1932, bills itself as the oldest creationist movement in the world, but Answers in Genesis's United Kingdom branch is probably of greater influence; a new group called Truth in Science (TiS) is effectively using IDC-style rhetoric, although its leadership tilts toward YEC. In September 2006, TiS sent packets of creationist teaching material, including two IDC DVDs, to the science heads of every secondary school (of which there are about 5,700) in the United Kingdom, provoking a national controversy; the government declared the material unsuitable for science classrooms (Randerson, 2006), although not so resoundingly as to allay all concern (Williams, 2006). A national controversy erupted previously in 2002 when it was alleged that Emmanuel College, a Christian secondary school run by the Vardy Foundation under a public/private partnership scheme, taught creationism along with evolution (Branigan, 2002). These allegations continue to dog the foundation's efforts to expand its schools, especially in light of the fact that Emmanuel College's head of science was until recently a director of TiS (Marley, 2006).

In European countries where, as in Britain, Protestantism is dominant or on a par with Catholicism, the level of acceptance of evolution is also generally high, especially in the Lutheran countries of Scandinavia (Tables 10.1 and 10.2). The biologist Ulrich Kutschera of the University of Kassel, who takes a particular interest in creationism in the German-speaking world, reports that the "God created human beings" option of the Gallup question was preferred by 21.8 percent of respondents in Switzerland, 20.4 percent in (majority Catholic) Austria, and 18.1 percent in Germany (Kutschera, 2003). There are various creationist organizations in these countries, of which Germany's *Wort und Wissen* (Word and Knowledge) may be the largest; its creationist textbook *Evolution: Ein kritisches Lehrbuch* (Evolution: A Critical Textbook), now in its sixth edition as well as in Russian, Serbian, Finnish, and Portuguese versions, is described as "the most important production of the European anti-evolutionists" (Kutschera, 2003, p. 17). From time to time a politician or government official expresses skepticism of evolution or sympathy for creationism—in Denmark in 2002 (Numbers, 2006, p. 411), in the Netherlands in 2005 (Enserink, 2005), in Germany in 2006 ("German Scientists," 2006), following the revelation that two public schools in Hesse were teaching creationism in science classes—but usually without any lasting or widespread consequence. Nevertheless, Kutschera recently edited a collection titled *Kreationismus in Deutschland: Fakten und Analysen* (Creationism in Germany: Facts and Analysis), which is apparently without precedent in the non-English-speaking world (Kutschera, 2007).

In Catholic Europe, the level of acceptance of evolution is also generally high (Tables 10.1 and 10.2), especially in France, whose citizens, Numbers remarks, seem to "have cared little" about the debate (Numbers, 2006, p. 411). Relevant, of course, are the views of the Pope. John Paul II acknowledged "the recognition of the theory of evolution as more than a hypothesis" by the scientific community (1997, p. 382), while still insisting on the immediate creation of the soul. In 2005, Cardinal Schönborn, the archbishop of Vienna, published a commentary deprecating neo-Darwinism and seemingly sympathetic to IDC (Schönborn, 2005), provoking speculation of a change in the Catholic position, because Schönborn is close to the new pope, Benedict XVI. The situation is still in flux, although it seems unlikely that the Vatican is going to embrace creationism (Heneghan, 2007). There are creationist groups in France, Italy, and Poland, but they have limited influence. In 2004, a plan to eliminate evolution from middle school curricula in Italy was thwarted (Numbers, 2006, pp. 411–412), although it is unclear whether creationism was a factor. In 2006, the Polish deputy minister for education described evolution as a lie, eliciting protest from the Polish scientific community (Graebsch, 2006); the deputy prime minister Roman Giertych belongs to the same political party and reportedly shares his view. Giertych's father, Maciej Giertych, is a YEC and member of the European Parliament; in 2006 he organized a seminar, featuring American, German, and French creationists, at the European Parliament in Brussels (Graebsch & Schiermeier, 2006; Kutschera, 2006).

The level of acceptance of evolution in Orthodox Europe is generally lower than in Catholic and Protestant Europe (Tables 10.1 and 10.2); a 2005 poll reportedly found 26 percent of Russians accepting evolution and 49 percent accepting creationism (Bigg, 2006), but a 2003 poll reports that 44 percent agreed with the statement "Human beings are developed from earlier species of animals" (National Science Board [NSB], 2006, vol. 2, table 7-10), a result that places Russia slightly ahead of the United States. Numbers suggests that the fall of the Berlin Wall in 1989 enabled evangelical missionaries to "sweep into the formerly communist East," bringing creationism with them; he notes the presence of creationist organizations in Romania, Serbia, and the former Soviet Union (2006, p. 412), particularly Russia and Ukraine. In 1998, the Romanian ministry of education was unsuccessfully lobbied to revise textbooks to avoid contradictions with creationism (Stan & Turcescu, 2000, p. 1478). In 2004, evolution was briefly banned in Serbian primary schools at the behest of the education minister, Ljiljana Colic, who also expressed support for teaching creationism ("Serbia Reverses Darwin Suspension," 2004); she subsequently resigned. The prospect of a Scopes trial in reverse surfaced in St. Petersburg, Russia, in 2006, when schoolgirl Maria Schraiber sued to force the teaching of creationism; despite moral support from patriarch Alexius II (the patriarch of Moscow and the spiritual leader of the Russian Orthodox Church), Schraiber departed the country and the suit was dismissed ("St. Petersburg Girl Quits School," 2007; "St. Petersburg Court," 2007).

Beyond the Anglophone world and Europe, the amount of available data declines sharply. There is little polling information available for Latin America. In Mexico, 60 percent of respondents described the statement "Human beings developed from earlier species of animals" as definitely or probably true; in Chile, 70 percent described it as definitely, probably, or (without qualification) true (Table 10.2). According to a report of a 2005 poll using a version of the Gallup questions (Massarani, 2005), 31 percent of Brazilian respondents preferred the "God created human beings" option, with 54 percent preferring the "God guided process" option, and 9 percent preferring the "God had no part in the process" option. Additionally, 89 percent of respondents supported teaching creationism alongside evolution, and 75 percent supported teaching creationism instead of evolution. There are active creationist organizations in Argentina, Brazil, Bolivia, Ecuador, Mexico, and Peru (Numbers, 2006, p. 417), often sponsored or encouraged by American YECs from the ICR, AiG, and the Seventh-day Adventist Church. A Mexican scientist is sanguine about their lack of effect in his country, commenting, "Only twice during my thirty years of teaching about evolutionary biology and research into the origins of life, have I encountered religious-based opposition to my work" (Lazcano, 2005,

p. 787). Juan De Gennaro (2002) reports that during the mid-1990s the treatment of evolution in the Argentine national curriculum was undermined at the hands of the Catholic Church; in 2004, the governor of the Brazilian state of Rio de Janeiro authorized the teaching of creationism in confessional religious classes in the public schools (Martins & França, 2004).

There is almost no poll information available for Sub-Saharan Africa; a survey of Christian Kenyan teenagers found that 68 percent of respondents held the view that Christianity is essentially committed to YEC, and 57 percent believed that Christianity is essentially committed to biblical inerrancy (Fulljames & Francis, 2004). Numbers mentions only a single African creationist organization, in Nigeria and now apparently defunct; he speculates that throughout Sub-Saharan Africa, "conservative Christianity had grown so strong that creationists rarely found an evolutionist establishment to attack" (2006, p. 420). In South Africa, evolution was removed from the curriculum during the reign of the proapartheid National Party (Lever, 2002); it began to return after the African National Congress came to power in 1994, though not without protest from a variety of conservative religious organizations (Chisholm, 2002). In 2006, the National Museums of Kenya were under pressure to downplay their famous collection of hominid fossils, which include the most complete skeleton yet found of *Homo erectus*, unearthed by Richard Leakey's team in 1984. Bishop Bonifes Adoyo, chair of the Evangelical Alliance of Kenya, which claims to represent churches of thirty-five denominations with nine million members, said, "Our doctrine is not that we evolved from apes, and we have grave concerns that the museum wants to enhance the prominence of something presented as fact which is just one theory." Leakey described Adoyo's plan to pressure the museum as "the most outrageous comments I have ever heard" (Pflanz, 2006).

Polling information is scarce for Asia: Seventy percent of Chinese, 64 percent of South Koreans, and 78 percent of Japanese in 2001 agreed with the statement "Human beings are developed from earlier species of animals" (NSB, 2006, vol. 2, table 7-10); 49 percent of Filipinos regarded it as definitely or probably true (Table 10.2). In India, a 2003–2004 survey found that 19.7 percent of male and 14.5 percent of female respondents accepted "biological theory" as the answer to "How did human beings/man evolve?" with 44.1 percent and 37.9 percent preferring "monkey" (doubtless a powerful distractor) and 11.8 percent and 12.8 percent preferring "Brahma/Adam"—the full text of the question and choices was not provided (Shukla, 2005, p. 129). Numbers writes, "the [South] Koreans have emerged as *the* creationist powerhouse" (2006, pp. 418–419, emphasis in original) in Asia, and also mentions creationist organizations in Taiwan, the Philippines, Japan, and Hong Kong, where almost half the schools are run by Christian missionary organizations, many teaching creationism (Clem, 2005). Inroads in China are rare, due to official hostility toward Christian evangelism, although two IDC publications have been translated. Although the ICR's Duane Gish appears as Eugene Dumsday, evangelizing in India, in *The Satanic Verses* (Rushdie, 1988, pp. 75–76), Christian forms of creationism are apparently rare in India. Vedic creationism—according to which both the earth and the human species are billions, or even trillions, of years old—is derived from Hindu scripture, particularly the *Bhagavad Gita*, and promoted by the Hare Krishna movement (Cremo & Thompson, 1993; see Brown, 2002, for discussion). Despite its affinities with Hindu nationalism, it is more popular in the West than at home (Nanda, 2003, pp. 119–120).

In Israel, a recent survey reports that only 28 percent of respondents agreed with "man is a result of evolution," with 59 percent preferring "man was created by God" (Yaar, 2006). In a previous survey, however, 54 percent of respondents described the statement "Human beings developed from earlier species of animals" as definitely or probably true (Table 10.2). Although creationism is a minority position within Judaism, there is a creationist faction among Orthodox Jews, both in Israel and in the United States (Cherry, 2006; Robinson, 2006), which accepts a literal interpretation of the Torah and of Genesis in particular; it also invokes a variety of ideas from the Talmud and rabbinic tradition. The intended audience for Jewish creationism is typically Jewish itself, although the books of the Orthodox physicist and immigrant to Israel Gerald Schroeder (e.g., Schroeder, 1990) are published by secular publishers and seem to be aimed at a wider audience. Formal presentations of Jewish creationism are, like Schroeder's, usually forms of OEC, but YEC is to be found, too. Numbers (2006, pp. 429–430) notes a 1993 episode in which a dairy in Israel was threatened with withdrawal of its kosher certificate because it distributed dinosaur stickers, thereby encouraging children to reject a YEC chronology. In 2005, a group of ultra-Orthodox rabbis in Israel denounced and banned the books of a colleague, Nosson Slifkin, who affirmed the compatibility of evolution and Judaism. A letter upholding the ban complained, "He believes that the world is millions of years old—all nonsense!" (Rothenberg, 2005).

For the Islamic world, too, polling information is scarce. With a 27 percent acceptance of evolution, Turkey trails Europe and even the United States (Table 10.1), and as a secular republic, it is presumably exceptional in the Islamic world. The NSB (2006, vol. 2, table 7-10) reports that 61 percent of respondents in (majority Islamic) Malaysia chose the correct response "Man, as we know him today, originated from an earlier animal species"; it overlooks, however, the fact that the correct response was bizarrely deemed to be *false* (Malaysian Science and Technology Information Centre [MASTAC], 2004, pp. 18, 50), so the actual level of acceptance of evolution is presumably less than 39 percent. Christian forms of creationism are apparently rare in the Islamic world, but the spectacular rise of the Islamic creationist organization Bilim Arastirma Vakfi or BAV (Science Research Foundation) deserves extended attention. Founded in 1990 in Turkey, BAV is headed by Adnan Oktar, who writes (so prolifically that it is clearly not a solo effort) under the pseudonym Harun Yahya.—The pseudonym is religiously significant, as Harun (Aaron) was the spokesman for Moses and Yahya (John) was the forerunner of Jesus. BAV originally adopted its arguments from the ICR's YEC, discarding claims about a young earth and a global flood not vouched for by the Qur'an or Islamic tradition (Edis, 1999, 2002). BAV later evinced a degree of sympathy for the less committal IDC, using the phrase "intelligent design" as equivalent with "creation" and employing IDC catchphrases like "irreducible complexity" (Harun Yahya, 2002), but eventually denounced IDC as insufficiently Islamic (Harun Yahya, 2005).

After the coverage of evolution in Turkish textbooks was improved in 1998, BAV launched a campaign in response, which faltered when Oktar was imprisoned on blackmail charges (Koenig, 2001). But in the long run, it may have succeeded: Biologists have complained that in Turkey evolution is now downplayed in textbooks (Graebsch & Schiermeier, 2006; Heneghan, 2006) and that Islamic creationists have in effect won (Ortega, 2005). BAV's efforts were not confined to Turkey: Numbers reports, "Initially BAV focused its missionary activities on Muslims in the

Adnan Oktar is a Turkish creationist who runs *Bilim Arastirma*, a group that promotes creationism around the world.

Turkic Republics and in the Balkans, but it quickly expanded to reach Muslims throughout the world" (2006, p. 425), with speakers dispatched to Singapore, Brunei, Malaysia, Britain, South Africa, and the United States (Shipman, 2006), and with a number of elaborate multilingual websites to boot. Nor were its efforts confined to Muslims: In 2007, copies of Harun Yahya's lavishly produced *The Atlas of Creation* were distributed in France, the Netherlands, and possibly elsewhere (den Boer, 2007; Morin, 2007). In 2005, Mustafa Aykol, a former acolyte of Harun Yahya, testi-fied in Kansas in support of a set of state science standards rewritten at the behest of local IDCs (Ortega, 2005). Such campaigns are likely to continue, especially if, as Taner Edis argues (2007, pp. 115–163), Islam is likely to be distinctively recalcitrant to accommodating evolution. On the lighter side, the Japanese game of Pokémon was reportedly to be banned in Saudi Arabia in 2001 in part because it was considered (wrongly) evolutionary (Hawley, 2001).

A few miscellaneous forms of creationism deserve mention. First, there are forms of creationism associated with indigenous peoples in the Americas, Australia, and elsewhere. The main exponent of Native American creationism was the Standing Rock Sioux activist Vine Deloria, Jr. (1995, 2002; Brumble, 1998, is critical); there are also forms of indigenous creationism in Canada (Barker, 2004), Australia (Layton, 2004), and West Africa (Awolalu & Dopamu, 2005, pp. 54–72). Second, there are forms of creationism associated with religions concerned with race. Numbers notes a form of Black Muslim creationism according to which blacks have existed for tens of trillions of years, with whites emerging only recently in a sinister breed-ing experiment (2006, pp. 430–431; Binder, 2002, compares Afrocentrism and cre-ationism). Similarly, white supremacist movements often involve a form of creationism; in Identity Christianity, for example, nonwhites are supposed to be descended from pre-Adamic "beasts of the field" and Jews from the union of Eve and Satan (Kaplan, 1997, pp. 47–48). Third, there is a plethora of New Age forms of creationism. Raëlians believe that instead of evolving, life on earth was created seriatim by extraterrestrial aliens (Pennock, 1999, pp. 234–242); their public endorsement of IDC (Raëlian Movement, 2002)—which officially is not committed to the supernatural—ought to have been, but was not, welcomed by proponents of IDC. Waldorf schools base their pedagogical approach on Rudolf Steiner's anthroposophy; it is alleged that Steiner's idiosyncratic views on creation have also been taught, unconstitutionally, in publicly funded Waldorf charter schools (Scott, 1994) in the United States.

The limitations of the present survey are obvious, both with respect to the material used and with respect to the topics unaddressed. Although polls offer the prospect of objectivity, the amount of data they provide is meager. Moreover, polls are sometimes wittingly or unwittingly skewed (Bishop, 2003; Mooney, 2003), and their results seem to be highly sensitive to changes in the wording of their questions even in the same language (Bishop, 2006), a problem heightened in translation (see Asghar, Wiles, & Alters, 2007, on the challenges of preparing a questionnaire about evolution for use in Indonesia and Pakistan). Coverage of creationism in the media tends to be sporadic and undetailed; even in the United States it is often uninformed and misleading (Mooney & Nisbet, 2005; Rosenhouse & Branch, 2006), and the situation is apparently not better elsewhere. Accounts by creationists and their opponents, although often detailed, are potentially biased; academic studies are valuable but comparatively rare outside the context of creationism in the United States. Thus the farther away from the United States, the closer the treatment verges on the anecdotal. In part, of course, the problem is that the survey here relies primarily on Anglophone sources, reflecting the fact that the literature on creationism is both mainly in English and mainly about creationism in English-speaking countries—not for nothing was a recent anthology on creationism subtitled *Anti-Evolutionism in English-Speaking Countries* (Coleman & Carlin, 2004). But it seems likely that the literature's emphasis in part reflects the reality that creationism is distinctively salient in the Anglophone world.

Creationism in the United States is a complex phenomenon, involving not only religion—in its staggering American variety—and science, but also education, law, and politics, all interacting in a complex web over the course of history from the initial reception of Darwin's ideas in the 1860s to the present day. There is no reason to think that the cultural milieu is any simpler in the rest of the world, even in areas where creationism is not so prominent a phenomenon. Nevertheless, the present survey is resolutely ahistorical, confined almost entirely to discussing events since the turn of the twenty-first century (for the global spread of the "creation science" form of YEC from the 1960s to the 1980s, see Numbers, 2006, pp. 355–368; the increasing literature on the comparative reception of evolution, [e.g., Numbers & Stenhouse, 1999] is also partly relevant). Out of necessity, it neglects the different religious, cultural, political, educational, and legal factors in the countries under discussion. Moreover, it neglects the transnational trends— such as the advent of the Internet as a cheap and easy means of communication and publication, the increasing hegemony of the English language, the burgeoning of Christianity and Islam in the global South, the political currents affecting the ways in which public education is governed, and the perceived need to upgrade science education in a rapidly technologizing world—that are clearly relevant to the present standing and future fortunes of creationism. Despite these limitations, it is possible to offer a few predictions.

It is useful to think about the future of creationism in terms of secularization, which the sociologist Steve Bruce defines as a social condition manifest, in part, in "the declining importance of religion for the operation of nonreligious roles and institutions such as those of the state and the economy" (Bruce, 2002, p. 3). Creationism, as a rejection of evolution motivated by religion, thus constitutes a challenge to secularization, particularly with respect to expositions of evolution such as in public education. In societies that are already secularized, it is not likely that creationism is going to enjoy a serious and lasting triumph: Educational policymakers are typically going to defer to the views of secular experts, such as the local national academy of science. (In 2006, sixty-seven national academies of science were signatories to a statement expressing concern that "within science courses taught in certain public systems of education, scientific evidence, data, and testable theories about the origins and evolution of life on Earth are being concealed, denied, or confused with theories not testable by science" and listing a number of key facts "established by numerous observations and independently derived experimental results from a multitude of scientific disciplines," including the age of the universe and of the earth, the change of the earth over time, and the common ancestry of life on earth (Interacademy Panel on International Issues, 2006). Even in episodes in Europe where antievolutionary action was actually taken, as in Italy and Serbia, the actions were quickly reversed owing to the negative reaction of the scientific community, the media, and the public.

Is the United States a counterexample? After arguing that the religiosity of the United States is both overstated and already transformed in response to secularization, Bruce concedes that it is still high in comparison with the rest of the industrialized world. The disparity, he suggests, is due to the "the federal and diffuse structure of the USA [which] allows conservative Christians the freedom to construct distinct subcultures" in which their faith prevails (Bruce, 2002, p. 204). With regard to education, two such subcultures are private fundamentalist schools and the home schooling community, in both of which creationism is frequently taught along with or instead of evolution. In addition, local public school districts sometimes become dominated by conservative Christians who then seek to promote creationism (as in the *Kitzmiller* case), often relying on materials and organizations that attempt to make a secular case for creationism. These efforts rarely survive scrutiny before a wider secular tribunal, however, whether a federal judge (as in *Kitzmiller*, but see Newman [2007] for worries about the effects of George W. Bush's appointments to the federal judiciary) or a state electorate (as in Kansas), and the few victories that creationists are justifiably able to claim tend to be merely symbolic. Creationism is unlikely to overcome the forces arrayed against it, but it is symptomatic of the climate of ignorance of, skepticism about, and hostility toward evolution pervading the United States, which is certain to remain a threat.

There are potential opportunities for creationism where secularization is not so advanced or in retreat, however. Philip Jenkins argues that through the twenty-first century, Christianity is going to boom in Africa, Asia, and Latin America, and he emphasizes that what he calls "the new Christian world of the South" is not as secularized as its Northern counterpart: "prophecy is an everyday reality, while faith-healing, exorcism, and dream-visions are all basic components of religious sensibility" (2002, p. 8). Already open to signs and wonders, it may be open to creationism, too, abetted by the continuing efforts of creationist missionaries from the North. Jenkins also argues, "Muslims stand to benefit from exactly the same global demographic trends that are producing the unimaginably rich harvest for Christians" (2002, p. 165). Islamic creationism is affiliated with antimodernist ideologies of reform in Islamic countries (Edis, 2007; Ernst, 2003, pp. 158–161), and there is reason to suspect that creationism will therefore accompany the global expansion of Islam. Insofar as the public exposition of evolution continues and increases in the global South, then, controversies such as those in Brazil, Kenya, and Turkey are likely to recur and intensify. In both religions, of course, existing forms of creationism will surely be adapted and transformed to serve the needs of its local adherents. And there are already indications that American creationism is in turn influenced by versions of creationism imported from abroad: Witness in particular the activities of Ken Ham and Mustafa Aykol. As the quip goes: "Creationism evolves, even if nothing else does."

Acknowledgments

My debt to the scholarship of Ronald L. Numbers is obvious. I additionally thank Jon D. Miller, Matthew C. Nisbet, and Mark Perakh, and my colleagues Charles Hargrove, Peter M. J. Hess, Eric Meikle, Carrie Sager, and Eugenie C. Scott, for their assistance and comments.

PART III

Evolution, Religion, and the Classroom

The Battle between Creation and Evolution in the Classroom: An Historical Perspective

by Edward J. Larson

In this selection, historian and legal scholar Edward J. Larson traces the battle between Darwin and the Bible in the classroom. The teaching of evolution, as he points out, has gone from a benign neglect of the subject following the trial of John T. Scopes in 1925, to the evolution of various strategies by creationists and advocates of Intelligent Design to remove the subject of evolution altogether, balancing it with some form of creationism, or teaching that evolution is "only a theory." The result, as he points out, is that the dispute continues to play out in the judicial system and is likely to continue to do so for the foreseeable future.

The American controversy over creation and evolution is primarily fought over what is taught in U.S. public high school biology classes. Virtually no one disputes teaching the theory of evolution in public colleges and universities or using public funding to support evolutionary research in agriculture or medicine. And there is no serious debate over the core evolutionary concept of common descent among biologists. It is the minds of American high school students that are at stake, and opponents of evolutionary teaching typically ask for (1) removing evolution from the classroom, or (2) balancing it with some form of creationist instruction, or (3) teaching it in some fashion as "just a theory." Actually, these three strategies, although always present to some extent, also neatly play out chronologically as to when they have dominated to create three discernable phases of antievolutionism. Allow me to deal with the first two as prologue to the current third phase.

Phase I

First comes the phase of antievolutionism characterized mainly by efforts to remove evolution from the high school biology classroom altogether, highlighted by the 1925 trial of John Scopes. Importantly, this effort coincided with and arose out of the so-called fundamentalist crisis with American Protestantism, when many mainline Protestant denominations—the Presbyterians, Methodists, American Baptists, and others—were deeply divided between the so-called modernists who adapted their traditional beliefs to current scientific thinking, and a new breed of fundamentalists who clung even tighter to biblical literalism in the face of new ideas.

No idea split the modernists from the fundamentalists more than the Darwinian theory of human evolution—and the rift was aggravated by the seeming rise in agnosticism within the cultural and scientific elite. From the first, the fundamentalist–modernist controversy raged over the interpretation of Genesis in the pulpit. By the 1920s, both sides had carried that theological dispute into the classroom. Neither side wanted the other's view taught as fact in public school biology courses. In 1922, fundamentalists across the land began lobbying for laws against teaching the Darwinian theory of human evolution in public school, leading to the passage of the first such statute in Tennessee during the spring of 1925. Lesser restrictions had already been imposed in other places and, like the current debate over intelligent design (ID), the issue had gained national attention.

From the outset, the so-called antievolution crusade was seen as evidence of new and profound cleavage between traditional values and modernity. I use the term "evidence" advisedly. The antievolution crusade did not cause the cleavage— it simply exposed it. Go back a generation or two before the twenties, and Americans tended to share common values (or at least those Americans of Protestant European roots that set the tone). There were atheists, agnostics, and deists in mid-nineteenth-century America, but they were marginal, and theological disputes among Christians rarely disrupted denominational harmony. Even the academy was a conventionally religious place—that is, until the rise of positivism, biblical higher criticism, and Darwinism late in the nineteenth century. By the early twentieth century, surveys and studies began detecting a widening gap between the God-fearing American majority and the disbelieving cultural elite. It was not that the elite wanted to reject God or biblical revelation, commentator Walter Lippman explained at the time; it was rather that the ascendency of rational, naturalistic modes of analysis make them unbelievable. Indeed, it was the scientific method as applied to all facets of life more than any particular scientific theory that lay at the heart of modernity—but Darwinism was critical in applying that method to the key issues of biological origins and human morality.

The Tennessee antievolution statute thus struck a chord that resonated widely. The nationwide attention garnered by its passage soon focused on Dayton when a local science teacher named John Scopes accepted the invitation of the ACLU to challenge it in court. The media promptly proclaimed it "the trial of the century" as this young teacher (backed by the nation's scientific, educational, and cultural establishment) stood against the forces of fundamentalist religious lawmaking. For many Americans at the time and ever after, the Scopes trial represented the inevitable conflict between newfangled scientific thought and old-fashioned supernatural belief.

Like so many archetypical American events, the trial itself began as a publicity stunt. Inspired by the ACLU's offer to defend any Tennessee school teacher willing to defy the new antievolution statute, Dayton civic leaders saw a chance to gain attention for their struggling young community by hosting a test case of the law. "The town boomers leaped to accept as one man," journalist H. L. Mencken noted at the time. "Here was an unexampled, almost a miraculous chance to get Dayton upon the front pages, to make it talked about, to put it upon the map." Scopes became their willing defendant at the invitation of school officials. The young teacher was neither jailed nor ostracized—and spent much of the time until his trial traveling and talking with reporters. Of course the ill-conceived scheme quickly backfired on Dayton when the national media indicted the town for indicting one if its teachers—it was simply too good a story to pass up. The real story, however, was that Tennessee had passed its anti-evolution statute in the first place, and that one had long roots.

Ever since Charles Darwin published his theory of evolution in 1859, some conservative Christians objected to the atheistic implications of its naturalistic explanation for the origins of species, particularly of humans. Further, some traditional scientists—most notably the great Harvard zoologist Louis Agassiz—promptly challenged the very notion of biological evolution by arguing that highly complex individual organs (such as the eye) and ecologically dependent species (such as bees and flowers) cannot evolve through the sort of minute, random steps envisioned by Darwinism. Although the scientific community largely converted to the new theory due to its ability to explain other natural phenomena that appear utterly senseless under a theory of design or creation (such as the fossil record and the geographic distribution of similar species), religious opposition remained, with these religious opponents often invoking the earlier scientific arguments against evolution. These religious objections naturally intensified with the spread of fundamentalism during the early twentieth century. The legendary American politician and orator William Jennings Bryan, a political Progressive with decidedly orthodox religious beliefs, added his voice to this chorus during the twenties, as he came to see Darwinian survival-of-the-fittest thinking (known as social Darwinism when applied to human society) behind World War I militarism and postwar materialism. Of course, Bryan also held religious objections to Darwinism and he invoked Agassiz's scientific arguments against it as well, but his fervor on this issue arose from his social concerns. Equate humans with other animals as the product of purely natural processes, Bryan reasoned, and they will act like apes. With his

Progressive political instinct of seeking legislative solutions to social problems, Bryan campaigned for restrictions against teaching the Darwinian theory of human evolution in public schools, leading directly to the passage of Tennessee's antievolution statute in 1925. He then volunteered to assist the prosecution when his law was challenged in Dayton—foreseeing the pending show trial as a platform from which to promote his cause.

The prospect of Bryan using the trial to defend biblical religion and attack Darwinism drew in Clarence Darrow. By the twenties, Darrow unquestionably stood out as the most famous criminal defense attorney in America. His trials were sensational, with Darrow pioneering techniques of jury selection, cross-examination, and the closing argument to defend his typically notorious clients in bitterly hostile courts. Outside the courtroom, Darrow used his celebrity status and oratorical skills to challenge traditional morality and religion. At the time, most Americans clung to biblical notions of right and wrong—with Darrow's defendants usually quite wrong. Darrow, however, with his modern mind, saw nothing as really wrong (or right); everything was culturally or biologically determined. For him, dogmatic beliefs springing from revealed religion were usually the real culprit, by imposing narrow standards, dividing Americans into sects and making people judgmental. Just as Bryan hailed God as love and Christ as the Prince of Peace, Darrow damned religion as hateful and Christianity as the cause of war. Indeed, Darrow saw rational science—particularly the theory of organic evolution—as offering a more humane perspective than any irrational religion. This left no grounds for compromise between the two on this issue. Both men were affable enough, and actually cooperated on some issues, but their world views were at war.

The prospect of Bryan and Darrow litigating the issues of revealed religion versus naturalistic science and academic freedom versus popular control over public

Both Darrow and Bryan were affable enough, and actually cooperated on some issues, but their world views were at war.

education turned the trial into a media sensation then and the stuff of legend thereafter. It attracted hundreds of reporters to Dayton and generated front-page stories around the world. Broadcast live over the radio, in time it became of subject of Broadway plays, Hollywood movies, and Nashville songs. Clearly *Scopes* remains the best-known misdemeanor trial in American history. Despite Darrow's eloquent pleas for academic freedom and his humiliating cross-examination of Bryan, Scopes ultimately lost the case and Tennessee's antievolution statute was upheld. In large part, this resulted from the fact that the U.S. Supreme Court had not yet extended the constitutional bar against government establishment of religion to public schools.

When it was all over, most neutral observers viewed the trial as a draw so far as public opinion was concerned. America's adversarial legal system tends to drive parties apart rather than to reconcile them. That certainly resulted in this case. Despite Bryan's stumbling on the witness stand (which his supporters attributed to his notorious interrogator's wiles), both sides effectively communicated their message from Dayton—maybe not well enough to win converts, but at least sufficiently to energize those already predisposed toward their viewpoint. If, as the defense claimed, more Americans became alert to the danger of placing limits on teaching evolution, others (particularly evangelical Christians) became even more concerned about the spiritual and social implications of Darwinian instruction.

Consequently, the pace of antievolution activism actually picked up after the trial (especially in the South), but it encountered aroused popular resistance everywhere. Arkansas and Mississippi soon followed Tennessee in outlawing the teaching of human evolution for example, but when one Rhode Island legislator introduced such a proposal in 1927, his bemused colleagues referred it to the Committee on Fish and Game, where it died without a hearing or a vote. A forty-year standoff resulted in which a hodgepodge of state and local limits on teaching evolution coupled with heightened parental concern elsewhere led most high school biology textbooks and many individual teachers virtually to ignore the subject of organic origins voluntarily. As a result, after the state supreme court reversed Scopes's conviction on a technicality, courts did not have another chance to review antievolution laws until the 1960s. By then, the legal landscape had changed dramatically.

The change began in 1947, when the U.S. Supreme Court grafted the First Amendment bar against religious establishment to the liberties protected from state action by the Fourteenth Amendment. Suddenly the Establishment Clause took on new life. Whereas Congress had rarely made laws respecting an establishment of religion prior to 1947 (so that there was little case law on point), states and their public schools had been doing so right along—hence a torrent of Establishment Clause litigation. Soon *Scopes*-like legal battles over the place of religion in public education began erupting in communities across the land giving the old trial new relevance everywhere.

Phase II

The first of these cases did not address restrictions on teaching evolution but they surely implicated them. In successive decisions beginning in 1948, the U.S. Supreme Court struck down classroom religious instruction, school-sponsored prayers, mandatory Bible reading and, in 1968, antievolution laws. These old laws simply banned the teaching of human evolution—they did not authorize teaching other theories. Indeed, in his day, Bryan never called for including any form of creationist instruction in the science classroom because no scientific alternative to evolution then existed. Even he believed that the biblical days of creation symbolized vast ages of geologic time, and said as much on the witness stand in Dayton. But with the publication of *The Genesis Flood* in 1961, Virginia Tech engineering professor Henry Morris gave believers scientific sounding arguments supporting the biblical account of a six-day creation within the past 10,000 years. This book spawned a movement within American fundamentalism, with Morris as its Moses leading the faithful into a promised land where science proved religion. The appearance of so-called creation science or scientific creationism (its proponents use both terms) launched the second phase of the antievolution politics: the phase associated with seeking balanced treatment for creation science.

Creation science spread within the conservative Protestant church through the missionary work of Morris's Institute for Creation Research. The emergence of the Religious Right carried it into politics during the 1970s. Within two decades after the publication of *Genesis Flood*, three states and dozens of local school districts had mandated "balanced treatment" for creation science along with evolution in public school science courses. It took another decade before the U.S. Supreme Court unraveled those balanced treatment mandates as unconstitutional. Creation science was nothing but religion dressed up as science, the High Court decreed in the 1987 decision, *Edwards* v. *Aguillard* (in which Justice Scalia dissented), and therefore was barred by the Establishment Clause from public school classrooms along with other forms of religious instruction. By this time, however, conservative Christians were entrenched in local and state politics from California to Maine, and deeply concerned about science education.

Phase III

Then along came University of California law professor Phillip Johnson and the third phase of the creation–evolution controversy. Johnson is (or at least then was) no young-earth creationist, but he is an evangelical Protestant with an uncompromising faith in God. His target became both the philosophical belief and methodological practice within science that material entities subject to physical laws account for everything in nature. Whether called "naturalism" or "materialism," such a philosophy and method excludes God from science laboratories and classrooms. "The important thing is not whether God created all at once [as scientific creationism holds] or in stages [as progressive creationism or theistic evolution maintain]," Johnson asserted. "Anyone who thinks that the biological world is a product of a pre-existing intelligence . . . is a creationist in the most important sense of the word. By this broad definition at least eighty percent of Americans, including me, are creationists." Darwinism may be the best naturalistic explanation for the origin of species, he stresses, but still wrong. If public schools can not teach creation science because it promotes the tenants of a particular religion, then scientific evidence of design in nature or at least scientific dissent from evolution theory should be permissible, Johnson argues. After all, evolution is "just a theory," he says, "and not a very good one."

Johnson's books have sold nearly a half-million copies, and it is no wonder that his kind of arguments now show up whenever objections are raised against teaching evolution in public schools. They were apparent in the U.S. Senate in 2001 when Pennsylvania senator Rick Santorum offered legislation encouraging teachers "to make distinctions between philosophical materialism and authentic science and to include unanswered questions and unsolved problems in their presentations of the origins of life and living things." That language, penned by Johnson, passed the Senate as an amendment to the No Child Left Behind education bill and eventually became part of the conference report for that legislation. Similar proposals surfaced as stand-alone bills in over a dozen state legislatures during the past four years. None have passed, but similar language has made its way into state and local school guidelines around the country, most famously in Kansas and Dover, Pennsylvania.

Another popular authority on this topic is Lehigh University biochemistry professor Michael Behe, a devout Catholic who wrote his own best-selling book challenging Darwinist explanations for complex organic processes and, most recently, who served as the star witness for defense in the challenge of the Dover school guidelines. If Johnson is the modern movement's Bryan, then Behe is its Agassiz reviving the arguments for design based on evidence of nature's irreducible complexity. Behe has never developed his arguments for intelligent design in peer-reviewed science articles. Indeed, he does not actually conduct research in the field and, along with other leaders of the ID movement, concedes that there is not as yet much affirmative scientific content to their so-called design revolution. The preface to the 1998 book *Mere Creation*, which featured contributions from most leading ID theorists, contained the prediction that a National Science Foundation-funded, design-based research program could be up and running within five years. Eight years later, it has not happened.

So far, ID theorists remain simply critics of the reigning paradigm in biology—doggedly poking holes and looking for gaps in evolution theory. Those gaps are best filled by design, they argue, and would be if science did not a priori rule supernatural explanations out of bounds. ID advocates now propose broadening the definition of science from dealing solely with naturalistic explanations for physical phenomena to include any account that draws on physical, observable data and logical inferences. At least, they add, design-based criticism of evolution, divorced from biblical creationism, should be a fit subject for public school science education. With this approach, they have expanded the tent of people willing to challenge the alleged Darwinist hegemony in the science classroom beyond those persuaded by Morris's evidence for a young earth.

Yet every public opinion survey suggests that the bedrock for antievolutionism in the United States remains the biblical literalism of the Protestant fundamentalist church, where there is typically greater concern about the earth's age (to which the Bible speaks) than about such intellectual abstractions as scientific naturalism. In *The Genesis Flood*, for example, Henry Morris stresses the theological significance of utter fidelity to the entire biblical narrative. Thus, when Genesis says that God created the universe in six days, he maintains, it must mean six 24-hour days; when it says that God created human and all animals on the sixth day, then dinosaurs must have lived alongside early humans; and when it gives a genealogy of Noah's descendants, believers can use it to date the flood at between five to seven thousand years ago.

Despite judicial rulings against the incorporation of scientific creationism into the public school biology curriculum, public opinion surveys suggest that approximately four out of every ten Americans accept biblical creationism of the sort espoused by Morris and his Institute for Creation Research. If not propagated in the public schools, then creationism must spread by other means—and conservative Christian religious organizations have the necessary structures in place. Fifty years after its initial publication, *The Genesis Flood* (now in its 42nd printing) continues to sell well in Christian bookstores, but it is now only one in a shelf full of such books. Christian radio and television blankets the nation with creationists broadcasts and cablecasts, such as Ken Ham's "Answers in Genesis," which is now heard daily on over 750 radio stations in 49 different states and 15 different countries. Although still relatively low in absolute terms, the number of students receiving their primary and secondary education at home or in Christian academies has steadily risen over the past quarter century, with many such students learning their biology from creationist textbooks. At the postsecondary level, Bible institutes and Christian colleges continue to grow in number and size, with at least some of them offering degrees in biology and science education in a creation-friendly environment.

All this creationist activity is nearly invisible outside the churches and religious communities where it occurs, but that has not stopped some evolutionists from striking back. To be sure, most biologists simply ignore religion. But some of them—ardent in their evolutionism and evangelical regarding its social implications—have taken a Darrowesque dislike to biblical Christianity. The British sociobiologist and popular science writer Richard Dawkins leads this particular pack.

In *The Blind Watchmaker*, published to great acclaim in the midst of legal wrangling over Louisiana's creationism law, Dawkins (1986) takes aim at what he calls "redneck" creationists and "their disturbingly successful fight to subvert American education and textbook publishing." Focusing on the philosophical heart of creationism, rather than simple biblical literalism, Dawkins challenges the very notion of purposeful design in nature, which he calls "the most influential of the arguments for the existence of God." In a legendary articulation of this argument in 1802, British theologian William Paley compared living things to mechanical watches. Just as the intricate workings of a watch betrayed its maker's purposes, Paley reasoned, so do the even more intricate complexity of individual organs (such as the eye) and of organisms prove the existence of a purposeful creator. Not so, Dawkins counters. "Natural selection, the blind, unconscious, automatic process which Darwin described, and which we now know is the explanation for existence and apparently purposeful form of all life, has no purpose. . . . It is the *blind* watchmaker." By banishing the argument for design, Dawkins proclaims, "Darwin made it possible to be an intellectually fulfilled atheist." Renown Harvard naturalist and science writer E. O. Wilson makes similar assertions. "The inexorable growth of [biology] continues to widen, not to close the tectonic gap between science and faith-based religion," Wilson wrote in this latest book. "The toxic mix of religion and tribalism has become so dangerous as to justify taking seriously the alternative view, that humanism based on science is the effective antidote, the light and the way at last placed before us."

Organized science has sought to defuse this controversy by affirming the compatibility of modern evolutionary naturalism and a personal belief in God. The National Academy of Sciences, a self-selecting body of the nation's premiere scientists, had asserted as much in a glossy brochure distributed to school teachers during the 1980s in reaction to the creation-science movement. In 1998, the Academy mass-produced a new booklet reasserting that, although science is committed to methodological naturalism, it does not conflict with religion. They simply represent separate ways of knowing. "Science," the booklet states, "is limited to explaining the natural world through natural causes. Science can say nothing about the supernatural. Whether God exists or not is a question about which science is neutral." To Dawkins, such an approach represents "a cowardly flabbiness of the intellect." Johnson dismisses it as rank hypocrisy. If they agree on nothing else, Dawkins and Johnson agree that Darwinism and Christianity are at war—and, with their writings and talks, they help stir popular passions over biology education much as Darrow and Bryan once did. We see its fruit even now in pending lawsuits and legislation.

With a solid majority of the people in some places believing creation science and an added percentage everywhere accepting intelligent design, teaching the theory of evolution inevitably becomes highly controversial in some places. Five years ago in Kansas, for example, creationists on the state school board succeeded temporarily in deleting the Big Bang and what they called macroevolution from the list of topics mandated for coverage in public school science classrooms. Last year, they took the further step of adding an ID-friendly definition of science to their educational standards. In 2004, the Cobb County, Georgia, school board decreed that biology textbooks should carry a disclaimer stating that evolution was just a theory. In 2005, the Dover, Pennsylvania, school board mandated not only an oral disclaimer akin to Cobb County's written one but also recommended intelligent design as an alternative explanation of biological origins. In cases that made front-page news across the country and overseas, federal district courts recently struck down the Cobb County and Dover restrictions. Although one remains under appeal, both rulings are instructive.

Responding to the concerns of local parents and taxpayers, the Cobb County school board had mandated that biology textbooks carry a sticker stating, "Evolution is a theory, not a fact, regarding the origin of living things. This material should be approached with an open mind, studied carefully, and critically considered." Similar disclaimers have appeared in Alabama textbooks for years without sparking lawsuits and are under consideration elsewhere but, perhaps because the diverse nature of the county's population and its visible location as a bedroom community for Atlanta, the disclaimer immediately encountered stiff opposition in Cobb County. The Georgia ACLU promptly filed suit on behalf of some local students and their parents.

In his judicial opinion, Judge Clarence Cooper tackled antievolutionists' "only a theory" argument. Of course evolution is only a theory, but it's not a hunch or a guess, he noted, adding: "The sticker targets only evolution to be approached with an open mind, carefully studied, and critically considered without explaining why it is the only theory being so isolated as such." In light of the historic opposition to the theory of evolution by certain religious groups, Judge Cooper concluded that "an informed, reasonable observer would perceive the school board to be aligning itself with proponents of religious theories of origins." As such, the sticker constituted an impermissible endorsement of religion under prevailing constitutional standards, the judge ruled.

Although Judge Cooper did not expand on the point, he identified the group benefited by the sticker as "Christian fundamentalists and creationists," not theists generally. Many people see the controversy this way, which helps explain its depth. Millions of American Christians and other religious believers accept the theory of evolution. For some theologically liberal Christians, evolution is central to their religious worldview. Even many theologically conservative Protestants and Catholics accept organic evolution as God's means of creation. They see no conflict between it and a high view of scripture. Theistic theories of evolution have a long and distinguished pedigree within evangelical Christian theology. By cautioning students against all theories of evolution, some saw the Cobb County school board lining up on one side of a dispute among religious believers and in doing so, unconstitutionally entangled church and state. Judge Cooper agreed—and held this as a second legal basis for striking the stickers.

The Dover case, like the Cobb County one, involved school guidelines built on the ID argument that students should be told that evolution is a controversial and unproven theory. "The theory is not a fact," the Dover disclaimer stated. "Gaps in the theory exist for which there is not evidence." This alone conveyed an unconstitutional endorsement of a religious viewpoint, the court ruled. Unlike the Cobb County sticker, however, the statement read to Dover students added, "Intelligent Design is an explanation of the origin of life that differs from Darwin's view. The reference book, *Of Pandas and People,* is available for students who might be interested in gaining an understanding of what Intelligent Design actually involves." This text, the court found, contained creationist religious material, including the affirmation that basic kinds of living things (such a birds and fish) were separately created. As such, its use in a public education violated the constitutional bar against religious instruction.

The decision went further, though. During a six-week trial, Judge John Jones heard extensive testimony on intelligent design to determine whether it could be presented as an alternative explanation of origins in a public school science class. Here his decision broke new ground. "After a searching review of the record and applicable case law," Judge Jones ruled, "we find that while ID arguments may be true, a proposition on which the Court takes no position, ID is not science." He gave three reasons. First, unlike science, ID invokes supernatural explanations. Second, it rests on the flawed argument that evidence against the current theory of evolution supports the design alternative. Third, scientists have largely refuted the negative attacks on evolution leveled by ID theorist. ID, the judge stressed, has not been accepted by the scientific community, generated peer-review publications, nor been subjected to testing and research—all points that Michael Behe conceded under cross-examination. Indeed, after offering an alternative definition for science that ID could meet—"a proposed explanation which focus or point to physical, observable data and logical inferences"—Behe admitted that astrology would also qualify as science. This alone probably sealed the decision, but evidence that school board members acted with a clear religious purpose and then tried to cover up their tracks also turned this judge, a no-nonsense conservative appointed by President George W. Bush, against the school policy. "The breathtaking inanity of the Board's decision is evident when considered against the factual backdrop which has now been fully revealed through this trial," Judge Jones concluded.

In Dover, as in Cobb County, the school board's decision to adopt the antievolution disclaimer polarized the community. It divided families, neighbors, and churches. In an election held before the court ruled, voters replaced eight members of the school board with candidates opposed to the policy, guaranteeing that it will not appeal the court's ruling. When Americans on either side of this controversy watch what happened in Cobb County or Dover, they know that they are looking in a mirror and wonder how it might play out in their own hometown and among their friends and fellow Christians. Of course the media took notice—making these cases top stories.

That, in brief, is where the creation–evolution teaching controversy stands today—still making news eighty years after Dayton, Tennessee, gained headlines by prosecuting John Scopes. It resurfaces periodically in countless Daytons throughout the United States over everyday episodes of science teachers either defying or deifying Darwin. Such acts generate lawsuits and legislation precisely because religion continues to matter greatly in America. Public opinion surveys invariably find that more than nine in ten Americans believe in God—just as they have found since surveys began polling on such matters in the 1950s. A recent survey indicated that over three-fourths of all Americans believe in miracles and that three out of five now say that religion is "very important" in their lives. It troubles many Americans that science does not affirm their faith and outrages some when their children's biology coursework seem to deny their biblical beliefs.

As a diverse people, we have learned to seek middle ground whenever possible. As a species, however, we instinctively respond to stirring oratory. Darrow and Bryan had mastered that craft and used it in Dayton to enlist their legions. They tapped into a cultural divide that deeply troubles this national house of ours, offering us no middle ground. And as we all know either from the Bible or a Broadway classic, "He that troubleth his own house shall inherit the wind." That wind has sporadically touched off maelstroms over the past eighty years—storms that sorely test our tradition of tolerance. If history is any guide, dark clouds remain on the horizon.

The Problems and Challenges of Teaching Biology in the Twenty-First Century

by Steve Randak

Steve Randak has been at the forefront of efforts to defend the teaching of evolution and real science in secondary schools. Here he emphasizes the importance of science for solving our contemporary problems, while bemoaning the problems he and others have had trying to teach evolution. He notes, that political pressures have denied evolution its place as a central tenet of all biology. Randak argues that "creation science" threatens the whole idea of science because science itself is badly misunderstood, pointing out that "fairness" or "teach both sides" are concepts with no relevance to science or science-teaching. He notes that evolutionary theory is under attack from both the political right and the political left, and that opposition has come not only from politicians, parents, and some students, but even from teaching colleagues. He criticizes university faculty for their failure to support the teaching of evolution in secondary schools while bemoaning the fact that biology commonly is taught so badly that students get no sense of wonder, core concepts, or the ongoing process—rather than facts—of science.

Based on "The Children's Crusade for Creationism," by S. Randak, 2001, *The American Biology Teacher*, 63(4), pp. 226–230; and Dr. E. O. Wilson's acceptance speech at the 2000 Kistler Prize Banquet.

When I started teaching biology forty years ago, I thought my job was important. Today I think it is absolutely crucial. What changed? The world changed some, but my perspective changed profoundly. I now realize that human destiny and survival are intimately tied to reach of mind. Echoing the sentiments of evolutionist E. O. Wilson, we must explore the universe embracing the ideas that there are no limits to the power of mind and no boundaries that restrict our reach. If we do less, we threaten the future of our species. Unfortunately, our evolutionary path has restricted our mental reach, because evolution by natural selection does not produce perfect organisms. We function well only in a very small envelope of time and space. We evolved to pursue short-term gain expressed in a generation or two, within a small circle of kith and kin, and within limited real estate. We evolved as a tribal species. We remained shortsighted and tribal as we dismantled the environment. Vanishing resources and increased competition pushed us toward tribal warfare. As the population exploded, we became warrior nations. Hectare by hectare we converted natural resources into wealth. Wealth unevenly distributed escalated the conflict. Today we are reaching the critical mass of human population size. The world is an increasingly dangerous and hostile place. We live in large shadows of climate disruption, new and old plagues, ethnic and religious hatred, and the greatest mass extinction since the demise of the dinosaurs. We must now seriously ask, how shall we survive the future?

There is hope. That hope is found in education and free scientific inquiry. The accumulation of scientific knowledge gives a long-term perspective, a focus that extends our view across many generations, both into the past and into the future. As individuals we seem hopelessly trapped with the tribal shortsightedness. As a people, science gives us a farsighted window into the future. But, too few have developed the long-range scientific perspective; and those that have, recognize the general lack of wisdom necessary to make good choices. Wisdom comes with age and we are only toddlers in the transgenerational foresight game. We may see farther than our predecessors, but we are still Paleolithic tribespeople. Another issue compounds this dilemma: A growing population of creationists long for the end of humans' reign on earth—the sooner the better. They are restricting the teaching of natural selection and scientific inquiry in classrooms across America and increasingly around the world. If future generations are not even exposed to the science that gives the long-term perspective, how can we ever expect to achieve the critical mass of thinkers required to develop the wisdom necessary to make good choices about our future?

To make choices that allow for our long-term survival, we must objectively study human nature and nature in general. To successfully accomplish this, we must employ the idea of natural selection. There is no idea that is more important to the understanding of life and the universe in general and no idea better supported. However, many students and their parents see evolution by natural selection as a most controversial and dangerous idea. Despite the importance of evolution, most high school biology teachers don't teach it or teach it as a reduced separate unit, not as the central and unifying theme of biology. You can hardly blame them; there is little or no support to do otherwise. Where can they look for support? It is much easier to say where *not* to look.

Colleges and university science departments don't give reasonable support. Few treat natural selection as the unifying idea in biology. Philosopher Daniel

Dennet suggests that if an award were given for the best idea anybody ever had it should go to Charles Darwin's idea of natural selection. If he is right, we should treat it as such. Why then is it seldom mentioned? It is possible to get a degree in biological science and hardly discuss natural selection. Most college-level courses are textbook driven. So much time is spent digesting the huge volume of facts that little time is spent on the unifying idea of natural selection. In addition to my high school instruction, I teach a science education class at a small liberal arts college. Senior students come to me with little understanding of evolution or the nature of science or how to teach them. The student teachers I mentor from the large local university are exactly the same. If natural selection is the most important idea crossing all of our artificially created boundaries in the biological sciences, why is it seldom mentioned?

Scientists give little support. Most see the efforts of creationists as misdirected and trivial. When our school's curriculum was undergoing attack by creationists, we received support from only one scientist at the local university. That institution could easily have been hundreds of miles away instead of just across the river. Biologist Dr. Ken Miller of Brown University is one of the exceptions to this rule of inaction. He takes an active role as defender of evolution and free inquiry. Many more need to follow his lead. Creationist efforts are misdirected, but they are not trivial. Most scientists have misjudged and underestimated the influence of fundamentalist Christian creationists. They are politically conservative and very active. They may be losing the battle in the courts, but they are winning the battle for hearts and minds. They fear that Darwin's idea will unravel the moral and social fabric of America. They want to legislate the teaching of religious doctrine in the science classroom, first under the guise of "creation science" and more recently

In response to a question about the 1999 Kansas School Board's ruling that removed the teaching of evolution from the state's science curriculum, President Bush went on record as favoring the balanced classroom treatment of Darwinian theory and creationism.

with the introduction of the concept of "intelligent design." Creation science rejects almost all of modern science including the idea of old earth, the Big Bang, and transmutability of species. Intelligent design followers accept more science but believe cells, organs, and organisms bear the unmistakable signs of being fashioned by a divine hand. President George W. Bush went on record, during the Kansas school board of education debate in August of 1999, as favoring the balanced classroom treatment of Darwinian theory and creationist ideas. He also supports charter schools, public funding of private academies, and a maximum amount of autonomy for local school boards. If these last three initiatives had been in place in 1999, the Kansas debate over the inclusion of evolution in the state science standards would have been meaningless. Each school would have taught whatever bastardized version of biology it preferred. Science content and teaching would be localized and politicized to the point that many students would receive inferior instruction. State and national science standards would be meaningless. To someone in education these initiatives all look very much like an attempt to kill public education.

You might think that the secular left is more likely to embrace Darwin's idea; not necessarily so. Many in that camp think the struggles between rival scientific ideas are decided by sociopolitical power, not evidence, and that male, white, Western science has been used to suppress women, minorities, and workers. With political suspicion on the left and fear of social and moral chaos on the right, who will stand up for evolutionary biology and insist that it be taught in public schools without censorship or dilution? It won't be Middle America. As the scientific worldview has become more authoritative and autonomous, it has created an avalanche of negative feelings and fears. The caring God of monotheism seems at odds with

Science, contrary to the biblical account of special creation, sees human life as one of many branches connected to the same tree all the way down to the roots.

the excessive waste and harshness of natural selection. Many ask, "Why would God find it necessary to create and destroy species, habitats, and ecosystems millions of times over in order to make our contemporary world?" The jury-rigging and poor design found everywhere in organic forms, from the human prostate to the Panda's thumb, suggest a God less immanent than the one hoped for by most of us. Mutations, the raw stuff of evolution, appear random, while evolution is reactive, and appears undirected. Most people of religious faith are unwilling to put God in the gaps or hide him in the chaos of quantum flux. We are good at living with such contradictions as long as our self-importance remains untouched. But, Darwin's light casts not the shadow of the favored species created in a garden world, a world placed here for us to use as we choose, but rather Darwin's light casts the shadow of just another branch of life connected to the rest of the tree all the way down to the roots—a branch that is ultimately subject to the same laws of pruning as all the rest. Nature's gardener shears are always sharpened, oiled, and ready for use. They are the shears named natural selection.

The challenge to science educators is to get our students to understand the unpopular idea of evolution by natural selection so we may have a more realistic picture of how we fit into the world and increase our chances of surviving. How are we expected to do this with little or no support? From the front lines of this educational dilemma it often seems hopeless. But, every challenge is an opportunity and this in no exception.

Biology is typically one of the last science courses that most Americans take. It is controversial and that makes it interesting to students. This gives biology teachers a wonderful opportunity to emphasize the teaching of evolution and to teach "the nature of science," using evolution as an example of the product of good science. Unfortunately, most biology classrooms are shrines to scientific facts. Too much time is spent memorizing information that is soon outdated or trivial. Noble laureate in physics Murray Gell-Mann said it memorably when he stated, "Today's science classrooms are like taking students to the world's greatest restaurant and force-feeding them the menu." It is more important today than ever to foster in students an understanding and an appreciation of science as a process. We are moving forward too fast to focus on the details. However, current educational initiatives seem to be pushing us in the other direction. I will discuss more on this topic later. Much of the factual content and investigative techniques generated by today's science are destined for obsolescence. Students need to understand and value the process that generates knowledge, so that they won't be overwhelmed or suspicious when new replaces old. They need to be aware that science is self-corrective and therefore dynamic. They must understand that changing knowledge is what we expect from scientific endeavor. It is essential for students to be able to distinguish science from nonscience. Most fail to understand that science is consistent, natural, predictive, tentative, testable, and peer reviewed. Few students recognize that the playground idea of fairness has no place in science and that peer review is often hostile. You frequently hear, "It is only fair that creation science be included." This argument is compelling if you don't understand how science works. The majority of Americans want the creation voice to be heard. Most don't understand that science is a rigorous competition of ideas based on evidence. Creationists want to skip the experimentation, the verification, the validation, and go right for the textbook inclusion. Students also need to know that complexity and theory-ladenness are fundamental sources of scientific uncertainty. The complexity of reality makes it impossible to consider all the factors that might influence an event. We can never be sure we have accounted for all the alternative explanations, but this complexity is also a source of hopefulness, because science makes progress by sorting out the complexity. Natural selection hews our universe from the complexity of chaos and guarantees that the work of science will never be finished. Despite this inherent uncertainty, science manages to produce ideas that are highly reliable, useful, and productive. That is because rather than insisting on absolute truth, scientists use a variety of criteria to decide which of the competing ideas is best. They decide which explanation conforms to patterns in the data, which is most predictive and parsimonious, and which handles best the anomalies and the exceptions.

Since the beginning of my career I have started each year with a unit of at least four weeks devoted to the nature of science, as previously described. For the rest of the semester we study ecology, cell study, and some genetics. During these units students use constructivist methods of learning and reinforce their understanding of the nature of science by spending 80 percent of their classtime in the lab. Second semester starts with genetics and finishes with evolution. I have chosen this order because by the time students get to the ten weeks of evolution, most understand what the product of good science looks like. Evolution fits that good product model. It has many parallel and converging lines of evidence. It unifies facts, hypotheses, laws, and observations. It is the best science has to offer. My methods and curriculum have matured, but they grew from the original seeds planted by exceptional mentors from my undergraduate studies, graduate studies, and from my teacher training. I feel I was one of the fortunate few. I have been teaching evolution as the central and unifying theme for forty years. On rare occasions I dealt with a creationist student or parent. And then the times changed. In 2000 the nightmare of every biology teacher happened at our school. Creationists petitioned the school board to have creation science added to the biology curriculum. The outcome was encouraging and enlightening.

Why did it happen at Lafayette Jefferson High School in the shadow of Purdue University? Our superintendent of schools thinks it happened because we taught evolution in depth and effectively. The class was team taught and student centered, and students tended to enjoy it. They were learning. If evolution is not taught, or is taught ineffectively, there will be no challenge. But, that doesn't explain why an organized creationist effort had not appeared before. I don't think it was the effectiveness of our teaching that caused the problem. The problem was that the creationists changed. Fundamentalist Christians already well organized were inspired by a president who saw the world as they did. A sizable portion of our nation no longer wanted the separation of church and state. This is a sad and dangerous truth.

At my high school the entire initiative to add creationism to the curriculum was student driven. No adult took an obvious role. We know that one of our chemistry teachers offered support for the creationist view. It seems possible and even likely that the petition was his idea or at least strongly encouraged by him. He spent the first several weeks each year teaching the creationist doctrine. He took the position that you had to accept Genesis or evolution; that you could not have it both ways. He appeared to have stopped because of administrative pressure. Then he invited Ken Hamm, who maintains the popular website Answers in Genesis (AiG), to lecture at a public meeting in the school auditorium. He also spoke in the chemistry class, but was asked to leave by the school's principal.

Exactly why it happened remains clouded, but what happened is vividly clear. The school's Christian club served as the springboard. These students organized and obtained signatures from half of the student population of 2,100 and thirty-five teachers on a petition requesting creation science be added to the biology curriculum. We found that even among faculty the argument "It is only fair that both sides be presented" was very compelling. Even two of our sixteen-member science staff signed the petition. The chemistry teacher's signature was missing. Those that signed did not realize that science has little to do with the playground idea of fairness. They fail to understand science is a competition of ideas where the strength of the supporting evidence determines which idea is accepted. The students that led the effort were good students who had taken biology. They should have understood the difference between science and nonscience. This taught me that students assimilate only what their world view allows them to seriously consider. We spent considerable time falsifying creationist arguments both with individual students and small groups. An interesting and unpleasant aspect of refuting creation "science" is that students take your criticism as an attack on their religion and not as an attack on a scientific idea. To quote one student, "It is bad enough that you teach the earth is old, you should not be able to attack my evidence that the earth is young." We often heard statements like "evolution is a religion," or "it is only a theory." They knew that acceptance in science is based on evidence and not on faith. They knew that a theory was the best science had to offer. I felt I had failed. It is humbling to see students in the midst of gaining critical thinking skills regress to using slogans. These statements were flags that showed the depth of the stress they felt. I came to realize they had a great deal to lose. To seriously consider evolution as an idea, they had to go against their parents, their church, and their God. For many, their very souls were at stake. If you were walking an old firing range and found a rusty hand grenade, would you pick it up? Would you pull the pin? For these students, evolution is a far greater danger than a rusty grenade. One parent told me she would rather see her child dead than to have her lose her faith; the influence of Deuteronomy 13:7–11, I supposed.

All was not despair. On the plus side, it energized all the students. The biology staff had more interest in the study of evolution and higher unit and post–test scores than ever before from a class that is not our strongest. The experience strengthened the bonds between the eight members of our biology department. In a small way we experienced the "band of brothers" effect. Because of this children's crusade for creationism our biology curriculum is better and stronger. We took each creationist criticism and addressed it in the curriculum. For example, Haeckel's embryo drawings are now accompanied by real embryo photos for comparison. We discuss how he was influenced by what he wanted to see, resulting in representations that were more similar than the real embryos. We now have a great embryo lab that helps teach nature of science.

What is most encouraging about this story is the way our school corporation responded. The superintendent immediately voiced his support for our curriculum and kept us informed of his actions. The biology staff mutually decided to maintain a low profile in the media. Our department head bravely gave the one newspaper interview, which resulted in the predictable misquotes. The superintendent educated the school board about the nature of science and the law and with the help of the science department head convinced the one wavering board member. The teachers, the administration, and the school board respectfully treated the students. At the public school board meeting, under the glare of national television lights, they were politely told that the curriculum would not be altered. It all worked the way a science educator would hope. The integrity of science education at Jefferson High School was preserved.

When things calmed down, I called Eugenie Scott of the National Center for Science Education. She had advised us throughout the entire ordeal. I was curious how our experience fit into the larger picture. What she told me was a shock. I assumed that student-led crusades for creation science were common. They are not. I assumed that school boards and superintendents often do the right thing. They do not. I was told that our situation was the ideal, not the norm. At that moment, I experienced more concern than any time during the many months of controversy. Children crusading for creation science or intelligent design in the name of fair play is a compelling idea. If the tactic is used in school corporations less ideal than ours, it will surely meet with success and science education will suffer.

What must we do to improve evolution instruction and block the creationist efforts?

Classroom teachers must teach evolution. This is almost an impossible task for many. They have neither supportive colleagues nor a school corporation behind them. In the current climate of active creationist and active lawyers, a single biology teacher could easily choose to avoid the controversy, in effect ducking under the fire. Many also feel they lack the necessary understanding of evolution to deflect creationist criticisms. Courage comes with numbers and knowledge. Join teaching associations. Attend conferences and workshops. Find like-minded teachers. Teach science as an evidentially based self-correcting process, not as a collection of facts. Don't challenge their faith and don't preach. Many teachers are theistic evolutionists. Stating that God is behind the process of natural selection is simply preaching your form of creationism. You are back to arguing points of view rather than considering the evidence. Keep the discussion to science.

The role of colleges and universities must change. Evolution must be treated as the central pillar of biology. It is not. Every college and university needs to teach a class titled Natural Selection and the Nature of Science to all undergraduates with a major in science. It is not just biologists who need a deep understanding of the ideas. As Daniel Dennett so aptly demonstrated in his book *Darwin's Dangerous Idea*, natural selection is fundamental to understanding all sciences. We have one observable universe and it is shaped by natural selection.

I think that current trends in high school reforms limit our chances of producing members for a scientifically literate democracy. A general or liberal education frees us, empowers us, and prepares us for those moments that define our lives. Through it we become persistent and patient agents of cultural transmission and change within our democracy. A liberal education permits us to have important conversations with those who came before, it encourages us to ask the big questions, and it helps us explore those questions across a wide variety of knowledge and experience. High school was the last bastion of a liberal arts education. The narrowing focus of study that is now typical of higher education is making its way into high schools. We are no longer producing generalists. Increasingly, schools have directives from above (not in the religious sense but in the bureaucratic sense) that are pushing classroom teachers in the wrong direction. Approaches such as Project Lead the Way seem designed to create high school graduates in biology that are ready to take their place at lab benches with knowledge of procedures but little insight into the nature of science or natural selection. Advanced Placement courses with the stress on covering content and rote memorization must sacrifice time spent doing science. We learn what science is only by doing it. Proficiency and graduation exams stress content that is soon outdated and not processes that generate new knowledge. We are headed down a dangerous path during dangerous times. We are creating a generation of specialists with narrow vision.

In Moravia 24,000 years ago, tribal humans battling regional extinction, left evidence of a profound cultural shift. The first permanent village of about one hundred people appeared. The switch away from the nomadic life of the smaller hunter-gather groups was a response to the climate's cold grip at the height of the last Ice Age. These large and first permanent villages allowed for the development of experts. Specialists made warmer clothes, sharper tools, and stronger shelters. These people prospered and their way of life spread, despite the challenges of the environment. We stepped out of the Stone Age and we strode into the present on the shoulders of specialists. This strategy definitely worked in the tribal society setting. It is obvious we cannot remain tribal and I suggest that we cannot remain specialized. In our addiction to specialists, are we losing sight of the wider perspective? What does this mean in the long run?

The Greek poet Archilocus wrote, "The fox knows many things, but the hedgehog knows one big thing." As a kid growing up in Montana I knew this truth, but my fox was a coyote and my hedgehog was a porcupine. The coyote is a generalist. It is intelligent, resourceful, adaptive, and resistant to the uncertainties and irregularities

The Greek poet Archilocus in his fable of the fox and the hedgehog wrote that "the fox knows many things, but the hedgehog knows one big thing." The moral of the story is that, in a rapidly changing world, it is better to be a generalist that can adapt to many situations, rather than a specialist limited to only one.

of everyday life. The porcupine, on the other hand, is devoted to a single system of survival—sharp points. In its reliance on this highly specialized system, it waddles through life bumping into trouble, but enthusiastic in its faith. The system-trusting porcupine is a specialist. I'm a Hoosier and coyotes are my new neighbors. On cool nights, when the windows are open, their howls slip in with the breeze. In my entire life, I've only seen two or three porcupine; all were Montanans. The coyote is a relative newcomer to the Midwest. Take the ancient insight of Archilocus and combine it with the modern ecological fact that coyotes have greatly expanded their range on this urbanized planet, whereas porcupines continue to lose ground in the face of habitat destruction and you can extrapolate an answer to the following question. Whose chances do you favor in the scramble to avoid extinction in a rapidly changing world—the specialist or the generalist?

An individual trained as a specialist is narrowly restricted to his or her small tribal envelope of time and space. That specialist has little chance of developing a transgenerational perspective. A world full of specialists will not likely develop the critical mass of thinkers required to develop the wisdom necessary to make good choices about the future. What is the fate of reach of mind in a world dominated by specialists? That fate is our fate.

Turmoil

by Laura Perras

Laura Perras, writing as a first-year college student studying evolution with a strictly religious, antievolutionist background, describes the turmoil the exposure has created in her personal understanding of the world. Her study, she adds, has undermined the pillars of her faith and created distance between her and her family and friends. She questions whether students her age are really ready to face the issues involved. She is also critical of the handling of related issues in her schools, wondering whether the education she received actually serves the needs of students, as opposed to overwhelming them with political controversy instigated not only by the schools but also by a battery of external political and economic forces.

Evolution or creationism? That is the ultimatum that has prompted the war over what should be taught in American classrooms. This ongoing battle, as chaotic as the primordial waters, has been brewing for many years now. The Scopes monkey trial in the 1920s was just a small glimpse of the controversy that would sweep across the country in the current era. The turmoil caused by these two ideologies has entered into America's courtrooms and public schools and it has shown no sign of being resolved quickly. Similar to a hurricane over the gulf, it keeps circling and striking land from numerous angles. The controversy of evolution versus creationism is here to stay and students are going to need more than rain ponchos to protect themselves from the crashing waves.

For approximately 150 years humankind has grappled with the questions proposed by creationism and evolution. Who are we? Where did we come from? These questions have not been fully understood or answered. Humans have come up with numerous answers ranging from aliens, special creation, and to, yes, even evolution. Americans are not alone in trying to discern where they came from. The conflict between these proposed answers, however, seems to have taken on a special degree of aggression among Americans.

Due to religious origins, particularly a strong Christian heritage, many individuals within this country cling to doctrines supporting special creation. Special creation, commonly known as creationism, allows individuals to believe in a higher being or beings that created them as unique creatures. Others believe strictly in biological evolution and so there is no need to introduce a higher being into the processes that created modern humans. Some individuals attempt to blend the two beliefs, which at times can incur criticism from the two major encampments. It is difficult for an individual to endorse both a creative being and evolution, and still to find sympathy, respect, or even camaraderie from committed evolutionists or creationists. Others, when considering this controversy, simply do not care. Although there is nothing wrong with any of these stances or an individual's entitlement to believe what he or she will, there is a problem when the major sides begin to battle for dominance in the realm of public education. Publicly funded education is being forced to rearrange curriculums to cater to the beliefs of particular groups.

For numerous years now the battle between what will be taught in public schools—evolution or creationism—has raged across the country. Some states, such as Kansas, have attempted to pass laws banning the instruction of evolution. Others have insisted on keeping religion out of science classes and keeping evolution in. Thus, the waters that served as the birthplace for life have ultimately been sent into turmoil over what middle school and high school students will be taught in science class. Will these students learn that the world around them was formed in six days? Or will they be instructed that it took millions of years of complicated processes to put them in those hard biology chairs?

As a college student, my view of the battle is perhaps distorted. I am no longer in the fray (public high school) listening to teachers complain about curriculum adjustments, nor am I in the educator's position of not knowing what should be taught or fearing what I say in case of lawsuits. My perspective is one that fluctuates from looking over my shoulder (and praying, "I'm glad I'm not in that position") to squinting into the future (namely, trying to ascertain what my children will be

Gordon Pollard providing my first exposure to the theory of evolution.

taught). I have come to the conclusion that the conflict between evolution and creationism is simply a mess. It is a mess forged from misconceptions, close-mindedness, and pride. The real loser in all of this is not the ideology that is ruled against in the courtroom; it is America's young minds. Students, due to the tumultuous time, are missing out on a well-rounded education that would help them understand the world around them.

Many of the young adults my age do not spend a lot of time contemplating this issue or the implications it will have. We hear about it on television or read about it in the newspaper, but oftentimes brush aside such reports. If a mere second is spent reflecting on this issue, most young adults utter one of three generalizations: (1) People are stupid. Evolution is the *only* explanation for life. (2) How can they discredit God like that? What is this world coming to? (3) This whole issue is stupid. Aren't there more important things to argue over? None of these responses show deep contemplation, but they do demonstrate the positions Americans often take. It is not enough, however, to simply "take a side" or murmur a generalization. All Americans, including my generation, need to stay on top of this debate. The current crop of college students especially needs to stay informed. After all, it is our children who will be affected in the years to come. Whatever is decided in court today may still be on the books when our children are middle and high school students. And, as the future caretakers and rulers of this country, we need to maintain the line between church and state. Such a distinction is prescribed in the Constitution, and it is important that such a line remain intact. Above all, we need to approach this debate with open-mindedness and a willingness to discuss the issues.

In many ways my own background parallels the history of this debate in America. Through my early years creationism was the only path suitable for me, but with age the tug and pull of both ideologies came to the forefront of my conscious. The parallel, however, ends there. America has not pulled itself out of the fog of confusion; I would like to think that I have.

I was raised Methodist in the northern part of this country, far from the Bible belt. That is not to say, however, that fundamentalism and literal interpretation of the Bible never had an impact on my young mind. For most of my childhood, right on up until my senior year of public high school, there was no other explanation for the origin of the world and all its wonders (for me) other than creationism. At the time I believed that a single divine creator, without the aid of evolution, had created the universe and all the biological life-forms present on the planet. It was not that I had never heard of evolution or been instructed about it in science classes; I simply refused to acknowledge its applicability.

I was raised in a fairly religious household. I went to Sunday school and church regularly and became involved in the choir and youth group. When I was old enough, I started teaching Sunday school and Confirmation classes. I adamantly believed that the universe and everything in it was made in six 24-hour days. There was never a mention of evolution and when there was, it was quickly disputed with claims about an incomplete fossil record, forged fossil finds, and an inaccurate definition of the word *theory*.

Those creationist beliefs did not stay within the confines of the church. It was also in my house. I remember one evening, when I was fairly young, a segment on evolution appeared on the evening news. The news reporter was relaying something about evolution; perhaps it was a new find or just another court battle. Not paying much attention, I was surprised with how upset my father became from hearing the latest news. I remember his eyes burning with anger and hurt, and a red flush spreading over his face. His war cry was, "No one is going to tell me I came from a ******* monkey!" Hopefully he will not disown me for writing this and the reader will excuse the foul language, but this mentality, while in my own home, was and continues to be in other homes. The influence exerted on individuals by creationist beliefs, however, is not the only reason as to why individuals become so defensive when they hear the word *evolution*. Misunderstanding is also a prominent factor.

Many individuals, myself included, have a huge misconception as to what evolution really is. For numerous years, I carried several monstrous misconceptions around. First and foremost, I believed that if I accepted evolution, any part of it, I was betraying my faith in God. I was convinced that if evolution was real, then God could not be. There is a belief in this country that it has to be one way or the other; that there is no middle ground. The fear of isolation and the lack of providence are also prevalent in this belief. The second misconception involved the evolutionary process itself. I thought that evolution meant we evolved from something else. Although humans did evolve, I expected that the "something else" would still be present on the earth. If we came from monkeys, why weren't there any half-monkey-half-human monsters walking around? It did not make sense to me that the intermediary form was not still present on earth. Lastly, it hurt my pride to consider I came from something as impish as an ape. I feared that if I was related to a monkey, I was not a special creation. I was not unique. I was nothing.

A final component that shaped my early years was the struggle I sensed between the church and the school. Each institution was telling me something else and each insisted that it was right. As a student (regardless of whether it is in Sunday school or science class), there is an innate tendency to please the teacher. The student wants to believe what the instructor believes. At this point, what the teacher says might as well be written on stone tablets. The problem for the student, however, comes when there are two sets of stone tablets with opposing views. To ask students at this stage in the development process to choose what they feel is right and applicable to life is useless. Students at this age have other issues to worry about. There are always immediate worries that overshadow curriculum concerns. Perhaps these young minds are occupied by studying for an upcoming exam, practicing for a basketball tournament, or coping with family issues. Whatever the concern is, evolution and the implications surrounding it are forced to take a back seat. Nevertheless, the whole point of education during these early years is to help the student shape a moral code to live by. Deep reflection is not an easy task for a young student.

From this initial point, deciphering what was right for myself in terms of belief only became more difficult. The tug-of-war between church and state is responsible for this "confusion or frustration" stage. It becomes apparent to some individuals that they are a pawn on a chessboard and their best interest may be sacrificed. Children, with no ability to demand a certain kind of education, are often moved around on the board, taught only what is on the square they happen to land on. This is precisely what happens in the war between evolution and creationism. Both sides are playing with education and it causes a great deal of confusion and frustration for the children that are caught in the middle of the struggle. These emotions could, and do, continue to survive well into adulthood.

My own public education, although exceptionally good, spawned these feelings of frustration and confusion. I distinctly remember a particular lesson in my seventh-grade science class. The teacher was showing us slides, describing different beliefs that humans have come up with in regard to human origin. The first was of a woman, a man, a tree, and a red sky. The instructor called it the "creation myth" and on hearing those words, I felt the hair on my arms stand on edge. I remember thinking: "Myth? What is he talking about? It is not a myth! He's wrong!" I was deeply confused by the fact that one of my teachers would try to discredit the lessons I had been taught in Sunday school. How could he call my religious beliefs a myth? And why did he use a particular tone of voice when he was describing special creation? Was I imagining things or did he seem partial to evolution? The perceived preference by a teacher raised a lot of turmoil in my young mind. It spurred the growth of an immense fear: that religion, that God, would be discredited. There are few anxieties worse than the fear of being told your life support, your religion, is no longer operating. Similar to the many other individuals afraid of being taken off life support, I adopted the use of a wall. This wall, similar to the Casparian strip in plant cells, prevents things from going in and coming out. I closed my mind to evolution, refused to learn about it, and kept telling myself that creationism was 100 percent correct.

The refusal to learn stayed with me for several years. It was not until my senior year of high school that my mind was finally opened. In my government class we were assigned a research project. This project forced us to define a controversial issue, write a paper on the issue, make some sort of visual, and present our findings and personal beliefs to the class. Being the overachiever that I am, I had to do something big. My mind set on religion because some wiseguy had made a crack about the Virgin Mary, my thoughts fell on evolution and creationism. There were some court cases that year and it had gotten some media attention. I wanted (and am ashamed of this now) to prove to my classmates that creationism did work and evolution was just a guess. I was in for the biggest surprise of my life.

At the onset of my research I was convinced that proving my argument would be simple. I would use the Bible, a few religious books, some Internet articles, and maybe anything else that crossed my path and was interesting. I started with the Bible. The first chapter of Genesis went well. It made for some quick reading; the creation of the earth and everything in it was neatly outlined in a six-day time frame. Yet, as my eyes wandered from the six-day schematic to Genesis Chapter 2, I felt them grow wider. At this point, things got sticky.

For all my years of Sunday school classes and listening to numerous sermons, no one had ever pointed out to me that Chapters 1 and 2 of Genesis do not correspond with each other. Chapter 1, as previously stated, is a neat six-day outline of the creation. Chapter 2, however, is not. The order of creation (what was formed first) is different as are some of the details. Wiping my eyes of disbelief, I tried my best to reconcile the deviating accounts. Perhaps one account was literal and the other metaphorical. Perhaps one was a mistake. Maybe Genesis 2 was one of the days presented in Chapter 1, simply in greater detail. I realized that the foundation for my argument had suddenly become unstable.

As impossible as it was for me to reconcile the two creation stories, the information about evolution was just as insurmountable. I looked through the library catalog and found no help. My school library did not have a single book on the subject. I then turned to religious doctrine. I leafed through various books (both Methodist and other) that yielded only ambiguous clues. The Internet, too, was of little help and was more nightmarish than anything. Most educators do not like the Internet because of the volumes of incorrect information online. As contradictory as some of my sources may have been, they all directed me to the same conclusion: Evolution did exist.

Where did this messy research lead me? A few weeks later, after Christmas break, I found myself standing up in front of the class presenting evidence that I myself did not truly comprehend. Using a hypothesis that I had stumbled on during my many hours of research, I claimed that the earth was made in six days. These days were not twenty-four-hour periods but instead consisted of vast quantities of time. I had constructed a chart depicting this hypothesis and used other handouts that indicated the verity of microevolution. I could not endorse macroevolution and used an old, familiar crutch as support: There was no convincing intermediary fossil evidence supporting macroevolution.

Today, although barely a year since that report was given, I am perhaps less confused and leaning further away from creationism. I believe in theistic evolution, and although some scientists disregard this, it is what I have reconciled myself to. There are numerous components of theistic evolution, and I do not adhere to all of the tenets in circulation. As of this moment, I continue to believe in microevolution but have progressed to the next level. I believe that macroevolution does exist and that human beings evolved from a common ancestor shared with other primates. Furthermore, I believe that there is a higher being behind every event that occurs. The ideologies of evolution and creationism are one in the same thing for me. Evolution exists and for some individuals such as myself, so does God.

There are numerous stages in personal development and following this observation is the fact that the approaches individuals take to resolve the questions of human origins will also be numerous and different from each other. But what should Americans do in light of the current controversy? Should we confuse adolescents by presenting the theory of evolution and attempting to discredit their religious faith? Should we teach them only a literal interpretation of the Bible that does not always make sense to scholars let alone everyday parishioners? Or should we take a middle ground that combines the two? I have labeled my own solutions to this problem (very creatively at that) solutions A, B, and C. Perhaps the best solution, however, is one that will be reached between the adherents to either ideology.

Solution A deals mostly with what religion can do to contribute to peace. First and foremost, religion should attempt to become more tolerant of scientific discoveries. Tolerance, in this sense, is the ability to observe the world and its beliefs. Tolerance also allows the individual to say, "This is what they believe over there. I have these beliefs. I am not threatened by their beliefs. They are entitled to those beliefs. There is no right or wrong; we are equally justified." Simply stated, it is okay to have differing views. Tolerance allows human beings to coexist in a cooperative and caring setting.

If tolerance is utilized by religious organizations, the next step is to accept the fact that science can exist in this world beside it. Religion and science do not have to be at war. If tolerance and acceptance were more widely employed, perhaps the two could help each other in discovering elements of the human condition and improving it. It is imperative to remember that science is a two-way street: It can prove evolution, but it can also prove biblical events. For instance, several scientists are currently researching Noah's flood using the latest scientific technology. Several of these researchers believe that the flood described in Genesis was not a world flood, but instead a localized flood caused by various environmental factors. The flood that these scientists are researching is not the traditional flood, but it is nonetheless a flood. Science could help religion explain phenomena such as Noah's flood, if it were allowed to do so. But cooperation in proving these biblical events is not what solution A calls for. Cooperation at this point is perhaps too much to ask for. What America and its students need right now is for religion and science to coexist without the vicious debate that is currently raging in numerous court-houses. We need peace.

Tolerance, however, may not be enough. More may be required of religious institutions. Religious institutions need to be confident that science will not discredit or disprove the validity of a particular faith structure. There is more to religion than what meets the scientific eye. God cannot be tested, sin cannot be tested, and salvation cannot be tested. There are elements of faith that simply cannot be touched by science or laboratory research. Religion needs to realize that science is a threat only if it allows it to be one.

Although these views may seem closed-minded, it is imperative to realize they are necessary. For various reasons, religious institutions have an innate tendency to be paranoid. Perhaps this paranoia for Christian sects traces back to the days of persecution at the hands of the Romans. Any statement or action that could be perceived as persecution may unintentionally make various sects nervous. Faith-based organizations, like organisms, are endowed with an instinctual desire to persevere; attacks, or perceived attacks, on faith networks trigger immediate responses. Thus, it is important to give faith-based organizations the confidence they need to thrive and to become stable enough to coexist and tolerate scientific theories. Closed-mindedness, in this case, may be a means by which science and religion can eventually coexist.

Within a faith organization it may be acceptable to teach certain doctrines, but religious institutions and their adherents need to realize that mandating creationist classes in public schools will not yield them the results they are hoping to achieve. There are many students who despise school and the subjects they are forced to learn. Is it really wise to expose students to the in-depth precepts of particular faiths in such a setting? If religious classes are mandated in public schools, such doctrines may open students up to an intolerance of religion in their lives. They may be inclined to steer away from church more fervently. Thus, in terms of education, science should be allowed to teach whatever it so chooses. Of course, the lessons of any scientific curriculum should be well grounded in the scientific method and extensive experimentation. Religion, then, must teach its doctrines within its own organizations and Sunday school classes.

Finally, it is also imperative that faith networks understand that teaching religion in public school is unconstitutional. There are countless individuals with belief systems that are different from the creationist classes that some individuals are trying to mandate. Is it fair that the children of these individuals be subjected to a faith that is not their own? Why should they be forced to learn a belief that is not entirely verified by science? The same amendment that protects the right of creationists to practice their religion also protects these students.

Now it is science's turn. Solution B is in many ways simply the converse of solution A. If religion must be tolerant of science, then science must be tolerant of religion. Science has a knack for threatening faith systems. Science is an innovative field that, due to its advanced methods and findings, scares individuals. Science seems to question the foundations of most houses, and religions are afraid that their house is going to fall. It is imperative that scientists, even if they themselves do not adhere to any particular religion, recognize this power. The only way to calm the fearfulness of certain religious networks is to recognize and calm such fear.

Relieving fear, however, should not mean forfeiting scientific practices. Scientists should pursue their craft faithfully. They should look at the natural world, explore it, test it, and see if they can produce answers to certain questions. Science is a wonderful field and it has made this country what it is today. Without inventions, and scientific theories or findings, our lives would be much more difficult. Science has made life easier. Yet, pursuing something faithfully does not mean pursuing it aggressively. It does not mean viciously attacking someone or his or her beliefs. If science does reveal a truth that is contrary to a belief system, that truth should not be flaunted or used to discredit the faith or the adherent. Truth should be presented with no bias and as professionally as possible. The idea behind this is to make science and religion comfortable with each other. An adult–adult relationship would be the healthiest alternative.

Above all, science should be tolerant of religious ideas that are not supported or grounded in scientific evidence. Again, tolerance is the ability to look at something and recognize its importance to another human being, but be able to calmly choose not to believe it for oneself. Science does not have to support religious beliefs; it simply has to tolerate their existence.

Last, solution C calls for science and religion to remain separate. For the time being, there is little evidence that can be used to peaceably link science and religion; thus, it is necessary in some cases to keep the two ideologies—like two children who are squabbling—far away from each other. Solution C is essentially a large time-out chair. If teaching evolution in public schools is seen as contrary to religious belief, then educational institutions should offer an elective course that discusses creationism or alternative explanations of how evolution and religion may possibly coincide. This class should of course be completely voluntary and respect the individual's right to religious freedom. Evolution, however, cannot be simply taken out of a curriculum. If anything, it needs to be more expounded on. There are far too many misconceptions being passed around in America today. It is necessary that some of those be dispelled. The future of a vibrant America is dependent on the well-rounded education of its younger generations. An understanding of evolution should be a core part of that education. And, if the student so decides, religious doctrine may also be included in the enlightenment process.

Science and religion should not be forever separated. They need to get along. If there are scholars who wish to someday pursue a unified theory of science and creationism, they must do so through sound scientific methods and in such a way that this research is not prematurely taught in classrooms. It should also not be forced on individuals who differ in thought. If there is ever to be true compromise, the story of human origin needs to be pieced together slowly and carefully.

The debate currently sweeping across America is a messy one. There is much fingerpointing, crying, and fear between both encampments. These actions and feelings are furiously spreading across the country in all directions. The controversy needs to be addressed now and a plan needs to be enacted so that the quality of education within American public schools does not deteriorate. It is imperative that students learn about evolution, but it is also important that they are given a chance to learn about their faith. Both needs are equal. Students do not deserve to be given an education that neglects one approach and asserts another belief that is contrary to their religious beliefs or scientific studies. Compromises can be made. The last thing America needs is more students graduating from high school without a basic understanding of evolution, their religious beliefs, and the significance of this controversy.

CHAPTER 14

Conclusions

by Mark Nathan Cohen

> *It is a mistake to think that good, healthy science needs to replace religion. . . .*
> *And it is an even bigger mistake to think that religion in general or Christianity in*
> *particular must define itself as antiscience. . . . Rather, the battle is over what*
> *constitutes good science and perhaps the definition of science itself.*
>
> —Hewlett and Peters, Chapter 4 of this book.

We have attempted to provide perspectives on the tension between beliefs in evolution and creation—and by implication between science itself and faith. As Hearn
pointed out, the position is a dangerous one because we are likely to be attacked
from both sides. As should be evident, we adhere strictly and wholly to neither the
scientific nor faith-based arguments. But a main theme throughout the book is that
the very appropriate refusal to permit creation "science" in science classes is quite different
from denying the importance of faith. Too often, people on both sides of the issues
ignore this important distinction. We believe, however, that at present, science and
faith intrude on one another far more than necessary, and it is these concerns that
we are addressing.

Our perspectives come from an anthropologist writing as a social historian,
describing the cultural embedding of both science and religion, with particular reference to the actual role of William Jennings Bryan (Robbins); a historian of law,
science, and evolutionary theory (Larson); a biologist defending evolution but also
considering its importance for broader areas of thought (Mayr); a biochemist and
evangelical Christian (Hearn) who refers to himself as both "a Christian serious
about evolution and a scientist serious about creation"; a biological anthropologist
defending evolution and science while considering other spheres of human need
and activity (Cohen); a molecular biologist (Hewlitt) and a theologian (Peters) working together to find a bridge between science and theology; a biologist interested
in controversies within evolutionary theory but also adamant about the separation
of science and religion (Gould); a lawyer and proponent of the theory of intelligent
design (Johnson, whose contribution was cut short by ill health); an anthropologist

writing as a historian of science exploring the origins of intelligent design theory (Marks); a student of the creationist movement and activist in defending science (Branch); a high school teacher trying to teach evolution (Randak); and a [then] first-year college student who finds herself caught among the evolutionary science she is learning, the absence of exposure to evolution in her earlier education, her friendship networks, and her own and her family's religious faith (Perras).

It should be clear that no one writing in this volume denies the importance of science, done and taught correctly (although some of the people discussed do). Johnson argues that the evidence for evolution is inadequate and that intelligent design will ultimately triumph, but even he suggests that real science itself should be pursued and will ultimately lead to that conclusion, without the intrusion of religious faith as part of the proof.

We recognize that science, improperly presented, can appear to promote atheism and materialism in the specific sense of focusing on the physical, tangible components of the world (not to be confused with another meaning of materialism (i.e., greed or the drive for personal wealth). But we do not believe that science, properly presented, can or should threaten faith or promote atheism, although it challenges the most literal interpretations of the Bible (an issue that clearly bothers Perras but is dealt with also by Hearn and others). But none of us believes that creationist beliefs are mere ignorance, as scientists often portray them, or that science and evolution are destructive processes and doctrines.

None of us believes that science can explain everything. None of us deny the importance of faith, morality, love, transcendent meaning, a sense of purpose, community; a need for a structure with which to organize the world; a need to explain the unexplainable; or a need for spiritual understanding. We disagree about whether these needs are natural parts of a human biological and cultural design that are in turn the product of evolution, or whether they are the results of divinely inspired faith.

I think that we would all agree that human behavior and human equality, emotions, and basic themes of social groups need not be explained by genes, and have meanings that transcend basic biology. We (particularly Robbins) noted the damage done to social institutions and people in the (misused) name of evolution. None of us accepts the socially destructive extensions of evolution, such as social Darwinism, eugenics, or racial "cleansing," nor, in full, do we accept modern genetic explanations of behavior (sociobiology and evolutionary psychology). We collectively do, and will continue to, fight attempts to revive any of these destructive doctrines. None of us believes, however, that these abuses are inherent in evolutionary theory properly understood. Moreover, we noted that the damage that results from science has to be balanced against the damage caused by faith. Both sides have contributed very significantly to the earth's troubled history, science providing the mechanisms, faith of various kinds providing the rationale.

We have sought various ways to mix faith and science for constructive purposes, whether we prefer to try to combine them, as in theistic evolution, agreeing to the existence of both God and evolution; to define separate but complementary spheres of need; to discuss primary versus secondary causation; to recognize different but equal ways of knowing (as in the separate magisteria of Gould); to seek truths versus Truth; to study proximate versus ultimate explanations; to discuss "how" as opposed to discussing "why"; to describe and explain different aspects of human experience important for different purposes and in different contexts; to distinguish between I-it knowledge (science) and I-thou knowledge (faith); or to distinguish between objective, impersonal science and faith that means personal involvement with spiritual reality.

Most of us, scientists and theologians alike, believe, however, that science and faith need to be kept, and taught separately, their qualities clearly distinguished, before they are compared or combined so that their respective qualities can be preserved and their complementarity fully understood. As Hearn pointed out, religion is very important and provides things that science does not, but airplanes need to be designed by scientists, not clergy with Bibles. None of us, other than Johnson, recognizes either creation science or intelligent design theories as legitimate science because they violate the definition of what science is and how it is done. In the eyes of Hewlett and Peters, they can be rejected on religious grounds as well.

Some of us have proposed that a distinction be made between creation as a single act and as an ongoing endeavor, and between God as creator—perhaps as creator of evolution—(whom both many scientists and most theologians accept) and God who has guided evolution through its history or who intervenes in the daily affairs of the world, a position defended by Johnson and Hearn in this book, but a position anathema to many theologians as well as by definition, to all or almost all scientists. Some of us believe (Hearn) and some of us deny (Cohen, Randak) that based on human history, there is a God who can be seen as a benevolent force in human affairs. (Where, Randak and I ask, in historic and modern human affairs, do we see signs of divine benevolence?)

Science and faith each have great power, but each has different or limited powers. If allowed, they might well complement one another to obtain the fullest understanding of human experience. All theologians and all scientists, including evolutionary biologists, in fact all people, actually operate by principles of both science and faith. After all, we live in a human social world that provides science and technology, but also provides purpose, morality, interaction, and faith in certain essential principles that do not come from science, whether or not they come from God. We cannot function without both kinds of thought and action. But each camp tends to blame the other for making a marriage of the two impossible. In fact, both sides bear significant responsibility for their inability to meld because blind faiths (including that of some scientists) tend to be mutually exclusive. Promoting self-examination and dissection of ideas, goals, and motives on each side is probably our most important goal. The point is not that religion and science can't coexist or mix; it is that some interpretations of each preclude the other.

Our efforts in this book are directed neither against science nor against faith. They are directed against people on either side of the evolution–creation debate (and either side of contemporary but unnecessary struggle between science and faith) who claim more than their side actually offers, who will not consider the legitimacy of the other side, and who would use one to distort or deny the other, rather than permitting them to work in concert. The problem we have addressed is how the debate and the tension between faith and science can be resolved in a manner that recognizes the vitality and essential nature of each and how to eliminate their potentially destructive inroads on one another. The critical point is that *science and creationist beliefs are each embedded in far larger matrices of beliefs, goals, egos, and politics that neither acknowledges, but that need to be understood and sorted out if any progress toward a solution to the controversy is to be found.*

Rationalism

As Marks pointed out, science falls in the larger category of *rationalism*, a principle dating from the Enlightenment that existed long before most modern science, scientific methods, and evolutionary ideas. Rationality claims that human minds, rather than simple faith, hold the solutions to our problems. It was a doctrine that, at the time, threatened a social order, held together in large part by faith, designed to maintain the status quo—a faith that reacted quite negatively to the rationalist threat. Science is a subcategory of rationalism designed to deal with a natural world that has specific rules of its own. It again threatens the social order and there is again a backlash.

As Randak, Hearn, and I each pointed out, science is a *process* that works in particular ways. Its workings need to be understood before much sense can be made of the issues of evolution and creation science. It is these workings, more than anything else, that need to be protected. In particular, science is a process of constant, open competition and potential replacement among ideas in a marketplace judged by principles of rationality, logic, and quality of fit with previous observations, hopefully resulting in the growth and improved accuracy of our understanding. It is a game that never precludes further competition, never precludes the possibility that ideas can change and new things can be learned as new arguments and evidence are brought to bear. Many examples of new ideas and evidence, causing scientists to rethink their positions, are scattered throughout this book. But, as I pointed out, the scientific marketplace is not as perfect as it might be because politics and ideology (both from within science itself and from the environment that surrounds it) can and have trumped its correct operating procedures, at least in the short run.

Uniformitarianism

All of science is based on one central assumption or axiom—uniformitarianism—which holds that all events and observations ultimately derive from known or knowable patterns and laws in nature and can be explained in those terms once we know enough. The fact that this principle is assumed or axiomatic is part of what critics refer to when they say that science is a philosophy or faith of its own. But, it is an axiom that is very consciously and explicitly developed in science, and one used constantly and successfully in everyday life. Despite the challenges, it has gained enormous strength from the power of its insights and its success in scientific endeavors and in the workings of everyday life. We could not function in any of our activities if it weren't true. Knowable, predictable natural principles are in fact the basis for almost all behavior of human kind, not just scientific inquiry. We rely constantly on predicting from previous experience, assuming that the basic rules will not change. Our experience is a reliable guide to future action. Why else do we have this ability? Why have we evolved or been granted the ability to think if it serves no purpose?

Science, *by definition*, demands uniformitarian thought. It is science's "way of knowing." Uniformitarianism explicitly denies magic, miracles, or divine intervention in human and world affairs. Scientists insist instead that explanations *must* invoke *only* known, or knowable, replicable, and reliable principles of nature. Science says that nothing is inherently unknowable, although all scientists would agree that there are many things we don't know or haven't figured out yet. Both scientific creationism and intelligent design involve appeals to miracles or unknowable forces. Neither plays by the rules of the scientific marketplace competition and uniformitarianism. Therefore, by definition, neither is science—a position shared by the theologians writing in this book as well as the scientists.

On the other hand, as scientists are well aware, our experience, gained over a very brief period of observation, is not a complete replication of natural rules many of which are still to be observed or understood. And we do sometimes misunderstand the experiences we observe, often because our period of observation has been so short, as in the case of the apparently static continents once so widely taken for granted, because without out very careful research we could not see them moving. Creationists, however, make the same mistake when they argue that macro (i.e., large-scale) evolution and the division of one kind or species into two—processes that involve thousands or even millions of years—cannot have occurred simply because we have not witnessed them in the very short span (less than two hundred years) in which we have been watching.

Evolution

Darwinian evolution is a uniformitarian principle. We see it operating constantly, and can presume its operation in past and future. As Randak pointed out, it is probably the single most important concept uniting the field of biology; and, I would add, geology, chemistry, physics, and their daughter sciences as well, because life is not the only system in which natural variation is contained by natural selection for stability, survival, and/or successful replication. But we must make a distinction between evolution as a source of all life, or as a mechanism by which life, once formed, becomes varied, complex, adapted, and mutable. This is a distinction on which evolutionary scientists are divided. Hearn, initially a biochemist, said, for example, that although he accepts evolution, he has gradually lost faith in proposed biochemical mechanisms to explain the emergence of life from nonliving compounds; and he has lost faith that science will ever solve the problem. The observation is clearly correct, in my opinion. Admittedly, demonstration of the process by which nonliving forms give rise to living ones has not yet been achieved to the satisfaction of all scientists. But Johnson's prediction that such a process will never be found is highly unlikely, in fact impossible, in the minds of most scientists.

Scientists have provided a great deal of evidence to show that the variety of life on earth, if not (yet) its ultimate origins, requires neither miracles nor intelligent design. The family tree of evolution was inherent in the work of Linnaeus who classified life-forms by similarity of structure, long before Darwin's model had been proposed. As Marks pointed out, other than by perceiving a family tree, how can we understand Linnaeus recognition of groups or families of organisms related more closely to one another than to other life-forms, in graded, nested groups of various sizes, larger categories encompassing smaller categories? We can and have demonstrated that life can and has evolved by natural mechanisms. The mechanisms of change exist and, we believe, are known in basic outline. Biological variation occurs spontaneously by DNA errors and, in sexual organisms, by genetic mixing. Family lines with the best variants tend to persist; others tend to be lost. We all know of branches of our families that for some reason or another have died out.

The mechanisms are obvious in our own experience in the evolution of modern families. Uniformitarian principles allow us, cautiously, to assume that the same processes were evident in the past. Families evolve because each generation of children tends to be a bit different from its parents; and siblings differ from one another because they get different mixes of their parents' genes. Siblings produce their own families generating various degrees of cousins with graded degrees of variation from one another, and the process continues generation after generation, multiplying the differences. Those same simple processes, multiplied by millions of generations, have, scientists argue, produced the variety we see today. We can see natural selection at work in modern populations in the form of changing frequencies of certain genes and the changing success of various groups of organisms, as environments change.

Have we ever seen one species actually change into another or divide into two different species, as is so obvious in the fossil record? We can easily observe the appearance of new forms in rapidly reproducing microorganisms (and must in order to fight disease). But because species are often defined by the inability or unwillingness to breed, the definition of *species* in asexual organisms is fuzzy.

Speciation is hard to observe in sexual organisms that breed more slowly because evolutionary change occurs over many generations, and we haven't been watching very long. I provided an example of two varieties of dogs, Great Danes and Chihuahuas, in which the mechanism of division into two species has already occurred because the two varieties can no longer interbreed as a function of their respective sizes. The division is almost complete. Our two kinds of dogs from a common ancestor now are essentially different species. The further evolution of one will no longer affect the other.

Most scientists believe that both the construction of our bodies and the fossil record demonstrate that evolution, involving gradual and occasionally very rapid change and the branching of family trees, has occurred. Radioactive dating techniques, well replicated and thoroughly checked against each other and other methods of counting age, establish that there has been time for millions of generations of life on earth. Despite the claims of creationists, there are numerous intermediate forms of fossils demonstrating both gradual change and the branching of family trees to be seen in the fossil record. Many of these fossils are found in multiple copies and their chronological position can often be cross-checked in many ways. As more fossils are found, the pattern is filled in, even though the record is not—and never will be—complete. Some of the best examples of intermediate forms come from the evolutionary tree of human beings themselves.

The bodies of organisms leading very different lives involve profound similarities of deep structure, including the basic genetic material itself—DNA—best explained as family resemblances. For a designer to use the same materials and designs for such different organisms and different function would be markedly inefficient.

Both fossil organisms and poor design point to a process that hardly appears to be the work of an all-knowing creator. The fossil record demonstrates that most family lines of organisms have died out or become extinct. Why waste the effort if this is grand design? Even those families that have survived display faulty structures (often those shared family traits that no longer function quite correctly for their new uses). In fact, the biological world—and people—are full of markedly *unintelligent* designs and events that argue against the operation of a divine hand. I called attention to the human spine and to high blood pressure and diabetes. Hewlitt and Peters pointed out that whatever the origin of the eye, we still need eyeglasses. Marks added acne, wisdom teeth, and cancer to the list of flaws that clearly don't point to divine benevolence, and the list can go on and on.

Sociobiology

Sociobiology—the attempt to find the genetic mechanisms and natural selective values underlying specific human emotions and behaviors, and to view people and animals as strategic machines promoting the defense and replication of their genes—was discussed most fully by Larson and by me. It can be a very powerful tool for stimulating new questions and new research. I argued that sociobiology combines good, in fact essential, questions with incorrect and/or inappropriate answers that violate the other explanations of human life and behavior far more than they need to. In a very basic way, sociobiology reduces many important human values such as love and altruism to selfish genetic manipulation. Larson and I described the arrogance of sociobiologists and their pretentious claims of displacing not only other branches of science but also the needs of faith and the importance of God. Sociobiologists and some other evolutionary scientists (Mayr and Crick as described by Larson) have overtly suggested or at least implied that science can and should replace religion and that atheism is appropriate and justified.

Most of us agree that sociobiologists have overstepped their data, and even their reasonable theory, in their attempts to suggest detailed genetic control of human behavior. They have tried in effect to extend evolutionary theory to the discussion of essentially all aspects of human behavior: people's motives, including selfishness and altruism; the way people—particularly men, women, and children—play particular roles; the way human societies work.

As I and others noted, sociobiology has many scientific problems, not least of which is its failure to recognize the degree of flexibility and imagination that the human brain possesses and the importance of culturally (or divinely?) inspired emotions as proximate motivations that do not always attend to genetic fitness. Several of us suggested that sociobiology has become something of a faith or dogma of its own, ignoring too many of its interpretive problems and contradictions in pursuit of foregone conclusions embedded in its own assumptions. Sociobiology has become an axiom from which to pursue answers (but it is a principle far more controversial and far less supported by knowledge and experience than uniformitarianism itself). Sociobiology also tends to be a very conservative doctrine, attempting to explain why things are, and should be as they are. The status quo becomes venerated by science just as it can be by faith. Sociobiology is not explicitly linked with any of the destructive social programs that have been encouraged by misinterpretation of science, but its logic of genetic determinism is not actually so far removed from the genetic determinism that fed them.

Criticisms of Science

Science, and particularly evolutionary science, is blamed for a number of our social ills. It is presumed by its critics to threaten the status quo and to imply change threatening comfortable circumstances; to promote materialism; to suggest that death and destruction are inherent parts of life's plan; to create a world too complex to comprehend; to expedite change at a speed that is too rapid for comprehension or comfort; to promote atheism; to promote social upheaval; to remove life's mystery; to challenge sustaining faith; to further immorality, or at least amorality, hence threatening ethical rules; to undermine principles of social interaction; to promote and justify inequality and promote racism; to eliminate a sense of purpose; to undermine the human soul; to result in loss of belief in immortality and loss of respect for human life; and more explicitly, somehow to condone infanticide and abortion. It threatens a sense of human uniqueness or oneness with God or the perfection of human design. (As Robbins pointed out, these issues, not evolutionary science per se, were inherent in the arguments of William Jennings Bryan at the time of the Scopes trial.)

Science clearly does challenge some cherished beliefs, and it can be very arrogant in the manner in which it does so. There is often a flavor of arrogance as well as logic in the way it dismisses creationism, often without making the rationale for rejection very clear. Evolution *does* suggest that our design is imperfect (for which there is abundant evidence); that teleology and purpose are not part of the pattern of life; and that we are not as unique, at least in physical form, in the animal kingdom as we like to think. Science and evolution do call attention to the fact that life is far more about failure, death, and destruction than people like to believe—but it is only occasionally the cause. The perception that failure, death, and destruction are not inherent in life has always implied a certain blindness to the world around us.

Science can hardly be blamed for abortion and infanticide, although it can make them safer and easier. Both infanticide and abortion are known to every culture on earth, regardless of its scientific sophistication. Whether or not the techniques are used is controlled by politics and religion. Effectively, infanticide was a major part of historic religious and government-run orphanages in Europe where death rates of children from neglect, hunger, and disease were extraordinarily high—far higher than in almost any known society, no matter how "primitive."

I would argue that science per se is a cultural unifier and a force for equality because results are judged on their own merits and scientists talk to one another cross-culturally, often operating *against* the divisiveness and discrimination of other cultural forces. But much of the rest of the problem represents misunderstanding of science, or scapegoating of science for social ills. The associations claimed are weak, overly fearful, or—dare I say—irrational. For example, evolution, natural selection, and the concept of fitness suggest that inequality of biological variants is defined only by the specific needs of the moment and that momentary success says nothing about the overall quality of the individuals. Biologists (but not social manipulators) know that we can't predict what will be fit in the future.

A more legitimate issue, discussed by several of us, is whether science is always what it purports to be (the objective pursuit of knowledge), and whether or not the domain of science, aside from its objective pursuit of knowledge, actually includes its own faith or dogma; a fixed political as well as theoretical agenda; a monopoly of permitted explanations; monolithic discrimination against other faiths; and denial of creation or intelligent design by simple fiat. As Robbins suggested, science has a far broader agenda than most scientists recognize. It fails to see its own cultural embeddedness and the breadth of its meaning to others. As noted, some contributors to this volume argue that evolution is embedded in a preexisting naturalistic or personal *philosophy* rather than in empirical science alone.

Science can clearly be entwined in politics, both within and without its own system. Internal politics temporarily prevented the most accurate ideas about maize evolution from being put on the table. A more famous example of external politics was the greatly misinformed model of evolution put forth by a man named Lysenko in Russia and maintained by Soviet governmental fiat for decades. All of these flaws, however, tend to be exaggerated and distorted in secondary or even tertiary description of science, combined often with deliberate misrepresentation by its critics.

Science has historically been wrong often enough to generate reasonable skepticism. Despite delays caused by poor observation or logic, internal squabbling, egos, preestablished beliefs, intimidation, or even politics, science, by definition, self-corrects temporary misdirection. But even temporary misdirection can often last long enough to do significant damage. Although delayed by politics, belated recognition that pellagra was a dietary, rather than infectious disease, finally resulted in the ability to eliminate it with relative ease. Skepticism is not hard to understand. Science is something to *do*, not something to believe. When science is simply believed as an article of faith, then it is no more scientific than any other faith. Science can in fact be described as having its own elite priesthood and as being very intolerant to those who do not share or succeed at its faith. The sense that science can and should be taken on faith (as it is often presented by scientists themselves) is one of the things that makes people (whether they know or believe scientific method) blindly and uncritically accept scientific results and then become upset and throw out the baby of science with the bathwater of results that later prove incorrect. As many critics have pointed out, which scientific statements (or statements popularly presented as if they were science) about proper diet should we obey?

At a more dangerous but less conscious level, scientists can be caught in assumptions that they themselves do not notice or question—so they never undergo critical analysis. All scientific endeavors, in fact all problem solving, begin with assumptions and premises. The solutions reached may be no better than the assumptions, no matter how faultless the reasoning or methods used to arrive at them. Some assumptions, like uniformitarianism as I have suggested, are explicit. Others are not, and there are undoubtedly other assumptions buried so deeply in our thinking that we don't even recognize their existence, yet they may still be skewing our thinking. What assumptions underlie science (or, for that matter various types of faith) that we don't recognize?

The Damage Coming from Pseudoscience

As Robbins, in particular, pointed out, *abuses* of evolutionary theory and science have often been inherent or at least complicit in many social and moral lapses. Darwin's theory of natural selection may have been intended as an objective, neutral description of the natural world, but it has been invoked (incorrectly) as a rationale for many inappropriate or even dangerous practices. And as he noted, it is most often distortions of science rather than the theory of evolution itself that are at the root of various problems.

In the hands of many individuals, and sometimes whole schools of thought, *abused* science has a history that is long and dishonorable. It has been invoked in the emergence of social Darwinism or the justification of class exploitation. It has also been used in promoting and defending the idea of different inherent worth and in the construction and denigration of racial categories (although good science shows very clearly that racial categories exist only in our minds). Abused science has also been used to justify eugenics and racial cleansing, or the overt elimination of whole groups of "inferior" people, like the destruction of the Jewish "race" by the Nazis.

Social Darwinism was used explicitly through the late nineteenth century and the early twentieth to demonstrate the superiority of upper classes and sanction destructive activities on the mistaken grounds that "fitness" referred to a person's "quality," wealth, or political clout—in other words, on sociopolitical dominance. Although the term is out of favor and explicit statements of it have dropped below the perceptual horizon, the idea is still very much alive and implicit in a great many actions taken by the wealthy and powerful, and by governments, including our own.

Eugenic policies (i.e., attempts to "improve" the human race, effectively by making everyone like the eugenicists themselves) were based on the presumption (with no basis, then, or even now) that mental and behavioral qualities were inherited genetically. (For a more explicit critique see Cohen, 1998, 2002.) This resulted in a policy to prevent the breeding of so-called inferior genotypes that took several forms: forced or secret sterilizations about which the recipients were not informed, far less given the ability to give or withhold agreement; preventing "inferior" beings (particularly from Eastern Europe) from immigrating to the United States, even at the height of the Nazi threat. (This practice ironically included Ashkenazi Jews whose IQ's are now rated as superior, whatever that means.) And, it resulted in mass extermination. Hitler's extermination policies were explicitly inspired by abuse of evolutionary theory that he actually learned from British and American eugenicists.

Similar abuses still exist in our society in explicit statements of genetic racial inferiority in the hands of twenty-first-century "scientists" such as Rushton (1999) and Sarich and Miele (2004) in their use of phony racial histories and absurd use of intelligence tests. They still exist in the use of IQ tests by more reputable, but I believe still misguided, scientists in their attempts to show that individual differences, and by implication group differences, in intelligence are largely heritable genetically as in the work of Herrnstein and Murray (1994). They persist in the common assumption that failures and successes are each rooted in the biology of the individual. And they persist in the pervasive, if usually unspoken, assumption that little investment need be made in the poor because poverty is inherent in their character.

Of course, as I have suggested, whether or not science, or even misinterpreted science, provides a rationale, it has never been sufficient on its own to promote any of the beliefs and activities involved. The forces required to promote such efforts are social, ideological (often religious), or political goals. Most of these ills have existed independent of science or in areas imbued with little scientific perception for centuries.

Faith and Religion

One of the first things to be noticed about the controversy between science and religion is that many, perhaps most, scientists do not see any contradiction, nor do many religions. Hewlett and Peters suggested that the Christian faith *demands* good science, because "through the eyes of science we can better view the wonder and majesty of God's creation." They also consider Darwinism "an incredibly fertile theory." Gould pointed out that both theologians and scientists acted as plaintiffs in a 1981 case challenging attempts to mandate creationism in public schools. I should point out that Darwin is buried in London's Westminster Abbey, the highest honor that the Church of England can bestow.

Faith is a human universal, as is belief in the involvement of some supernatural forces in human affairs, whether the supernatural is viewed as one god, many gods, spirits of nature, or even in the ghosts of the ancestors, whose relations to the natural world can take many forms. Most emphasize essential human involvement as part of the natural world and subject to its laws. Dominating nature is a Judeo-Christian model and, at present, a very dangerous one.

One value of belief in the supernatural, obviously, is a universal need to "explain" what appears otherwise to be random or inexplicable in human affairs, helping people deal with the enormous part of the world that defies analysis or understanding. Why did I get sick: germs or spirits (neither of which most people can ever see)? Why did crops fail? What can I do about that? Faith (whether or not faith in God) is an essential part of the makeup of every individual, and it seems even to be related to our physiology and health. It does help heal, whatever the object of the faith. Faith obviously also provides people with comfort, a sense of purpose and confidence; a feeling of control of their own lives and aspects of their environment; a sense of community through a shared belief system; a sense of self; of moral and emotional support; and of a guide for action in areas that science can't touch. Faith sets moral guidelines. It helps make and bolster decisions and helps solve problems (as well as creating many), particularly in the domain of human interaction.

Science does eliminate some of life's mystery as it progresses—but the supply of mystery is infinite and hardly threatened by the little progress that science makes. But, if science threatens faith in its explanatory power, it may also appear to threaten everything else for which people look to faith, although that connection is hardly necessary. Faith also has the very important value of inclusiveness. At the entry level, it is politically more egalitarian than science (at least in theory) and it clearly has fewer prerequisites for participation.

However, for many, faith is essentially antirationalist and antiscience, tending to "trust in the Lord," rather than bringing human intellect to bear on our decisions and actions. Uniformitarianism is scary because it implies that we are alone, with our own knowledge to solve our problems. We cannot wait and hope for divine intervention. It also takes effort, in fact a great deal of effort, to find explanations and solve problems, whereas faith often promotes easy fatalism. If the airplane fails, human beings must work to try to correct the problem—an effort much greater than that of praying. More practically speaking in the contemporary world, it is we, not God, who must control air and water pollution and stop the earth from overheating. Scientists at least can try, and they have more chance of success than faith, judging by the whole history of the world.

Faith, like science, oversteps its real boundaries and involves its own very serious abuses. Part of the problem is that, like any system of culture or science, the way faith in God and religion present themselves is far different from their actual operation, or the actions of their proponents. Faith attempts, unnecessarily, to enlarge the list of things that "defy analysis," preferring to keep things in the range of the supernatural to minimize the application of science, in order to preserve the political advantages of faith. The Catholic/Christian Church has a very long history of blocking scientific advance and persecuting its protagonists. One can easily argue that the church has done far more damage to science than vice versa. Religions have been far more active than science at promoting bigotry. Some branches of Christianity have even promoted an apocalyptic vision of the end of the world, in which they alone will reach salvation, others left to perish or worse (about as powerful an example of bigotry as there is). Such people may actively seek the destruction of the world, favoring the very problems that science hopes to correct, and impeding the efforts of scientists to solve them. That is a vision shared by members of our government. (A secretary of the interior under President Reagan was once reported to have said that we should strive to use up the earth's resources to promote the second coming of Jesus.)

Faith can actually promote more inequality than does science. It can be used to substitute obedience to other people for individual thought—and conversely as a means to control other people. It can provide a rationale for hatred and has done so on many occasions. It can intrude, inappropriately and dangerously, on the realm of politics, as is conspicuously the case in the United States in the early twenty-first century. Faith has hardly been a uniter of people. In fact, faith has been, and is now, a very powerful motivator of human divisiveness and violence. Science creates terrible weapons of war, but almost all of the wars of history have been conducted in the name of religious or cultural differences, or territorial or political aspirations, not scientific disagreements. People of faith, rather than science, can hardly claim the moral high ground, as they commonly attempt to do, judging by human history and contemporary events.

It often seems that religious zealots actually miss the most important message of their religion in their rush to judge others. They insist on very selective literal interpretation of what often seem the trivial and self-promoting rather than the most important messages of the Bible: Jesus' teachings of love and tolerance, and the actual contents of the Ten Commandments. It seems more important to some people to display the Ten Commandments than to obey them.

Creationism

As we have pointed out repeatedly, creationism is not the same as faith even if offered in the name of faith. Hewlitt and Peters pointed out that creationism takes many forms: whether or not, or how much, or what parts of the Bible one takes literally; whether attempts are made to justify ideas of creation through science; whether or not creationism refers to the variety of life-forms, or only life's origin; whether to accept microevolution (small-scale) within species although not macroevolution (large-scale) across them (i.e., the branching family tree); whether to recognize macroevolution guided by divine intelligence; whether to assume a young age for the earth, and whether a "day" is twenty-four hours as we know it, or a shorthand or metaphor for a very long period of time. The more the Bible is read as metaphor, the more compatible science and faith as descriptions of the earth become. The more literal the interpretation of the Bible, obviously, the greater the conflict with science. Creationists, tending toward very literal interpretations of selected biblical passages, assume that the variety of life is God's direct creation, done very quickly and very recently, with all species created separately more or less as they now are (allowing begrudgingly for slight microevolution within kinds). The story told is remarkably biblical, and is by definition neither challengeable nor refutable by any weight of evidence that can be brought to bear, other than Genesis itself. It's a "hypothesis" that precludes any known or knowable data or observation except the words of Genesis; and its defense is based almost entirely on Genesis, used in a circular manner as proof of its own assertion.

Creationists have made a few attempts to use science to prove tenets of their belief, such as attempting to establish a short chronology of earth history by refuting established methods of dating prehistoric events and substituting their own, by interpreting the earth's layers in unusual ways, or by pointing somewhat disingenuously at gaps in the fossil record. These efforts *are* commonly recognized in the scientific marketplace but easily dismissed, using the principles by which science operates. Despite those few weak attempts to offer scientific support for the theory, the argument consists almost entirely of attempts to show evolution as wrong apparently on the theory that if evolution is wrong, the *other* model must be correct, as if there were only two possibilities. As science, it is inconsequential at best, and part of the stress scientists feel is the necessity of defending real science by responding to such an absurd argument—again, and seemingly forever.

Creationism is a doctrine with a political message that is highly conservative doctrine, an attempt to use the Bible to defend the status quo and to freeze and defend social classes, as it once was used to protect the divine right of kings and the fixity of feudal life. (In this sense, it becomes remarkably similar to its nemesis, sociobiology.) It is an assertion of established, immutable knowledge over new ideas and learning and of the established social and political order over mutable social principles.

Intelligent Design (ID)

ID, a more modern and purportedly moderate version of creationism, accepts many of the arguments for evolution, including the basic idea of a macroevolutionary family tree. (See particularly Chapter 5 by Johnson.) In the eyes of many conservative Christian sects it is objectionable because it is "soft on" biblical inerrancy. It is an attempt to remove the debate on the role of creator from theological arguments and to place it squarely in the realm of science, effectively challenging scientists at their own game. One might see it as surrender to the failure of scientific method up to this point, rather than a continuing sense that natural answers are still to be pursued. The argument is that the idea of intelligent design should be considered as one of various scientific hypotheses under discussion. As Johnson argued, scientific research itself, done by its own rules, must ultimately arrive at the failures of evolutionary theory and the necessity of ID as a force in the design of organisms and people. Johnson pointed out that ID was never intended as a subject for public school science classes, but as an issue in the philosophy of science to be investigated in universities. (Davis, cited by Hearn, suggested that ID consists only of an interesting philosophical critique of the explanatory efficacy of Darwinian models. See Chapter 3.)

ID may appear as a vision far less threatening to science than strict creationism, but its ultimate assumption of divine guidance violates the essential principle of science, the requirement that only natural principles may be used. Like creationism, it will undermine understanding of scientific method. In Chapter 6, Marks saw ID as an attack on rationality and intellectual methods, not just evolution, and he argued that this is a legal, rather than a scientific, strategy.

The Judeo-Christian Bible

None of us denies the enormous significance of the Bible even though we understand its importance in different ways. Both theologians and scientists in this volume largely discount literal interpretations of all words of the Bible, because they deny or defy processes of nature that we know well, and substitute unknowable miracles that defy analysis. Hearn said that to take the Bible seriously as God's revelation is not the same as taking it literally, suggesting for example that the "days" of Genesis need not be interpreted as meaning twenty-four modern hours. Perras, who originally believed in the literal interpretation of the Bible, described being caught short when she realized that the two versions of creation in Genesis contradict each other in significant ways, making literal interpretation of both impossible.

Hearn pointed out that the Bible can be different things at different times and for different purposes; that it is a library of many different kinds of writing, and a "constitution" setting out broad patterns to be filled in and interpreted. Some of its passages are to be interpreted as poetry, some as history, some simply as correspondence, some as moral guidelines, some clearly intended as metaphor or symbol, some as divinely inspired truth that lays out the meaning of our lives. And he argued that in order to understand its meaning one has to interpret what it meant to its writers and original readers.

Teaching

As several of us, most explicitly Gould, have pointed out, it is of no concern what faith people hold, whether they worship in a synagogue, mosque, church, or at home. People as individuals need not believe in evolution or even science. The critical thing is that creationism not penetrate public policymaking or public (or private) school *science* classrooms and not be thought of by anyone as scientific knowledge. (Gould pointed approvingly to the example of Jehovah's Witnesses who confine creationist teachings to home and church, but do not try to force them on public schools.) Scientific understanding is hard enough without insisting on teaching as science things that have no relation to scientific principles, knowledge, or methods.

But questions do remain. Do we teach faith and science equally? Should we teach both in the same context? How should we discuss the relationship of science and faith? Student choice cannot exist without alternative possibilities, but the alternatives are not evolution and the pseudosciences of creationism or intelligent design. Students should be exposed to both science and faith as alternative and complementary ways of knowing. However, science classes have to be reserved for the scientific way of knowing.

Randak and I were perhaps most explicit about the need to teach evolution and science unadulterated by any taint of faith or creationist teaching. Even Hearn, the evangelical Christian, argued for the need to teach science correctly. Randak in particular focused on the central importance of evolutionary theory as the core and force of scientific reasoning that cannot be ignored in science classes as it is in many classes otherwise teaching serious science. He bemoaned the failure of most high school curricula to include serious teaching of evolution, and the absence of support for high school teachers from college and university professors of biology. (I agree. But it has been my experience that, when I make myself available there is little interest in my involvement, perhaps because science teachers in my region of the country don't feel besieged.) As do I, Randak feared the damage to scientific understanding that results from the intrusion of creationism into science classes, and/or the watering down of science curricula, often to the point of excluding evolution altogether. He asked whether the intent may not be to eliminate public education altogether.

As Randak said, we need to educate our students in the *process* of science as an ongoing inquiry of competitive ideas, rather than the facts, emphasizing that the facts and theory that are taught in class or presented in textbooks represent the current state of knowledge in the discipline, not "the truth." He argued that science can be threatened as much by sterile teaching of facts ignoring process, as by teaching faith—and that far too much teaching of evolution and of all science is devoid of understanding and interest. He also argued that science is threatened by the increasing tendency to teach skill without theory (a trend that seems to me to pervade all areas of higher education) and by the increasing emphasis on education for specializations rather than broad-based knowledge. The analogy he cited between how science is typically taught and exposing people to a wonderful array of food and then forcing them to digest, instead, the menu, is quite apt for what happens in too many science classrooms. Students should no more accept evolution as a matter of faith, than they should accept any other faith as a replacement for science. Moreover, as Randak pointed out (and I agree), students must be taught about the dynamic nature of how science works, rather than being confused and disheartened by the way in which one seeming "fact" is replaced by another.

Science needs to be taught in its own terms, but this does not require that all students accept those terms; it requires that students (in fact all people) understand what those terms are, how they work, and what they can do. Robbins also suggested that science classes might well be introduced by a discussion of the philosophy of science and the existence of alternative philosophies such as those of faith and creation, even though the content of the latter cannot be included in the science content itself.

In my own evolution classes, I make it quite explicit that students need not agree with evolution—even to get good grades—but they must understand how science works, what the scientific arguments are, how scientists judge them, and why most scientists believe the arguments for evolution, even as they repeatedly challenge one another. These students too have the right to challenge, but not to ignore. This does not deny the fear of some people of faith, that teaching evolution will undermine their children's faith and belief in God. Nor does it deny that some scientists have explicitly attempted to make science replace faith or even explicitly tried to use it to promote atheism. But in the minds of these authors, the solution is not simply to dilute scientific method and scientific conclusions but to permit or even require discussion of other human needs that science does not provide, and the role of faith as a legitimate means of fulfilling *those* needs. Our sense, however, is that whereas education should discuss the significance of faith, it should not, at least in public schools, be permitted to favor teaching of one faith over another, or even to require that students maintain faith in God (as some teachers are also guilty of doing). But scientists need to understand (and perhaps should be taught) the basis of faith, the various sources from which it can spring, and its grounding in other cultures as well as our own.

Teaching science need not offend. Hearn reminded us that teachers need to respect the religions and faiths of their students—and they should perhaps make clear in their teaching that science is limited to naturalistic explanations, important as those are. He pointed out that most parents would probably agree that no specific religious denomination should be taught in public schools, but would be offended by teaching that appears to put down faith—which can, after all, be considered inserting an individual dogma as offensive as any other. Most of us agreed with Randak that the implicit or explicit assertion that science is a superior and self-sufficient system, and the elitist assumption that people who do not believe it are ignorant members of lesser classes, is bound to offend others and contribute significantly to negative reactions and fears. He also pointed out that science need not be taught in a way that is overly dismissive of creationism as faith.

The dilemma about teaching was framed best by Perras, the sole student in our group. She described how jarring it was to be introduced suddenly to evolution at the college level when it had been dealt with so little in her earlier education; but she confessed that her perspective has been changed toward greater willingness to accept evolution by the college exposure. She described how scary it was to have her "life support system" (her religion of biblical literalism) threatened—clearly a problem that isn't being addressed by either side, because neither side recognizes the existence of a legitimate controversy with which students must struggle. The problem is exacerbated by what she described as an inherent need on the part of students to be at one with the teacher of the moment. (As Randak pointed out, the ability of students to assimilate is deeply embedded in their world view.) She stated that she suffers from the fact that for most of her education, her scientific education was badly distorted. Her overall sense was one of frustration and confusion that she is working through, based partly on the fact that she isn't being taught either side of the controversy very well. And she noted that presentations on either side tend unnecessarily to debunk one another by phrases such as the creation *myth* and by obvious body language or tone. She argued that trying to force religions into science classes won't yield the important results creationists are actually hoping to achieve. Perras described the problem of isolation from both sides that comes from trying to balance the two. She suggested that most students face too many distractions and personal problems for deep reflection, and simply aren't paying enough attention to care very much or listen very carefully, when, in fact staying on top of the tensions between faith and science should be part of everyone's education. She described being, as a student, the object of a competitive game not only framed by education but also by legal and political intervention egged on by lawyers and the omnipresent media (and, Gould would add, textbook publishers) in which neither she and other students, nor perhaps prospective students, are actually being considered much at all. And, according to Perras, forcing creationism into science classes will not accomplish what people of faith want.

In essence, Perras argued that nobody's education is being served very well. She argued that it is very important for both science and faith to be more tolerant of each other, and more introspective about their own intolerance. She and I agree that both areas must be taught, but be taught separately, and faith must be taught in a way that does not insist on the importance of any specific faith or denigrate students with alternate faiths. Many of us agree, however, that evolution is not always taught correctly as science, but often presented as fact or faith, often no better than the presentation of any other faith. Although appreciating science, Hearn suggested that science presented as scientism or Darwinism actually is a faith like any other ism. He suggested, more generally that a good deal of the tension between science and faith or creationism could be resolved by correct labeling of positions. Hewlitt and Peters, and Gould also suggested that some interpretations of Darwinism and evolution approach faith in the uncritical zeal with which they are presented.

Teaching Outside of Science Classes

Most of us agreed as well that students must be exposed to issues and discussions of morality, faith, and an idea of purpose and spirituality but with a clear sense that these might come not only from religious faith, but perhaps also from other sources, including the society. The juxtaposition and comparison of scientific and faith-based approaches to problems should ideally be involved. These issues must be taught in contexts other than science classes so that there can be no confusion between the two. This might take the form of general education and/or elective courses in the humanities, with the understanding that these are not to insist that content be religious or favor any one religion over others. An ideal form might be a (required?) class in "two cultures" modeled after arguments presented by C. P. Snow, although focusing on a different dichotomy than Snow defined.

Overzealousness of Exclusion

In our writings we agreed that there are, or should be, perfectly legitimate contexts for the teaching of religion on college campuses. And we agreed that some recent actions by college campuses have been overzealous in their proper desire to maintain separation between church and state. Religion and its importance are important topics, as is exposure to the thought and history of individual religions; but, like science these must be taught in a nonsectarian manner that requires understanding but does not demand belief or religious participation.

Democracy, Fairness, Equal time, and Academic Freedom

Randak and I both emphasized that fairness, free speech, equal time, academic freedom, and democracy, although important in other contexts, have nothing to do with decisions about what is to be taught in science classes. Science is neither about fairness nor democratic vote; it is about competition among theories that abides by very specific rules. (See my own Chapter 1.) Outcomes reflect the quality of evidence and arguments and the judgments of trained professionals. We do not teach math or languages by democratic arguments; we teach what we think is correct. We do not want majority vote to decide which is the most popular airplane design; nor do we think that we should include good and bad airplane designs to be fair. We want them to be designed by people trained in scientific methods and scientifically proven designs. We need to teach the processes of science with that in mind.

As I pointed out, the 'right' to teach creation science or intelligent design in a science classroom does not exist. Freedom must always be balanced by judgment and responsibility, and it must be curtailed in accordance with those other principles. Privileged and licensed positions always carry with them some limits to freedoms that other people enjoy. The privilege and license to teach carry with them an obligation to teach the subject matter as defined. One cannot claim freedom to teach a topic wrong, whether it be science, math, or grammar.

Government Involvement, and Parental or Student Pressures

In accordance with what has just been said, government or court mandates, school boards, parental pressures, and pressures from student groups simply should have no bearing whatsoever on the proper content of biology (or any science classes) and evolution is too central to the cores of theory in biology classes to be left out. The fact that a president or other holder of political office favors a particular position is irrelevant and should never be given the weight of the ideas of someone involved in the correct conduct of the professional activity. Ideally, they should never be voiced in a public, apparently authoritarian context. The fact that Ronald Reagan and George W. Bush both mindlessly jumped into the debate on the side of creationism is not relevant. Would we want our presidents to make pronouncements on grammar or geography? Would we accept their versions of spelling or pronunciation just because they were presidents?

This is not an issue of "balance" as I pointed out, because there are many creation stories from around the world, most of which did not have the benefit of being written down and maintained in our cultural history. Each has been put forward by people with the same emotional and ethical needs and with the same sense of something divine that we have. Are they so easily dismissed? Even Islam, which draws its roots from a Judeo-Christian God but sees creation differently? How many stories or theories do we discuss? How do we honestly choose?

Why the Popularity of creationism?

Gould once suggested (reprinted in this volume) that creationism as science was a peculiarly American phenomenon not shared by European nations. But he still held that American scientists were significantly underestimating the importance of the movement. Like Gould, I have had the experience of interviewing and/or being interviewed by people from several European countries. I have talked recently to people in two very Catholic countries, Portugal and Spain, as well as in France and England. All found the whole creationist movement puzzling. They were aware of no serious counterpart in their own countries and were curious to hear about our experiences. Peters and Branch, however, described the enormous worldwide (but not particularly European) increase in fundamentalist opposition to evolution. And he thinks that Gould significantly underestimated its growing world impact.

As Gould pointed out (and I concur), for the vast majority of people involved the issue may not be about religion at all, at least under the surface; it is (also) about fear; anger; psychological and social needs; class (and opposition to class disdain that people feel); wealth; religion (quite independent of creationism itself); education; geography; and even politics, both of party affiliation and of local versus national control of affairs.

Both in the Third World and in the West, resurgent creationism may represent a kind of "revitalization movement." That term, very well known to anthropologists, describes a situation in which people feel that their own culture, values, and belief system are threatened or have been significantly undermined by other people (typically people who have colonized them). They feel they have been relegated to second-class citizenship in a new social order, and want some of the wealth or privileges that they see others enjoying and that they feel more properly belong to them. As a result they make a relatively sudden, dramatic, but often peaceful move to reject the culture of the colonizing group and to reestablish not so much their actual independence (which may be impossible) as their group identity and group pride. People of faith may well see science itself as a colonizing force, particularly because science does commonly present itself as a superior system, those of faith representing a lower class of uneducated people. (There is even an implicit, occasionally explicit, quasi-racist sense in discussions, by some scientists, that the others are not only ignorant but not very bright.)

Creationism may in part be based on its revitalization qualities. It is something with which to identify; something to own; something to share; something with which to bind a community. It provides a mechanism with which to oppose the system that threatens; to hate; to rebel symbolically; to thumb one's nose; a team for which to root. It is a way of rejecting social change and the modernization that science implies. It is a way to find authority and a justification for a return to (what was) the status quo—or perhaps, more accurately, a romantic perception of what was once the status quo. I emphasize the romantic perception, in this case, because in blaming science and evolution for social ills, people of faith and religion tend to ignore the enormous difference between the ideals of their faiths and the actual history of faith-related institutions. These institutions, as I have mentioned, have probably been the cause of far more social ills than has science. (It is interesting that in the Third World, where the movement is generally being made in the name of Christianity, it is desired to return not to a pre-Christian status quo, but perhaps to a world in which spirituality, a feature common to both Christianity and the religions it replaced, is not dominated by material and technological concerns.)

We must delve into what might be called creationism's latent (i.e., unspoken, even unconscious) functions and the nonreligious as well as religious needs it fulfills for so many of its adherents. And we must be willing to address them. All of us must try to understand what is going on in terms of those other pressures. Learning these things and reminding ourselves and others that there are two separate and equal cultures that need not intrude on one another may be the only recourse we have to resolve this. The larger issue isn't evolution; it is the survival of science. And in terms of the world's problems, both natural and cultural, there isn't much time to resolve the issue or reassert the valuable functions of science. I personally think that the existence of a separate culture of faith (although not its contents) must be mentioned in science classes, and that establishments of faith must make clear their appreciation of science; that the two cultures must be a very central part of everyone's education.

The bottom line, I believe, is that both science and faith must "deconstruct" themselves or become conscious of their parts while deigning to look at the values and needs of the other system. If that occurs, true science can separate itself from its overextensions into human needs. And faith could separate itself from inappropriate attempts to quell science.

Adami, C., Ofria, C., & Collier, T. C. (2000). Evolution of biological complexity. PNAS, 97(9), 4463–4468. Retrieved from http://pnas.org/ cgi/content/full/97/9/4463

Allen, E., Beckwith, B., Beckwith, J., Chorover, S., Culver, D., Duncan, M., et al. (1975). Against "sociobiology." New York Review of Books, 22, 42–44.

Alphonso, C., & Séguin, R. (2006, October 25). Teach Darwin, Quebec tells evangelicals. The Globe and Mail, p. A6.

Alters, B. J., & Alters, S. (2001). Defending evolution in the classroom. Boston: Jones & Bartlett.

Arnold, M. (1977). Natural hybridization and evolution. New York: Oxford University Press.

Asghar, A., Wiles, J. R., & Alters, B. (2007). Discovering international perspectives on biological evolution across religions and cultures. International Journal of Diversity, 6(4), 81–88.

Awolalu, J. O., & Dopamu, P. A. (2005). West African traditional religion (Rev. ed.). Nigeria: Macmillan.

Barker, J. (2004). Creationism in Canada. In S. Coleman & L. Carlin (Eds.), The cultures of creationism: Anti-evolutionism in English-speaking countries (pp. 85–108). London: Ashgate.

Barnes, B. (2002). Scientific knowledge: A sociological analysis. London: Athlone Press.

Barnett, S. (2006, April 15–21). By accident or design. The New Zealand Listener, 203(3440).

Baslaugh, G. (2006). SSHRC—We have a problem. Humanist Perspectives, 157 3–4.

Behe, M. (1998). Darwin's black box: The biochemical challenge to evolution. New York: Free Press

Berra, T. M. (1990). Evolution and the myth of creationism. Stanford, CA: Stanford University Press.

Bigg, C. (2006). Russia: Creationism finds support among young. Radio Free Europe. Retrieved from www.rferl.org/featuresarticle/2006/03/c847984f-4125-404f-9f71-7d22c229112c.html

Binder, A. J. (2002). Contentious curricula: Afrocentrism and creationism in American public schools. Princeton, NJ: Princeton University Press.

Bishop, G. F. (2003). Intelligent design: Illusions of an informed public. Public Perspective, 14(3), 5–7.

Bishop, G. F. (2006). Polls apart on human origins. Public Opinion Pros. Retrieved from www.publicopinionpros.com/features/2006/aug/bishop_printable.asp

Bloor, D. (1991). Knowledge and social imagery. Chicago: University Of Chicago Press.

Branch, G. (2005). President Bush addresses "intelligent design." Reports of the National Center for Science Education, 25(3–4), 13–14.

Branch, G. (2006). Defending the teaching of evolution: Strategies and tactics for activists. In E. C. Scott & G. Branch (Eds.), Not in our classrooms: Why intelligent design is wrong for our schools (pp. 130–152). Boston: Beacon Press.

Branigan, T. (2002, March 9). Top school's creationists preach value of biblical story over evolution. The Guardian, p. 3.

Brook, S. (2000, February 1). Sex an evolving pleasure. The Australian, p. 6.

Brown, C. M. (2002). Hindu and Christian creationism: "Transposed passages" in the geological book of life. Zygon, 37(1), 95–114.

Brown, S. D., & Delodder, J. (2003). When is a creationist not a creationist? Appreciating the miracles of public opinion polling. Canadian Journal of Communication, 28(1), 111–119.

Bruce, S. (2002). God is dead: Secularization in the West. Oxford: Blackwell.

Brumble, H. D. (1998). Vine Deloria, Jr., creationism, and ethnic pseudoscience. American Literary History, 10(2), 335–346.

Bryan, W. J. (1922, February 26). God and evolution. New York Times, p. 84.

Buffon, George-Louis Leclerc, Comte de (1749–1789). Histoire Naturelle, Generale et Particuliere. Paris: L'Imprimerie Royale. See also http://personal.uncc.edu/jmarks/Buffon/Refs. html

Cherny, R. W. (1985). A righteous cause: The life of William Jennings Bryan. Boston: Little, Brown.

Cherry, S. (2006). Crisis management via biblical interpretation: Fundamentalism, modern orthodoxy, and Genesis. In G. Cantor & M. Swetlitz (Eds.), Jewish tradition and the challenge of Darwinism. (pp. 166–187). Chicago: University of Chicago Press.

Chisholm, L. (2002). Religion, science, and evolution in South Africa: The politics and construction of the Revised National Curriculum Statement for Schools (grades R–9). In J. Wilmot & L. Wilson (Eds.), The architect and the scaffold: Evolution and education in South Africa (pp. 51–59). Human Resources Research Council.

Clem, W. (2005, October 22). Each-way approach evolves in HK. South China Morning Post, p. 5.

Cohen, M. N. (1998). Culture of intolerance. New Haven, CT: Yale University Press.

Coleman, S., & Carlin, L. (Eds.). (2004). The cultures of creationism: Anti-evolutionism in English-speaking countries. London: Ashgate.

Collins, F. S. (2002). Human genetics. In J. F. Kilner, C. C. Hook, & D. B. Uustal (Eds.), Cutting edge of bioethics. Grand Rapids, MI: Eerdmans.

---

*Note on publication dates: While different contributors have often cited the same book (e.g. Ronald Numbers The Creationists), some have used an earlier version (e.g. hardcover 1992) while other have used a later edition (e.g. softcover 1993). For sake of consistency, we have cited the earlier date in each case.

Compas. (2000). *Hot button issues in the federal campaign.* Retrieved from www.compas.ca/data/001124-NPostHotButtonFederalElection-EP.pdf

Crapanzano, V. (2000). *Serving the word: Literalism in America from the pulpit to the bench.* New York: New Press.

Cremo, M. A., & Thompson, R. A. (1993). *Forbidden archaeology: The hidden history of the human race.* Denver, CO: Bhaktivedanta Institute.

Cuomo, M. (2004). In the American Catholic tradition of realism. In E. J. Dionne Jr., J. B. Elshtain, & K. M. Drogosz (Eds.), *One electorate under God? A dialogue on religion and American politics* (pp. 17–18). Washington, D.C.: Broutings Institution Press.

Daly, H. E. (1996). *Beyond growth: The economics of sustainable development.* Boston: Beacon Press.

Darwin, C. (1958) [1876]. The autobiography of Charles Darwin 1809–1882 with original omissions restored. Ed. Nora Barlow. Collins.

Darwin, C. (1964). *The origin of species by means of natural selection.* Cambridge, MA: Harvard University Press. (Original work published 1859)

Darwin, C. (n.d.). *The origin of species by means of natural selection, or the preservation of favoured races in the struggle for life.* Retrieved from www.talkorigins.org/faqs/origin/chapter14.html. (Original work published 1859)

Darwin, F. (Ed.). (1887). *The life and letters of Charles Darwin* (3 vols.). London: Murray.

Dawkins, R. (1976). *The selfish gene.* Oxford, UK: University of Oxford Press.

Dawkins, R. (1986). *The blind watchmaker: Why the evidence of evolution reveals a universe without design.* New York: Norton.

Dawkins, R. (1996). *Climbing mount improbable.* New York: Norton.

Dawkins, R. (2001). Foreword. In W. D. Hamilton, *Narrow roads of gene land: The collected papers of W. D. Hamilton* (p. 2). Oxford, UK: Oxford University Press.

Dawkins, R. (2006). *The God delusion.* Boston: Houghton Mifflin

"Dawn horse" is a good "ancestor" for rhinos discredits horse evolution? (n.d.). Retrieved from http://members.cox.net/ardipithecus/evol/lies/lie016.html

De Gennaro, J. (2002). Two worlds in conflict: Creationism & evolution in Argentina. In A. Chesworth, S. Hill, K. Lipovsky, E. Snyder, & W. Chesworth (Eds.), *Darwin Day collection one: The best single idea, ever.* (pp. 399–402). Albuquerque, NM: Tangled Bank.

Deloria, V., Jr. (1995). *Red earth, white lies: Native Americans and scientific fact.* New York: Scribner.

Deloria, V., Jr. (2002). *Evolution, creationism, and other modern myths.* Golden, CO: Fulcrum.

Dembski, W. A. (Ed.). (1998). *Mere creation: Science, faith & intelligent design.* Westmont, IL: InterVarsity Press.

den Boer, N. (2007). The atlas of creation. Radio Netherlands. Retrieved from www.radionetherlands.nl/currentaffairs/edu070227

Dobzhansky, T. (1963). Anthropology and the natural sciences—The problem of human evolution. *Current Anthropology, 4.*

Douglas, Mary. (1978). *Cultural bias.* Occasional Paper No. 35 of the Royal Anthropological Institute of Great Britain and Ireland. London: Royal Anthropological Institute.

Edis, T. (1999). Cloning creationism in Turkey. *Reports of the National Center for Science Education, 19*(6), 30–35.

Edis, T. (2002). Harun Yahya and Islamic creationism. In A. Chesworth, S. Hill, K. Lipovsky, E. Snyder, & W. Chesworth (Eds.), *Darwin Day collection one: The best single idea, ever.* (pp. 419–422). Albuqueque, NM: Tangled Bank.

Edis, T. (2007). *An illusion of harmony: Science and religion in Islam.* Amherst, NY: Prometheus.

Edwards, W. (2004). *A response to Locke's "The scientific case against evolution.* Retrieved from www.freethoughtdebater.com/FlockerRespons.htm

Eldredge, N. (1995). *Reinventing Darwin: The great debate at the high table of evolutionary thought.* New York: Wiley.

Eldredge, N. & Gould, S. J. (1972). Punctuated equilibria: An alternative to phyletic gradualism. In T. J. M. Schopf (Ed.), *Models in paleobiology.* San Francisco: Freeman, Cooper.

Enserink, M. (2005). Is Holland becoming the Kansas of Europe? *Science, 308*(5727), 1394.

Ernst, C. W. (2003). *Following Muhammed: Rethinking Islam in the contemporary world.* Chapel Hill: University of North Carolina Press.

Ewen, S. (1996) *PR: A social history of spin.* New York: Basic Books.

Forrest, B., & Gross, P. R. (2007). *Creationism's Trojan horse: The wedge of intelligent design* (Rev. ed.). Oxford, UK: Oxford University Press.

Fulljames, P., & Francis, L. (2004). Creationism among young people in Kenya and Britain. In S. Coleman & L. Carlin (Eds.), *The cultures of creationism: Anti-evolutionism in English-speaking countries* (pp. 165–173). London: Ashgate.

German scientists concerned about rise in creationist belief. (2006). Deutsche Welle. Retrieved from www.dw-world.de/dw/article/0,2144,2222454,00.html

Giberson, K. W, & Yerxa, D. A. (2002). *Species of origins: Americas search for a creation story.* Lanham, MD: Rowman & Littlefield.

Gish, D. (1995). *Evolution: The fossils still say no.* El Cajon, CA: Institute for Creation Research.

Goldschmidt, W. (2005). *The bridge to humanity: How affect hunger trumps the selfish gene.*

Goodman, S. (1995). Creationists in Canada. *NCSE Reports, 15*(1), 1, 10–11.

Gould, S. J. (1981). *The mismeasure of man.* New York: Norton.

Gould, S. J. (1989). *Wonderful life: The Burgess shale and the nature of history.* New York: Norton.

Gould, S. J. (1991a, August). Opus 2000. *Natural History, 100.*

Gould, S. J. (1991b, September). Unenchanted evening. *Natural History, 14.*

Gould, S. J. (1991c). William Jennings Bryan's last campaign. In *Bully for brontosaurus.* New York: Norton.

Gould, S. J. (1996). *Full house: The spread of excellence from Plato to Darwin*. New York: Harmony.

Gould, S. J. (1999). *Rock of ages: Science and religion in the fullness of life*. New York: Ballantine.

Gould, S. J. (2002). *The structure of evolutionary theory*. Cambridge, MA: Harvard University Press.

Gould, S. J., & Lewontin, R. C. (1979). The Spandrels of San Marco and the Panglossian paradigm: A critique of the adaptationist programme. *Proceedings of the Royal Society of London* (Ser. B, Vol. 205).

Graebsch, A. (2006). Polish scientists fight creationism. *Nature, 443*, 890–891.

Graebsch, A., & Schiermeier, Q. (2006). Anti-evolutionists raise their profile in Europe. *Nature, 444*, 406–407.

Hamilton, W. D. (1964). The genetical evolution of social behavior, I. *Journal of Theoretical Biology, 7*.

Hamilton, W. D. (1996) *Narrow roads of gene land. The Collected Papers of W. D. Hamilton* (Vol. 1). New York: Freeman.

Harun Yahya [pseudonym]. (2002). *Darwinism refuted*. New Delhi: Goodword.

Harun Yahya [pseudonym]. (2005). *The "intelligent design" distraction*. Retrieved from www.harunyahya.com/new_releases/news/intelligent_design.php

Hawley, C. (2001). Saudis to stamp out Pokemon. BBC News. Retrieved from news.bbc.co.uk/2/hi/middle_east/1249820.stm

Heneghan, T. (2006). Muslim creationism makes inroads in Turkey. Reuters November 22. Retrieved from www.msnbc.msn.com/id/15857761/

Heneghan, T. (2007). Pope says science too narrow to explain creation. Reuters April 11. Retrieved from www.reuters.com/article/topNews/ idUSL1015081120070411

Herrnstein, R. & Murray, C. (1994). *The bell curve*. New York: Free Press.

Hunt, K. (1994–1997). *Transitional vertebrate fossils FAQ*, Parts 1B, 2B, & 2C. Retrieved from www.talkorigins.org/faqs/faq/transitional/part1b.html

Hunter, G. W. (1914). *A civic biology presented in problems*. New York. American Book Company.

Huxley, T. H. (1997). Evolution and ethics. In A. P. Barr (Ed.), *The major prose of Thomas Henry Huxley*. Athens: University of Georgia Press.

Interacademy Panel on International Issues. (2006). *IAP statement on the teaching of evolution*. Retrieved from www.interacademies.net/Object.File/Master/6/150/Evolution%20statement.pdf

International Social Survey Programme. (2000). *Environment*. Zentralarchiv für Empirische Sozialforschung.

Ipsos MORI. (2006). *BBC survey on the origin of life*. Retrieved from www.ipsos-mori.com/polls/2006/bbc-horizon.shtml

Jenkins, P. (2002). *The next christendom: The coming of global christianity*. Oxford: Oxford University Press.

John Paul II. (1997). Message to the Pontifical Academy of Sciences. *The Quarterly Review of Biology, 72*(4), 381–383.

Johnson, P. E. (1993). *Darwin on Trial*. Westmont, IL: InterVarsity Press.

Kaplan, J. (1997). *Radical religion in America: Millenarian movements from the far right to the children of Noah*. Syracuse, NY: Syracuse University Press.

Kazin, M. (2006). *Godly hero: The life of William Jennings Bryan*. New York: Knopf.

Koenig, R. (2001). Creationism takes root where Europe, Asia meet. *Science, 292*(5520), 1286–1287.

Kuhn, T. (1961). *The structure of scientific revolution*. Chicago: University of Chicago Press.

Kutschera, U. (2003). Darwinism and intelligent design: The new anti-evolutionism spreads in Europe. *Reports of the National Center for Science Education, 23*(5–6), 17–18.

Kutschera, U. (2006). Devolution and dinosaurs: The anti-evolution seminar in the European Parliament. *Reports of the National Center for Science Education, 26*(5), 10–11.

Kutschera, U. (Ed.). (2007). *Kreationismus in Deutschland: Fakten und Analysen*. Musster: Lit-Verlag.

Lack, D. (1957). *Evolutionary theory and Christian belief: The unresolved conflict*. London: Methuen.

LaHaye, T. (1980). *The battle for the mind*. Grand Rapids, MI: Baker Book House.

Larson, E. J. (1997). *Summer for the gods: The Scopes trial and America's continuing debate over science and religion*. Cambridge, MA: Harvard University Press.

Larson, E. J. (2003). *Trial and error: The American controversy over creation and evolution* (3rd ed.). Oxford: Oxford University Press.

Larson, E. J., & Witham, L. (1997). Scientists are still keeping the faith. *Nature, 386*.

Layton, R. (2004). The politics of indigenous "creationism" in Australia. In S. Coleman, & Carlin, L. (Eds.), *The cultures of creationism: Anti-evolutionism in english-speaking countries*. (pp. 144–164). London: Ashgate.

Lazcano, A. (2005). Teaching evolution in Mexico: Preaching to the choir. *Science, 310*(5749), 787–789.

Lever, J. (2002). Science, schooling, and evolution in South Africa. In J., Wilmot & L. Wilson, (Eds.), *The architect and the scaffold: Evolution and education in South Africa*. (pp. 10–44). Pretoria, South Africa: Human Resources Research Council.

Lewontin, R. C. (1974). *The genetic basis of evolutionary change*. New York: Columbia University Press.

Lewontin, R. C., & Hubby, J. L. (1966). A molecular approach to the study of genic heterozygosity in natural populations: *Vol. 2. Amount of variation and degree of heterozygosity in natural populations of Drosophila pseudoobscura*. *Genetics, 54*.

Lippard, J. (2007). *Creationist finances: Some conclusions*. Retrieved from http://lippard.blogspot.com/2007/01/creationist-finances-some-conclusions.html

Lloyd, P. (2005, November 5). Evolutionists target views of creationists; 70,000 unite over "intelligent design." *The Advertiser* (Adelaide, Australia), p. 47.

Malaysian Science and Technology Information Centre. (2004). *Public awareness of science and technology Malaysia 2004.* Retrieved from www.mastic.gov.my/

Margulis, L., & Sagan, D. (2002). *Acquiring genomes: A theory of the origins of species.* New York: Basic Books.

Marley, D. (2006, November 24). Creationism tag puts academies at risk, says Vardy. *The Times Educational Supplement,* p. 8.

Martin, E., (1987). *The woman in the body: A cultural analysis of reproduction.* Boston: Beacon Press.

Martins, E., & França, V. (2004). Rosinha contra Darwin. *Época, 314,* 44–47.

Massarani, L. (2005). *Few in Brazil accept scientific view of human evolution.* Retrieved from www.scidev.net/News/index.cfm?fuseaction=read News&itemid=1885

Mayr, E. (1997). *This is biology: The science of the living world.* Cambridge, MA: Harvard University Press.

McKenzie, D. A. (1981). *Statistics in Britain 1865–1930: The social construction of scientific knowledge.* Edinburgh: Edinburgh University Press.

Meyer, S. C. (2006, January 28). Intelligent design is not creationism. *The Telegraph,* p. 24.

Miller, J. D., Scott, E. C., & Okamoto, S. (2006). Public acceptance of evolution. *Science, 313*(5788), 765–766.

Mooney, C. (2003). *Polling for ID. Doubt and about.* Retrieved from www.csicop.org/doubtandabout/polling/

Mooney, C., & Nisbet, M. C. (2005, September/October). Undoing Darwin. *Columbia Journalism Review,* pp. 30–39.

Morin, H. (2007, February 4). Un ouvrage turc antidarwinien diffusé en masse auprès de l'éducation nationale. *Le Monde* p. 8.

Morris, H. M., & Parker, G. E. (1987). *What is creation science?* (Rev. and expanded ed.). El Cajon, CA: Master Books.

Nanda, M. (2003). *Prophets facing backward: Postmodern critiques of science and Hindu nationalism in India.* New Brunswick, NJ: Rutgers University Press.

National Science Board. (2006). *Science and engineering indicators 2006* (Vol. 1, NSB 06-01; Vol. 2, NSB 06-01A). National Science Foundation.

National Science Teachers Association. (2005). *Survey indicates science teachers feel pressure to teach nonscientific alternatives to evolution* [press release]. Retrieved from www.nsta.org/pressroom&news_story_ID=50377

Nedin, C. (1996). *Archaeopteryx: Answering the challenge of the fossil record.* Retrieved from www.talkorigins.org/faqs/archaeopteryx/Challenge.html

Nesse, R. M., & Williams, G. C. (1998, November). Evolution and the origins of disease. *Scientific American, 90:* 86–93.

Newman, S. A. (2007). Evolution and the holy ghost of *Scopes:* Can science lose the next round? *Rutgers Journal of Law and Religion, 8*(2).

Numbers, R. L. (1982, November). Creationism in 20th century America. *Science, 5,* 538–544.

Numbers, R. L. (1993). *The creationists: The evolution of scientific creationism.* Berkeley: University of California Press.

Numbers, R. L. (1998). *Darwin comes to America.* Cambridge, MA: Harvard University Press.

Numbers, R. L. (2006). *The creationists: From scientific creationism to intelligent design.* Cambridge, MA: Harvard University Press.

Numbers, R. L., & Stenhouse, J. (Eds.). (1999). *Disseminating Darwinism: The role of place, race, religion, and gender.* Cambridge, MA: Cambridge University Press.

Ortega, T. (2005, May 5). Your OFFICIAL program to the Scopes II Kansas monkey trial. *The Pitch.*

Pennock, R. T. (1999). *Tower of Babel: The evidence against the new creationism.* Cambridge, MA: MIT Press.

Pennock, R. T. (2003). Creationism and intelligent design. *Annual Review of Genomics and Human Genetics, 4,* 143–163.

Pflanz, M. (2006, August 12). Evangelicals urge museum to hide man's ancestors. *Daily Telegraph,* p. 15.

Plimer, I. (1994). *Telling lies for God: Reason vs creationism.* Melbourne: Random House Australia.

Polanyi, M. (1958). *Personal knowledge*: Towards a post-critical philosophy. Chicago: University of Chicago Press

Polling the creationism/evolution controversy. (2004). *Reports of the National Center for Science Education, 24*(5), 19.

Putnam, R. (2000). *Bowling alone: The collapse and revival of American community.* New York: Simon and Schuster.

Raëlian Movement. (2002). *Raelian Movement supports ID theory* [press release]. Retrieved from www.prweb.com/releases/2002/11/ prweb50443.php

Randerson, J. (2006, December 7). Ministers to ban creationist teaching aids in science lessons. *The Guardian,* p. 10.

Redfern, M. (2007, April 14). Creationist museum challenges evolution. BBC News. Retrieved from http://news.bbc.co.uk/2/hi/programmes/from_our_own_correspondent/6549595.stm

Riddell, D. (2002). Creationism in New Zealand. In A. Chesworth, S. Hill, K. Lipovsky, E. Snyder, & W. Chesworth (Eds.). *Darwin Day collection one: The best single idea, ever.* (pp. 387–389). Albuquerque, NM: Tangled Bank.

Robinson, I. (2006). "Practically, I am a fundamentalist": Twentieth-century Orthodox Jews contend with evolution and its implications. In G. Cantor & M. Swetlitz (Eds.), *Jewish tradition and the challenge of Darwinism.* (pp. 71–88). Chicago: University of Chicago Press.

Rosenhouse, J., & Branch, G. (2006). Media coverage of "intelligent design." *BioScience, 56*(3), 247–252.

Ross, H. (2006). *Creation as science: A testable model approach to end the creation/evolution wars.* Colorado Springs, CO: NavPress.

Rothenberg, J. (2005, October). The heresy of Nosson Slifkin. *Moment* pp. 37–46, 58, 70, 72.

Ruse, M. (1996). *Monad to man: The concept of progress in evolutionary biology.* Cambridge, MA: Harvard University Press.

Ruse, M., & Wilson, E. O. (1985, October 17). The evolution of ethics. *New Scientist.*

Ruse, M. & Wilson, E. (2001). *The evolution wars: A guide to the debates* (Rev. ed.). New Brunswick, NJ: Rutgers University Press.

Rushdie, S. (1988). *The satanic verses.* New York: Viking Press.

Rushton, P. (1999). *Race evolution and behavior.* New Brunswick, NJ: Transaction Press.

Sarich, V., & Miele, F. (2004). *Race: The reality of human differences.* Cambridge, MA: Westview Press.

Schönborn, C. (2005, July 7). Finding design in nature [op-ed]. *New York Times,* p. A23.

Schroeder, G. L. (1990). *Genesis and the Big Bang: The discovery of harmony between modern science and the bible.* New York: Bantam Books.

Scott, E. C. (1994). Waldorf schools teach odd science, odd evolution. *NCSE Reports, 14*(4), 20–21.

Scott, E. C. (2005). *Evolution vs. creationism: An introduction.* Berkeley: University of California Press.

Scott, E. C. (2007). Creation science lite: "Intelligent design" as the new anti-evolutionism. In A. J. Petto & L. R. Godfrey (Eds.), *Scientists confront intelligent design and creationism.* (pp. 59–109). New York: Norton.

Seger, J. & Hamilton, W. D. (1988). Parasites and sex. In R. E. Michod & B. R. Levin (Eds.), *The evolution of sex: An examination of current ideas.* Sunderland, MA: Sinauer.

Serbia reverses Darwin suspension. (2004). BBC News. Retrieved from http://news.bbc.co.uk/1/hi/world/europe/3642460.stm

Shipman, P. (2006). Turkish creationist movement tours American college campuses. *Reports of the National Center for Science Education, 26*(4), 11–14.

Shukla, R. (2005). *India science report: Science education, human resources and public attitude towards science and technology.* New Delhi: National Council of Applied Economic Research.

Skocpol, T. (2003). *Diminished democracy: From membership to management in American civic life.* Norman: University of Oklahoma Press.

Smith, B. H. (2005). *Scandalous knowledge: Science, truth, and the human.* Durham, NC: Duke University Press.

Smith, J. M., (1995, November 30). Genes, memes, and minds. *New York Review of Books.*

Sonderstrom, M. (2000). Australopithecus or Adam's rib? *McGill News, 80,* 16–20.

Stan, L., & Turcescu, L. (2000). The Romanian Orthodox Church and post-communist democratisation. *Europe-Asia Studies, 52*(8), 1467–1488.

Steel, R. (2006). "All you need is love." New York Review of Books, Volume 53, Number 11 June 22.

www.nybooks.com/articles/article-preview?article_id=19100

St. Petersburg court rejects schoolgirl's suit over Darwinism. (2007). RIA Novosti. Retrieved from http://en.rian.ru/russia/20070221/61084667.html

St. Petersburg girl quits school and country over Darwinism suit. (2007). RIA Novosti. Retrieved from http://en.rian.ru/russia/20070130/59893374.html

Sugirtharajah, R. S. (2001). *The Bible and the third world.* Cambridge: Cambridge University Press.

Toumey, C. P. (1994). *God's own scientists: Creationists in a secular world.* New Brunswick, NJ: Rutgers University Press.

Updates. (2006). *Reports of the National Center for Science Education, 26*(3), 12–16.

Wade, Nicholas. (2000). Genetic code of human life is cracked by scientists. The *NY Times,* June 27

Watson, J. D. (1980). *The double helix: A personal account of the discovery of the structure of DNA.* New York: Norton.

Watson. J. D., & Crick, F. H. E. (1953). A structure for deoxyribose nucleic acid. *Nature, 171.*

Weikart, R. (2004). *From Darwin to Hitler: Evolutionary ethics, eugenics, and racism in Germany.* Hampshire, UK: Palgrave Macmillan.

Weinberg, S. (1999). *No to cosmic design.* Paper presented at the Cosmic Questions Conference, April 15.

Whitcomb, J. C., Jr., & Morris, H. M. (1961). *The Genesis flood and its scientific implications.* Phillipsburg, NJ: P & R Publishing.

Wiles, J. R. (2006). Evolution in schools: Where's Canada? *Education Canada, 46*(4), 37–41.

Williams, J. (2006, November 25). Combating creationism [Letter to the editor]. *New Scientist.* p. 23.

Wilson, E. O. (1975). *Sociobiology.* Cambridge, MA: Harvard University Press.

Wilson, E. O. (1978). *On human nature.* Cambridge, MA: Harvard University Press.

Wilson, E. O. (1994). *Naturalist.* Washington: Island Press.

Wilson, E. O. (1998). *Consilience: The unity of knowledge.* New York: Knopf.

Wilson, E. O. (2000). *Sociobiology: The new synthesis.* Cambridge, MA: Harvard University Press.

Witham, L. A. (1997, April 11). Many scientists see God's hand in evolution. *Washington Times,* p. A8.

Witham, L. A. (2002). *Where Darwin meets the Bible: Creationists and evolutionists in America.* New York: Oxford University Press.

Wright, R. (1999, December 13). The accidental creationist. *New Yorker.*

Yaar, E. (2006). *Science and technology in the Israeli consciousness.* Retrieved from www.neaman.org.il/neaman/ [summary in English; report in Hebrew].

Young, M., & Edis, T. (Eds.). (2006). *Why intelligent design fails: A scientific critique of the new creationism* (Rev. ed.). New Brunswick, NY: Rutgers University Press.

Young, R. M. (1971). Darwin's metaphor: Does nature select? *The Monist, 55,* 442–503.

Photo Credits

Index